MW01614490

"*Some communities suffer starkly different health outcomes than others. Across relatively small geographic areas, average life expectancy may vary by 15, 20, or even 30 years. This has led to the recognition that 'when it comes to health, your zip code matters more than your genetic code.' A root cause of poor community health is social isolation, disconnectedness, and exclusion. Low-income communities of color have faced segregation, disinvestment, aggressive policing, and political, social, and economic marginalization for generations in the U.S. This exclusion is often internalized and can literally alter people's physiology. Latino Health Access has discovered a cure that has the promise to revolutionize our understanding of health and health care. Through its dedicated recruitment, training, and development of a robust network of promotoras who form deep, lasting, and relevant relationships throughout Santa Ana, LHA has effectively rewoven the intricate tapestry of community by creating a powerful sense of belonging among families, neighbors, and residents. Belonging is a fundamental human drive that helps us find purpose and meaning in our lives. LHA begins by attending to our spiritual health and sense of shared humanity; by so doing, they bring deep healing that improves our physical health. By redefining health as connectedness to community and placing love in the center of their philosophy, LHA points us in the direction of potent community health solutions. Solutions that in 21st century America will resonate beyond just low-income communities.*"

—Tony Iton, JD, MD
    Senior Vice President of Healthy Communities, The California Endowment

"*This powerful book combines the wisdom of community and its 'homegrown leaders' with practical tools and principles honed by one of the foremost community institutions in the world. With emphasis on authentic participation, unlearning as well as learning, and providing strong, practice-based evidence, Latino Health Access and its promotores offer a critical new path to community-driven health equity processes and outcomes. Community organizers, community-engaged researchers, and others will appreciate this accessible and lively account of how a community institution, grounded in empowerment, critical thinking, and inclusiveness, can achieve sustainability and impressive health and social outcomes.*"

—Meredith Minkler, DrPH, MPH
    University of California at Berkeley

"This is a masterful work that describes in clarity and detail why promotores are so uniquely effective in leading individuals, families, and their neighborhoods to positive and sustainable health outcomes. This new offering published by Hesperian Health Guides shows us how it is done. For more than two decades, Latino Health Access has been training and integrating in their practice community members, most of whom are low-income immigrants. **Recruiting the Heart, Training the Brain** articulates brilliantly how the organization, in relationships based on dignity, respect, and mutual accountability, inspires its participants to recognize their own relational gifts, and to combine their neighborhood expertise with training and technical support. The results include remarkable successes in healthy behaviors, and individual, family, and community empowerment – the very foundation stones for building a healthy community.

"It has been my great joy to participate in shared learnings with Latino Health Access for more than 20 years. With characteristic wisdom and generosity, America Bracho and her colleagues have produced a book that will resonate deeply with other communities struggling against poverty and economic, racial, and linguistic marginalization. This book will speak directly to the hearts of its readers, and particularly to participants in other community-based promotora programs. **Recruiting the Heart, Training the Brain** comes alive with the voices of promotoras who share in their own words their sorrows, struggles, passions, and triumphs.

"**Recruiting the Heart, Training the Brain** will be a great contribution to health care institutions contemplating the integration of promotoras into their workforce. It underscores the necessity of appropriate institutional support, supervision, and respect for the integrity of their qualifications and for the unparalleled training they receive. It also strongly urges training of those institutions. There are profound lessons available to all readers from Latino Health Access' shining example. This book should be required reading for all who are interested in community health work."

—*Nancy Halpern Ibrahim, MPH*
   Executive Director, Esperanza Community Housing Corporation, Los Angeles, CA

"*LHA's story is one of remarkable organizational success, balancing an understanding of natural organizational development with a deliberate evolution from service delivery providers to champions of policy change. From the beginning, Latino Health Access has been a role model for working side-by-side with their community residents to create lasting change. Their experience shouts from the mountain top that the relationships we build with those we serve are fundamental and irreplaceable. It is through these relationships that the promotores move people into new spaces of civic engagement."

—*Harold Goldstein, DrPH*
   Executive Director, California Center for Public Health Advocacy

"The Canadian International Development Authority (CIDA) once evaluated their programs and concluded the single best predictor of success was the effective involvement of the people targeted by the program. In this book, America Bracho shows how true that is in a California community. Medicine is based on using the truth for a patient. Community health is based on using the truth for everyone, therefore, social justice is the driver. But Latino Health Access goes beyond social justice to social involvement, creating inspiring two-way bonds. Bracho demonstrates the power of coalition, where collective wisdom surpasses individual wisdom, where even children are involved in making individuals healthy within a healthy neighborhood, within a healthy city. Fatalism is replaced by power, with trust becoming the glue that holds it all together. Latino Health Access provides more than an inspirational story, it also provides an instruction manual for those interested in building dynamic and healthy communities. The good news is: There is hope!"

—William H. Foege, MD, MPH
  former Director, Centers for Disease Control
  Professor Emeritus, Rollins School of Public Health, Emory University

"*Recruiting the Heart, Training the Brain: The Work of Latino Health Access* is the powerful account of a bold approach to working collaboratively to improve the wellbeing of a community and its residents. The book's overarching narrative illustrates the successes that are possible when community members are engaged to tackle seemingly intractable issues. From recruiting promotores (community health workers) to successful health promotion programs to policy advocacy to create a healthy environment with playgrounds and walking trails, the stories within the larger narrative are exemplars of community engagement and collaboration, leadership development, and non-hierarchical ways of working. This book will leave the reader inspired, with renewed hope, and a sense of greater possibilities for social change."

—Salome Raheim, PhD, ACSW
  School of Social Work, University of Connecticut

"*Recruiting the Heart, Training the Brain* clearly represents and brightly illuminates both the needs and potentials of our communities. The book is an extraordinary treasure trove of LHA's experiences using the promotor model and deserves to be read by everyone interested in and committed to the process of building healthy, self-sufficient communities."

—Alexander Fajardo
  Executive Director, El Sol Neighborhood Center

"This is a must read for anyone who works with families and communities and dreams of changing the future. Based on years of hard won experience and discovery, America Bracho and her colleagues provide immediately useful guidance and practical tools for helping community members find their voice and advocate for their families, health, and quality of life. Interwoven with this practical content are thought-provoking and often profound ideas about what it means to work in partnership with vulnerable groups, and how we must rethink many of our most basic assumptions. I recommend you buy multiple copies – you will want to share this gem of a book with others."

—Lyndee Knox, PhD
  President and CEO, LA Net

"This clearly written and carefully conceived book will be a treasure for those struggling to achieve greater equity in health and in the community conditions that shape health."

—Paula Braveman, MD, MPH
  Director, Center on Social Disparities in Health
  University of California at San Francisco

"Ever since I was introduced to LHA's energetic and passionate approach to enabling change in communities that have been disenfranchised, I have been keen to know more. The principles of participation, collaboration, and partnership that guide their approach resonate strongly in my work in Australia, and in this exciting and long-awaited book, the concepts of empowerment through participation come alive. We see them in action. No longer abstract principles, they live in the practice, the people, and their stories of change. As a foundational text for anyone engaged in communities, **Recruiting the Heart, Training the Brain** will provide a companion on that journey, one that inspires and challenges, offering a rigorous account of how communities can become places of energy, change, and possibility. I have had the great good fortune to meet America Bracho and the LHA team of promotoras and am very excited that others now have the chance to know their work."

—Maggie Carey, Co-Director of Narrative Practices
  Adelaide, Australia

to Josepa

Recruiting the Heart, Training the Brain

The Work of Latino Health Access

America Bracho, MD, MPH
Ginger Lee, MPH
Gloria P. Giraldo, MPH
Rosa Maria De Prado, MFT
and the Latino Health Access Collective

hesperian
health guides

LATINO
HEALTH
ACCESS

Front cover photo: Norma, a *promotora* in the Emotional Wellness Program, does outreach in Santa Ana. As she gives away tortillas, she explains, "Tortillas are part of our culture. Violence is not." (Photographer: Josefina Jimenez, also a *promotora*)

Back cover photo: A family at a *Dia de los muertos* celebration inside the LHA building (Photographer: Moises Vazquez, also a *promotor*)

This book has been printed in Canada by Friesens, an employee-owned corporation, on FSC certified paper.

hesperian
health guides
Hesperian Health Guides
1919 Addison St. #304
Berkeley, California 94704 USA
www.hesperian.org

Credits

Editorial coordination: Todd Jailer
Editing: Cynthia Peters, Todd Jailer
Book and cover design and production: Kathleen Tandy
Production support: Kokaale Amissah-Aidoo, Rosy De Prado, Rosemary Jason, Miriam Lara-Meloy, Paula Worby
Proofreading: Sunah Cherwin
Photographers: Danny Cortez, Josefina Jimenez, Gloria Montiel, Tania Pantoja, Moisés Vazquez
Front cover photographer: Josefina Jimenez
Back cover photographer: Moises Vazquez
Ojo de Dios painting: Jesus Fajer

The Latino Health Access Collective

Guillermo Alvarez
Sarai Arpero
Teresa Baltazar
America Bracho
Adriana Brindis
Rosa E. Calderon
Patricia Cantero
Norma Ceballos
Alejandra Chavez
Noraima Chirinos
Norma Cordero
Iliana Coronado
Danniel Cortes
Luis Cortes
Rosy De Prado
Verenice Escobar
Elizabeth Estrada
Sandra Estrada
Antonio Flores
Guadalupe Galeana
Rosario Galeas
Angel Garcia
Catalina Garcia

Lupita Garcia
Victoria Garcia
Gloria Giraldo
Soledad Gomez
Maria Rubi Gonzalez
Bienvenida Guzman
Adriana Hernandez
Oscar Iglesias
Josefina Jimenez
Socorro Juarez
Francisca Leal
Ginger Lee
Suzi Lopez
Irma Macias
Mario Marin
Nancy Mejia
Hiromi Minakata
Adela Montañez
Gloria Itzel Montiel
Rafael A. Orozco
Hilda Ortiz
Ana Marcela Ortiz
Laura Pantoja

Tania Pantoja
Eduardo (Lalo) Perez
Maria de la Paz Perez
Luzy Piña
Rosalia Piñon
Celene Ponce
Esperanza Ramirez
Maricela Ramirez
Irma Rivera
Araceli Robles
Loreta Ruiz
Veronica Ruiz
Wilma Salomon
Flory Sowa
Gary Taylor
Gina Torres
Ana Urzua
Alejandro Vazquez
Moises Vazquez
Rosalia Vargas Villaseñor
Brenda Zeferino

Latino Health Access Board of Directors

George Avila
America Bracho
Modesto Diaz
Rita Cruz Gallegos
Victor Manuel Gonzalez

Herlinda E. Ramirez M.
Edwin Rivera
Catalina Santamaria
Dorothy Lane Siddall
Lilia Tanakeyowma

Acknowledgements

We would like to thank the community that has been leading these change efforts with heart and with unrelenting hope and energy for more than two decades. Many thousands of people have been involved in advancing the agenda of creating a healthier city, the process of which we have had the honor of capturing in this book. In addition to the current staff at LHA, whom we call *The LHA Collective*, we would be remiss if we did not thank all previous staff members, or our *LHA Alumni*, as we call them. They have invested their talents, dreams, and hard work in improving this community.

Kaiser Permanente and Winston F. Wong, MD, MS, FAAFP, Medical Director, Community Benefit, deserve special thanks for their encouragement and the Foundation's financial support of the writing of the manuscript. Their grant allowed us to carve out time to complete the book. Special thanks to Patricia Cantero, PhD, for her support and contributions to Chapter 10, and to Nancy Mejia, MPH, MSW, for her support and contributions to Chapter 1. Robert Ross, MD, CEO of The California Endowment, has been highly supportive of our work in the community and of the completion of this book. We thank him and The California Endowment for their phenomenal support, including a grant that allowed us to go to publication.

We are grateful to all foundations and sponsors that have made our work possible, particularly for the long term partnership and ongoing support of Marguerite Casey Foundation, The James Irvine Foundation, Hoag Community Benefits Initiative, particularly Dr. Gwen Parry, The Weingart Foundation, California Health Care Foundation, The California Wellness Foundation, The Orange County Community Foundation, St. Joseph Health and St. Joseph Foundation. We want to express our deep gratitude to Tom David who shared our vision of a better and more inclusive society, believed in our dream of creating Latino Health Access, and supported our efforts to make it a reality during its initial years through guidance and funding.

Finally, we wish to thank Alfonso Diaz from the Narrative Practices Collective in Mexico for his careful and thoughtful review of the near final draft, that allowed us to question some of our own assumptions and to clarify some areas of the manuscript.

It is with extreme gratitude that we acknowledge the team at Hesperian Health Guides for seeing the potential in our efforts, for their leadership in manifesting this book into the physical world, for their understanding of our philosophy during the editing phase, and for their encouragement along the way.

Contents

Preface *by Robert Ross* . . . . **ix**

Introduction: A Different Idea of Success *by America Bracho* . . . . **xiii**

1 Latino Health Access: An Institute of Community Participation **1**

Our theoretical underpinnings:
From global to local and from the past to the present 7

The first Healthy Cities project in Orange County 11
First things first: How did we translate
data priorities into action priorities? 12
The places: The anchor sites of Healthy Cities 92701 13

We cannot do it alone. 21
How do we work with other organizations? 23

Confluence of streams and riding the current 28

2 Participation Makes the Difference. **31**

Getting involved to generate solutions 32
If participation is so important, why is it not the norm? . . . 34
Are we missing opportunities to make
our communities healthier?. 35
Technical expertise is not enough 37

How do we re-learn to participate?. 38
Activating the participation and leadership of everyone . . . 38
What are the benefits of participating with others?. 39
If people see the value of participating, what are
their reasons for not participating? 42

Understanding where participants are:
The Participation Continuum 44
    Levels of Participation 44

How do we assess whether we are supporting the
participation of others? 48
    The worker for the job 49

3 Community Experts: Involving the *Promotores* of LHA 53

Promotores are community experts 54
    Promotores engage community strengths to
    address community needs 55

What do *promotores* do? 58

LHA's mission, strategic objectives, and
program outcomes by Areas 61
    Volunteer participation 71

Hope-Energy-Action Projects 73
    A model Hope-Energy-Action Project: The Children
    and Youth Initiative at Roosevelt Elementary School
    in Santa Ana, California 77
    LHA's work with children and youth today 84

**4 How We Work with *Promotores*: Recruiting the Heart
and Training the Brain 87**

Recruitment, co-learning/co-teaching, and
supportive supervision 88
    Characteristics of effective *promotores* 89
    Recruitment and selection in practice 91
    Educational level 95

Promotores as employees vs. *promotores* as volunteers 97
    The continuum from volunteer to paid employee 97

Training and learning with *promotores* at LHA 102
    Basic Training with *promotores* 107
    Promotores as trainers 109
    Commitment to ongoing learning 111

Should community experts be certified? 113
    Context of the debate about certification 113
    LHA's position on certification 116

Training community workers as part of the
health care team 117
If *promotores* are community experts,
who will certify them? 119
Supervision, coaching and support of *promotores*,
and the selection and recruitment of supervisors 123
Supervisors support *promotoras* in three main dimensions:
Human, technical, and financial/administrative 124

**5 What Have You Unlearned Lately? Paradigms for Learning
and Unlearning at LHA 131**
The Board of Directors of Latino Health Access 133
How do we learn and unlearn at LHA? 136
Re-cognizing and Re-naming 139
Paradigms analyzed and recreated 142

6 Principles of Practice: Guiding LHA's Community Work 145
LHA is not the community, nor is it an institution
separated from the community 159
Our participants are our co-workers 160
Validating the community's ways 163
Areas of tension with our own principles 167

7 The Personal and Professional 173
The workplace is a place where we spend part
of our lives together 174
Importance of stories 175
The responsibility to oneself 179

8 Our Work Performance: Competencies and Expectations 183
How do we improve, learn and unlearn, and become
increasingly competent at LHA? 191
Trainings 192
How do we validate and defend our model and our work? . . 197
How to innovate? 199

9 Sustaining Ourselves Financially.............................**201**

Partnering with foundations that share our philosophy 204
   Challenges in working with grants and contracts 207

Cross-training staff and fostering flexibility
in team members 213

Retaining a presence in the neighborhoods,
no matter what. 213

Investing energy in collaborative approaches. 215

Developing diverse means of financial support 215

Operationalizing fund development within LHA. 220
   Challenges in the fund development function 221

10 The Tangible and the Intangible: Finding New Ways to Measure...223

Evaluation is not research. 225
We value our system of communication across
the agency 226
We use a centralized database 227
We strive for balance 228

How do we develop and utilize appropriate methods
of evaluation for the type of work we perform? 229
   Reaching agreements with staff 230
   Outcome data: qualitative, quantitative, or both? 231

What are the roles of the *promotores* and the community
in evaluation? 233

**11 Reflections: For Institutions Working or Wanting to
Work with *Promotores*** **237**

What if we treated communities like institutions? 239
   Some practical advice about managing the intersection
   of community with institutions. 240

Final words: The people of my city 244

Bibliography **249**

Preface

by Robert K. Ross, MD

I first met the remarkable America Bracho and the good folks at Latino Health Access in 1999, and what a treat it was. At the time I was about to wrap up a seven-year stint as Health and Human Services Agency Director in San Diego County, and poised to embark on a new career in health philanthropy. The half-day site visit taught me more about the future of public health than any graduate course I had taken, book I had read, or article I had reviewed. In fact, the visit began the process of opening my eyes to the new public health – years after receiving an Ivy League education, completing a pediatric residency, and running two major-sized urban public health departments.

Here's why, and here's how. Under America Bracho's stewardship, Latino Health Access has emerged as the leading pathfinder in community-based public health practice and community empowerment. Those of us who are engaged in the battle for health equity and the reduction or elimination of health disparities tend to talk a really good game about "community empowerment" and "community engagement" – but we often fall short of reaching meaningful heights on both fronts.

Latino Health Access begins every health journey and every health battle (and make no mistake, addressing health inequity routinely involves battle) with the idea of participation. Neighborhood residents, parents, young people, the elderly, the poor, the non-poor, immigrants, citizens, butchers/bakers/candlestickmakers – are respectfully but assertively reached out to and engaged. It is as if the members of Latino Health Access have discovered that there is something fundamentally therapeutic about civic engagement – the path to health equity and healing begins with participation in the process. Key words and phrases soon follow: leadership, outreach, strength, training, learning, commitment. The chapters of the book you are about to immerse yourself in will challenge you to think deeply about these concepts.

There is an adage that community organizers and youth organizers often utilize, that goes something like this: "Nothing about us, without us." America Bracho and LHA have mastered the art and science of community health by putting community first and foremost. This is the first critical lesson about the new public health: community participation is not a box to be checked; it is, in fact, the fuel that drives the car on the road to health equity. Data and research help with understanding how far the car must go, but the fuel of community participation and empowerment is what gets it there.

While LHA did not invent the *promotora* model of community health improvement, they darn sure make it work here in the U.S. Their approach is the quintessential "assets-based" model; every participant has something meaningful to bring to the table, and every cultural tradition or practice is a potential lever in advancing towards a state of wellness. I recall a story related to me by several *promotoras* during one of my visits there.

It seems that several of the LHA *promotoras* – during the course of their community visits in diabetes and chronic disease management – were picking up clear indications of domestic violence occurring in several of the homes in a certain neighborhood in Santa Ana. They also observed that suspicious bruising increased after a weekend featuring a big boxing match on television, as the sport of boxing is cherished by many Mexican and Mexican-American men.

The *promotoras* had deciphered the epidemiologic trail of these domestic violence incidents: a big boxing match is scheduled for television, a group of men agree to join one another at a bar or someone's home, beer and liquor flow freely, and inebriated men later unleash frustrations on their partners or spouses at home. The *promotoras* engaged one another and devised a simple approach to begin the process of addressing domestic violence as a local public health problem.

The intervention in this case was for LHA, working with local leaders and involving a church, to host the next televised boxing match, making it a family affair featuring children, families, tamales, and alcohol-free beverages. This simple but brilliant approach demonstrated a family-friendly, culturally anchored alternative to the boxing-beer-brutality problem – a disruptive innovation of sorts – and its success also paved the way for the *promotoras* (and *promotores*) to develop a men's support group on family violence. This approach was embraced by the women in the community because a campaign encouraging battered women to "just dial 911" on their husbands was not the desired outcome here – particularly when matters of immigration and poor relations with law enforcement tainted this approach as a viable strategy.

As a former public health official, I can say with assurance that no one who has ever worked for me in a local public health department would have conceived the idea of using a televised boxing match to catalyze a community-based domestic violence prevention strategy. Such is the wisdom of community.

Recruiting The Heart, Training the Brain is a powerful reminder that addressing inequality in our nation – in this case, through a health lens – indeed requires the discipline of data collection, science-based analysis, and carefully constructed prevention and early intervention strategies. But even more importantly, it calls upon those of us in health and public health settings to engage, to listen, to be willing to look into someone's heart and allow their story to be told. As a mentor of mine advised me early in my public health career: If you are embarking on moving a health strategy or policy forward, "no numbers without stories and no stories without numbers." Engagement and storytelling by marginalized and disenfranchised communities not only provides meaningful data, but empowers health as well: health activism, health advocacy, and community health organizing

Dr. Robert Ross and America Bracho at the Latino Health Access Gala in 2014

are unleashed. What soon follows are more and safer community parks, healthier food options in stores and schools, and health-promoting policies in city, county, and regional plans.

America Bracho tells us how the road to health equity in our nation begins with meaningful community engagement, trust building, data gathering, and action oriented power building. Welcome to the new public health for our nation.

Robert K. Ross, MD
President and CEO
The California Endowment

Introduction:
A Different Idea of Success

by America Bracho, MD, MPH

It is an immense privilege to present this book to you. It brings
together discussions, learnings, and recommendations growing out
of the community work that Latino Health Access has carried out
for more than 20 years. We invite you to consider the ideas, lessons,
and questions resulting from our individual and team experiences,
and the collective wisdom built from living and interacting with
our communities. Our goal in writing this book is to share our
experiences and to provide ideas and inspiration to all those who
want to start or improve their own community practice.

 The entire organization contributed in one way or another
to making this book. A smaller group participated in the writing
process. It took us seven years. Throughout these years, as we wrote
the first drafts and shared them with the team at Latino Health
Access (LHA), something marvelous happened: We were led to
contemplate our work as spectators, to look with outsiders' eyes and
reflect upon what we do, trying to understand why and how we
were doing it. At first, we had to confront the difficulty of writing
about ourselves and sharing our internal tensions, lack of consistency,
and imperfections. During this process, we questioned the things that
do not work as well as those that do. We discovered that the most
difficult part of the process was not the recognition of our failures,

but the validation of our successful practice by analyzing, naming, and defining it, and then daring to put it in writing.

The process of stopping to reflect and share our lessons, beliefs, doubts, fears, and successes has not been easy, particularly since our work is immersed in a society that privileges money, power, prestige, the exclusive, the individual, academic theories, recognition and professional titles, one-size-fits-all interventions, impressive triumphs, and gigantic successes. Writing this book invited us to think about the social value and the lack of social value given to community work with low-income families who are often unaware of their own power. The more we talked, the more we uncovered and reaffirmed our different idea of success, one based on our different way of doing community work. We share with you a model of building leadership, of an inclusive practice that involves ongoing dialogue, in which the academic and scientific co-exist with the experience and wisdom of common people, where everybody is an expert, and where all successes are important.

We embarked on the task of investigating our most successful internal practices in order to elevate them as "best practices" for the entire organization and encourage their use in all our programs. Our successes are dependent on a deep connection with the women, men, youth, and children in our neighborhoods. Our community constantly reminds us of what is relevant and what is important. We believe in the right of our families to be heard and to be treated in a caring, respectful, and equitable way, in safe environments where they are trusted and not intimidated. It is clear to us that regardless of how many important interactions we have on a daily basis, the most important ones are those with individuals from our communities that surround us. They are our priority and we need to devote time and love to them. Our team is convinced and operates under the assumption that we all are leaders, not because we have followers, rather because we are all owners of the capacity to make decisions: staff and community members alike. The *promotora* who arranges safe afterschool programs for kids, the mother who makes tamales to pay her rent, and the woman who prays with others when they lose a loved one. All are leaders.

The creation of this book helped us to write our own definitions, to improve and re-commit to the principles that guide our organization. Since our inception, we have been committed to developing and documenting the principles and values that guide our organization, and in this book you will find the 20 principles that guide our work. These principles allow us to confront ourselves when we behave in ways that do not honor what we believe is fair or appropriate. They allow us to see what is aligned with our philosophy, or what has nothing to do with it, and to make decisions accordingly.

We have also tried to be transparent about our assumptions in these pages. For example, we say, "Assumption: People in our communities want the best for themselves and their families." This is an assumption under which we work. Others may assume something different. Whatever the assumptions are – whether or not we believe in the capacity of people without formal education to be leaders, that we all are leaders, that participation in every aspect of one's life is a right – those assumptions, sometimes conscious and sometimes not, greatly influence the ways we work – in particular, the ways we do community work and the ways we evaluate our successes.

LHA is a very special place and organization. It opens its doors and embraces children, youth, and adults, and invites them to build community. Our work is guided by a heart that feels love for our community and expresses that love through acts of solidarity. It is a heart that gives us courage to fight for what we think is right and fair. It is a heart filled with compassion but not pity; it suffers with the pain of others and the lack of justice and opportunities for our families, but it does not despair. It is a heart that compels us to share our time, resources, and stories in solidarity so we all can become stronger. Obviously, our work is also guided by the brain and the many experiences, lessons, and skills that exist among team members and outside LHA. Still, we have seen how difficult it is to connect and mobilize our neighbors, to invite them to be part of improving their communities when the call comes only from the brain.

At LHA we make every attempt to recruit loving hearts: the woman who came to manage her diabetes but by the second class was offering support to others; the man who is a recovered addict and approaches individuals battling addictions with a profound sense of love and respect; the woman who came to us to figure out how to stop violence at home and now offers her home to other women in similar circumstances; the women who cook beans and tortillas to provide a snack so our kids can eat during our very underfunded children's programs. We recruit hearts that allow people to be creative, find solutions, find each other, work together, and overcome barriers and conflicts during difficult times. At LHA we recruit the hearts and train the brains. This does not mean that we operate in a mythical land of perfection and balance. It only means that we let the love for our people, for our vulnerable communities, our immigrants, our many moms, dads, kids, sisters, brothers, and friends trying to live happy, healthy lives in very difficult circumstances to become central in our strategies. It means that we do not apologize for letting love be central to our work, and we do not let our brains be embarrassed by our hearts.

We started our work in Orange County, California, in 1993. Since then we have developed different strategies and programs to carry out our mission of partnering and supporting working families so they can have the resources and the environment they need to enjoy health and prosperity, actively encouraging the participation of every person in the processes of learning and transformation by which we measure success.

In this strong partnership that LHA has with our communities, we carry out our strategies in teams of staff and neighbors that include experts in a variety of areas. Our community experts are the *promotoras*. They are people from our communities, many of whom came to LHA as participants in our programs, after which they became volunteers and later on health promoters or *promotores* (known in many places as community health workers). We began with a few volunteer *promotoras*. Now, 41 out of 67 employees are paid *promotores* working in different communities throughout the county, finding community members everywhere – in laundromats and on the streets, at bus stops and in markets. They visit families in their homes and invite people to participate. They educate and they serve.

The families and neighbors from our communities arrive daily to our offices and programs. We make sure they understand that our facility is theirs and that we are there to serve them. They come to participate in programs, to talk about their lives, to seek help or share their successes, to volunteer, to exercise their leadership, and most importantly, to become community with us and among themselves.

At LHA, we acknowledge our many successes, both large and small. These successes give us energy. They help us get out of bed every morning. They give us the strength to continue moving forward when problems arise, when we face difficult moments inside or outside the organization. We succeed every time we share a health, wellness, or prosperity message with our communities; when we meet our neighbors; when a woman leaves a violent relationship; when a man decides to enter a recovery home rather that hit his partner again; when a young person engages in advocacy; when moms and kids raise funds to go to the local aquarium.

We are successful when an older adult is contacted by our door-to-door *promotor* team and connected with services and other seniors. We are successful when a person with diabetes learns to manage her condition and prevents blindness or improves her sight after receiving low-cost or free eye surgery from our volunteer doctors. We are successful when our breast health outreach team connects a person to life-saving treatment; when an individual accepts and learns to live with her mental condition or to effectively manage her emotions thanks to our Emotional Wellness Program; when a group of parents improve their relationships with their children thanks to our Mother-to-Mother Program.

We have been successful in creating open spaces and changing institutional and government policies with the guidance and incredible effort of LHA's Community Engagement and Advocacy Department. After 11 years of organizing, advocating, and fundraising in a joint effort with community and business partners, they succeeded in establishing the *Familias Corazones Verdes* Park and Community Center so our children and families can finally play and enjoy themselves in a safe space.

We are successful every time we recruit an adult or young neighbor as an employee of our organization and support their quality of life through the opportunity to help their neighbors improve theirs. Likewise, we are successful when we recruit talented individuals with skills gained through higher education who are willing to share their knowledge and experience. We are successful when we bring financial resources to support local jobs and programs. More than anything, we have been successful defending our inclusive, committed, and respectful way of doing community work.

We have had success in attracting national media to help increase awareness about the reality of our communities. We have made inroads into local media to share the cultural expressions flowering in our communities, and to challenge the negative and disempowering portrayals of Latinos and low-income people that bombard us relentlessly from the mass media.

LHA works with the community to solve immediate problems and provide short-term relief while at the same time helping the community propose and advocate for longer-term solutions. Creating healthier communities in situations characterized by inequity, lack of opportunity, and social injustice is a complicated proposition requiring complex responses. It is necessary to nurture the seeds of change along the way, and doing so is a success, too.

We support the creation of healthier communities where families can raise their kids safely with opportunities to develop their potential; where every person can aspire to enjoy life and become a productive, prosperous individual with a decent job that doesn't turn off their mind, break their body, destroy the environment, or leave them in poverty; where neighbors enjoy mutual support; where local government is accountable and committed to the benefit of all the people they represent; where threats of deportation and police violence are unacceptable; where local participation and leadership is so common that decision-making and accomplishment are seen as collective events. These are some of the successes we have achieved and will continue to achieve through our brand of organizing that builds capacity and multiplies leadership. How can we not be successful when our communities are bursting with so much strength, talent, energy, wisdom, and love?

Our communities are calling for transformative leadership that can help us build social and economic justice as the path toward a better life for all. It's not easy. It requires vision, patience, persistence, consistency, long-term commitment, discipline, self-awareness, mutual respect, and a profound faith in one's self and in one's community. We accept this challenge with humility and joy.

This book represents the experience of LHA in taking responsibility for creating change. If you are already a part of such change, or have already decided to lead efforts for making change in your community, or if you are considering embarking on such an adventure, we hope this book will give you some tools you can immediately use, adapt, and improve upon, as well as other ideas that you can file away for later. We offer this with the understanding that every community's context and realities are different. Ours is one framework of many that are improving health around the world. Latino Health Access is a non-profit organization engaged in public health work in a relatively large U.S. city, with community members inside and outside of the organization leading this change. We humbly acknowledge the richness of the many approaches to improving health in diverse communities around the world. We all can learn from each other. We don't purport to have the one and only way, but rather a way that has worked to move us toward having a healthier community where we live. We offer what we have done in Santa Ana, California, in the hopes that some parts will be useful to you, and would love to hear about your own experiences and successes.

Now, and with all our love, we share with you this book that tells the story of Latino Health Access, a beautiful story of growth and of personal, professional, and community transformation. Enjoy!

America Bracho, MD, MPH
President and CEO
Latino Health Access

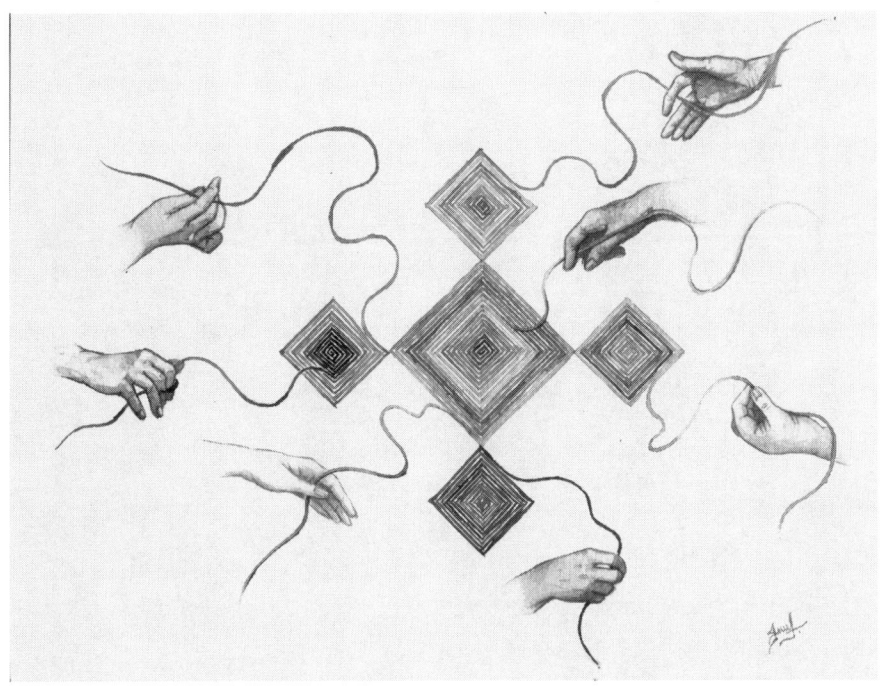

"Ojo de Dios" by Jesus Fajer

Ojo de Dios is Spanish for "Eye of God." The *Ojo de Dios* is an ancient indigenous symbol found in several cultures, including the Cora and the Huichol. God's Eye is symbolic of the power of seeing and understanding that which is unknown and unknowable, the Mystery. It is believed to offer protection. When a Huichol child is born in Mexico, the central eye is woven by the family. Later, one layer in a different color is added to the eye for every year of the child's life until the child reaches the age of five. Then the *Ojo de Dios* is presented to the child, who adds a color for every birthday. When the child comes of age, at about age 11, he or she gives the *Ojo de Dios* back to the tribe for safe keeping. This sends a message to the tribe, a reminder of the duty to take care of the children. Likewise, it sends a message to the children that, while they have a say, they are in the care of the tribe. Latino Health Access chose this symbol as our logo because it represents our commitment to creating mechanisms for all of us to care for our youth and our entire community.

(Adapted from en.wikipedia.org/wiki/God's_eye and stories from LHA families.)

LATINO HEALTH ACCESS

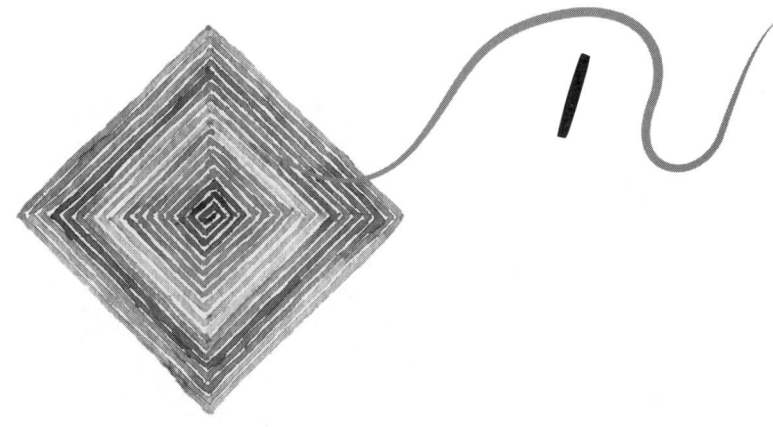

Latino Health Access:
An Institute of Community Participation

"Now that my sons are adolescents, parenting is harder. It is nerve-wracking as a parent to know that your children cannot leave the house because it is not safe out there; not the next street over, not the next neighborhood. It is not safe! Not because we need more police officers but because we need more activities in which youth can feel valued and involved. It really hit home when Moises, a young community health worker, said, 'One needs more than the love of one's parents to not get involved with the wrong crowd.' I am trying to be a very loving mother, to build good communication with my children, and to keep up with their lives, but my surroundings conspire against us by putting my children at risk at every moment."

—Sarai, *mother of four and promotora, Santa Ana, California*

This is the voice of a mother in Santa Ana, California, but it could be the voice of a mother in almost any community in the world affected by poverty. We know well that our children – your children and my children – have dramatically different opportunities in life depending on where they were born and in which country, state, province, county, city, or ZIP code they were raised. The differences in life chances by geographical place are striking and are

1

A mother with her children attends a community meeting.

seen worldwide. The members of society most affected by poverty have higher levels of illness and die earlier. But poor health does not afflict only people in poverty. In countries at all levels of income, health and illness follow what is called a "social gradient" which means that the lower the socioeconomic position, the worse the health. A girl born in Switzerland in 2012 can expect to live 85 years (World Health Organization, 2008), but a girl born in Sierra Leone can only expect to live 46 years (World Health Organization, 2014). In the United States, a girl born in Marin County, California, can expect to reach her 85th birthday; however, if she happens to be born in Perry County, Kentucky, she can only expect to make it to 72 (Institute for Health Metrics and Evaluation, 2013). These remarkable differences are not the result of biology; they are the result of unequal conditions in which people are born, grow, learn, work, play, and age. These conditions are called social determinants of health, and differences in these conditions contribute to abysmal differences in life opportunities and in how long a person will ultimately live.

This is not new information. If you are reading this book, chances are you already know this either because you have read countless reports and attended thousands of meetings, or because you live in a place challenged by inequality. You may also believe that this reality does not have to be this way, that it is not right that your ZIP code can predict your opportunities in life. You may wake up every day to fight for social justice in your own life or go to work every day to try to change the current reality because you have joined so many around the world who believe that "social injustice is killing people on a grand scale" (World Health Organization, 2008). If that's what you do and that's how you think, then we have a lot in common. And we would like to share with you what we are doing about it, and how the work of challenging injustice has motivated us to remain involved. We would like to share our story.

Our Beginnings

Latino Health Access was created in 1993 with the idea of responding to the health needs of Latinos and under-served communities in Orange County, California. The idea of the organization was born from the observation that in Orange County, as in many parts of the world, the communities affected by poverty had a long list of needs that co-existed with a very low level of political influence. The low level of engagement of the community contributed greatly to the continuation of all kinds of health and social problems, and stood as the major obstacle to the creation of healthier communities.

These low-income communities in Orange County were home to hundreds of thousands of Latino families, many of them immigrants in need of resources and services. In 1993, a group of us, immigrants ourselves and raising our own families in the U.S., conducted the first study to assess the health needs of Latinos in Orange County (Delhi Community Center and *Bienestar Familiar* Project/HERR Coalition, 1993). We were painfully aware of the need for culturally appropriate, accessible health services in our communities, and the study in a sense ratified and amplified our own first-hand knowledge of the community's health needs, the gaps in health services, and the insufficiency of resources to close those gaps. We were also well aware of the discrimination and constant harassment that were victimizing our families. We knew that no stopgap measure would provide a fix. We could see that no single resource would address our community's needs. So we started to consider creating an organization that could provide ongoing services to low-income individuals and families, as well as help us find, with the community, new ways to address the systemic injustice they were facing.

Our initial conversations included an analysis of the most-needed services, such as programs to prevent and manage chronic diseases. We also discussed the important behaviors that we all need to practice in order to have healthier lives and create a healthier community, including healthier eating and active living as important behaviors. We also began to think about participation as a health behavior, and what might happen if we really were successful in expressing our opinions and taking action to improve the health of the community. We understood from day one that we needed to make room for our community members' many strengths and talents and include them. We agreed that, from a strategic point of view, we needed to re-learn how to participate and invite others to do so as well. The rationale of our conversations went like this: "When we participate, not only can we accomplish many things, but we can do them faster. We can have more programs and better outcomes, and we can do all of that while building capacity to create the changes our families and communities want to see." We compared this cooperative and inclusive approach with the traditional ways that other organizations brought projects into communities. Many projects had good intentions, but only dealt with a single issue, such as tuberculosis, drug treatment, or smoking cessation. The program staff worked to help individuals in need, and individuals were indeed helped. But the conditions that created the health issues in the first place were left untouched.

Therefore, the central questions in our minds during these conversations were: How much healthier will this community be in 30 years with a traditional intervention? What could happen if, instead, we created spaces to multiply leadership so more of us could participate in the improvement of our health, the strengthening of our families, and the transformation of our communities?

As the founding group of LHA, we asked ourselves the following questions:

- How can we build an organization that can offer leadership to multiply leadership?
- How can we create a healthier community and offer services at the same time?
- How can we include people from the most vulnerable sectors of society in all aspects of our process in a way that honors their wisdom and strengths?
- How can we create an organization committed to the philosophy that every person has the right and duty to articulate her thoughts, use her voice, and take a leading role in the changes she wants for her life?

We were challenged to find answers to these questions while at the same time addressing the realities facing Latinos in Orange County. All of us in the group were public health practitioners dealing with unmet needs that were now documented in the first health report about Latinos, needs that required immediate action. Therefore, offering and connecting families with health services was recognized as a responsibility and obligation. The community needed programs for health promotion, and for disease prevention and management. We had the strength and talent in the community to provide the services. We decided to start our work by creating a program that could offer a very important and needed service: helping people with diabetes who did not have health insurance. We started the first Diabetes Self-Management Program conducted in Spanish in Orange County in 1994. During the implementation of the program, we were able to identify participants who were particularly caring, responsible, respectful, and helpful. This was our opportunity to recruit the first group of community experts, also called *"promotores"*[1] and "community health workers," to support the program and become trainers. People learned how to manage their condition and how to help others.

---

1 *Promotoras* and *promotores* are women and men community health workers. Throughout the book, we have chosen to use the feminine (*promotora*) and masculine (*promotor*) forms of the noun interchangeably.

Sure enough, the Diabetes Self-Management Program was a success in the hands of a team that included experts in public health and community experts (people with diabetes from the same community). Positive clinical outcomes were reported. When it came to serving people with diabetes, *promotores* were accomplishing what other institutions and programs had not been able to do.

Simultaneously, *promotores* and participants started discussing the desperate conditions in which they were living. They spoke of the difficulty they experienced trying to follow nutritional recommendations due to lack of food. They described over-crowded living conditions, such as a family of five living in a garage with no place to cook. They started to share their experiences and perceptions: their fear of walking, jogging, or getting any kind of exercise in the streets because the neighborhood was not safe; the absence of nearby parks where they could play with their children; their inability to consistently come to class or to arrive on time because they were working 60 hours per week; their inability to come on their own because they lacked transportation and did not know how to navigate the public transportation system; their fear of coming alone because they could not read the names of the streets; and their high level of stress due to family problems, economic hardship, loneliness, and more. Participants were explaining the conditions that influenced their opportunities to be healthier – known in public health as "the social determinants of health" (World Health Organization, 2008). They were surrounded by conditions that interfered with their ability to prevent and manage chronic diseases. Residents of the 92701 ZIP code, one of the lowest-income areas in Orange County, made up the majority of our initial group of participants.

LHA responded to our participants with solidarity. We provided food, connected people with resources, provided transportation and child care, and created opportunities to help participants find solutions. Two years later in 1996, LHA started the first place-based project in Orange County, known as "Healthy Cities 92701." LHA recruited and hired new *promotoras* to expand the work. They were deployed as outreach workers, service providers, and community organizers in the 92701 ZIP code. We started a process of identifying opportunities and problems. *Promotoras* provided the necessary leadership to create LHA's first Emotional Wellness Program. We added more *promotores* to our staff. They became the heart of the organization, allowing LHA to respond in real time to crises arising in our neighborhoods. Their feedback and observations guided LHA to develop new programs and strategies. A few years later, LHA created a policy department to structure our advocacy work. We started advocating for policy changes in schools, health care, and city and county governments. This became our "multiplying leadership" approach, answering some of the questions we had raised at our inception in 1993.

Since 1993, LHA's programs have achieved many successful outcomes and made tangible changes at the community level and in the lives of thousands of participants. Throughout this time, LHA has made participation central to its work and the *promotores* the driving force at its core. Since our inception, we knew that we needed a framework to guide us. We are privileged to have been showered with ideas from all over the world, as well as wisdom from around the block.

Our theoretical underpinnings: From global to local and from the past to the present

Wisdom from around the world

"Healthy Cities" and "social determinants of health" are terms that have become part of the daily conversation of public health. These terms have been recycled through different eras of public health but were born again, so to speak, in a major way since the 1970s. In international arenas, from the late 1970s all the way to the mid-1990s, there was much excitement about setting the course to achieve "Health for All" by the year 2000. Global conventions brought forth landmark proclamations such as the Alma-Ata Declaration of 1978, which emerged as a major milestone of the twentieth century in the field of public health. It identified primary health care as the key to attaining the goal of "Health for All" (World Health Organization, 1978). A few years later, in 1986, the Lisbon meeting of 21 European cities launched the Healthy Cities project (Ashton, 1992). These world events, conferences, and declarations shaped a new era in public health, which liberated the concept of health from the constraints of the biomedical model and redefined health as a process intertwined with prevailing social, political, economic, and environmental conditions. These declarations and definitions are important because they express the consensus of people around the globe who are fighting to end health inequity.

Wisdom from around the block

From this global perspective, let's adjust our lens and zoom in on Orange County, California, which itself was in the midst of a demographic and sociopolitical transformation in the 1980s. A quick look at history shows that Orange County's urbanization and industrialization moved forward at a dizzying pace. A recent report by the University of California at Irvine and the University of California at Los Angeles Labor Centers provides a great historical summary of the region, highlighting that before World War II, the county had a population of 130,000 and was a predominantly rural area with an agriculture-based economy. Today, Orange County is one of the most urbanized counties in California with a population of more than 3.1 million. In the last two decades, Orange County's economy has shifted toward reliance on the service and information sectors, with a particular emphasis on tourism. Small manufacturing plants and the tourism and service sectors created jobs that paid much lower wages than the large plants there previously had offered; hence this labor force demand was filled by immigrant labor. Much of the county's population growth from the 1950s to the 1970s was driven by domestic and international migration. Today, immigrants make up one-third of the county's population, with more than 922,000 immigrants from every region of the world. Among immigrants, 21% arrived since 2000, and another 58% arrived between 1980 and 2000. Today, fewer than half (43%) of Orange County residents self-identify as non–Hispanic white, while 19% identify as Asian or Pacific Islander (API), and 34% identify as Latino (Waheed, Romero, and Sarmiento, 2014). Based on the latest census data, there are 1,065,112 Latinos who call Orange County home (U.S. Census Bureau, 2014).

When Latino Health Access began, the statewide political context in California was marked by anti–immigrant sentiment evidenced by legislation such as Proposition 187, also known as the Save Our State (SOS) initiative. This ballot initiative was passed in 1994, but was later ruled unconstitutional by a federal court. If allowed to go forward, this law would have required California police, health care professionals, and teachers to verify and report the immigration status of all individuals, including children, who sought their services (Martin, 1995).

It is in this context that LHA founding members came together with a vision of forming an organization in Santa Ana, the heart of Orange County. We embraced a holistic model of health and saw health as determined in large part by social conditions. We were influenced by global public health movements and work experiences in communities around the world, in inner cities in California, and in Orange County itself. When we created LHA, we had a long-term vision of community transformation. The vision begged a strategy that incorporated the participation of those most affected by social inequities. The community members, the *promotoras*, and the founding board members at LHA worked together to generate questions, including:

- How can we solve the problem of obesity if we don't have parks where people can exercise?
- How do we reduce violence if we don't reduce access to alcohol and drugs?
- How do we address the emotional and mental health situations affecting individuals involved in violence and drugs?
- How do we increase safety if we don't invest in prevention, work to strengthen neighborhood leadership, and improve coordination with law enforcement?
- How do we create policies that benefit our communities if we don't vote?
- How can our vulnerable children, youth, and families have better opportunities in life if social institutions do not invest in and protect our communities?

These were and continue to be complex questions. While we do not claim we have a magic formula, we have found coherence in a paradigm and a framework to guide our work. The two approaches to public health that have anchored us philosophically are the Healthy Cities model and its ever-present companion, the social determinants of health. These frameworks have helped us situate ourselves from the beginning in the physical places where people live, work, and play, that is: where health is created, promoted, or inhibited. It is in these places that people's lives unfold and health outcomes are determined, depending on access to income, quality education, health services, power, favorable immigration status, and many other social conditions. What is the Healthy Cities model exactly? Here is a good working definition:

> "A locality-based strategic and systemic approach of social, physical and individual determinants of health and disease incorporating the full involvement of communities in the formulation, implementation and evaluation of policies and interventions aiming at equity in health and sustainable development."
>
> —Takano, 2003

Another way of explaining this model is to ask people what they think a healthy city is. People do not generally have any difficulty coming up with answers. All they have to do is think about where they want to live and how they want to raise their family. After posing the question to thousands of people in the U.S. and around the world, here is what they say:

> "A healthy city is a place that is clean, calm, and pleasant, with safe streets, high quality child care, and decent schools. It is a place where arts and culture are part of daily life, where diversity is appreciated, and there is freedom of belief and expression. It is a place where people have medical insurance and good health care, people are friendly, the community is involved in what happens in the city, and no one is excluded from civic engagement. It is a place where people can grow fruits and vegetables, free of factories that damage health, where everyone has access to safe drinking water, and where you can enjoy safe parks. It is a place with employment opportunities that offer a living wage, where people can find decent affordable housing and aren't homeless, where everyone knows their neighbors and can share with them. It is a place with a sense of community, where people are united, where there are no liquor stores near schools and no immigration raids, where police are friendly and helpful, where there are enough garbage bins, where industrial zones are well separated from residential zones, and where politicians work for the people and are accountable to the residents. This is what a healthy city is."

Evidently, people know what a healthy city looks and feels like. They have an idea of what it would be like to live in one. The question is: Where do we start? How is a healthy city built? The academic experts tell us there are three main pillars upon which we can build a healthier city:

1. local data, including place-based data;
2. community engagement (genuine participation); and
3. multiple stakeholder collaboration (World Health Organization, 1995, 1997).

Community experts tell us, "Go find your people, create relationships, involve them with common purpose, increase their participation, and you will transform your neighborhoods into healthier places."

At LHA, we listened and learned from both the academic and community experts.

The first Healthy Cities project in Orange County

LHA started its first Healthy Cities project in 1996. We launched it in five low-income neighborhoods in the 92701 ZIP code of Santa Ana, California. The total population of the city was 293,742 with approximately 60,000 people in this particular ZIP code. At that time, Latinos made up approximately 70% of the city's population, and the percentage was higher in the 92701 area. We selected 92701 because it was the most impoverished ZIP code in Orange County; the median annual income at the time was between $15,000 and $20,000, compared to the whole county's median, which was about $66,000 (Ovanessian, 1996; Alberts and Bermudez, 2001).

The academics say local data is a key pillar in the building of Healthy Cities. Yet during the early 1990s, health data about the city of Santa Ana was unorganized and unavailable, and specific data for the partner neighborhoods of our Healthy Cities project was absent. So our first step was to collect health data at the neighborhood level. To do this, we partnered with the Orange County Department of Health to gather the data. A local foundation, the Sisters of St. Joseph Healthcare Foundation, funded the data collection. LHA's *promotores* participated in developing the questions and conducting the surveys, first in 1996 and again in 2000 (Ovanessian, 1996; Alberts and Bermudez, 2001). In both cases, data from the neighborhood not only came from the survey but from the observations, testimonies, and photographs taken by *promotores* and other members of the team. The data confirmed what we already knew: there was over-crowding, very low levels of education, and a high concentration of low-income families surviving with minimal resources. The first survey showed that the average number of people living together was 5.6, sometimes in a one-bedroom apartment. More than half of the respondents had six years or fewer of education, 86% were immigrants from Mexico, and 46% worked in labor or service occupations. The most commonly reported health concerns were diabetes, high blood pressure, and asthma (Ovanessian, 1996).

After we analyzed the survey and produced the report, we knew the information wouldn't lead to any changes unless we shared it with the people of the 92701 ZIP code. So we took the results into the community at the beginning of 1997, sharing them with approximately 300 neighbors in a conference room at a local church. The issues of safety, alcohol abuse, violence, lack of afterschool activities for youth, and lack of parks and other open spaces were front and center. The next step was to ask attendees to think about solutions and to share their talents, skills, and ideas. People completed forms expressing a willingness to help improve their community. LHA followed up with them, creating the first group of committed neighbors who guided services and activities.

First things first: How did we translate data priorities into action priorities?

The recommendations and partnerships created during these initial years through surveys, events, community gatherings, and consultations were critical in the development of multiple programs and strategies in the years that followed. We were able to attract funding to bring relevant programs into the community, such as asthma and diabetes management, nutrition education, immunization, home safety, mental health, awareness about alcohol abuse and misuse, afterschool programs for children and youth, and policy work around the creation of open spaces and safer communities, just to mention a few. These programs and strategies evolved from a focus on services only to a combined focus on services and policy change, with a strong community engagement component as prescribed by the Healthy Cities model. And then Santa Ana became a healthier city. End of story.

Not quite. If that had been how it worked, we never would have written this book. But as you can see, this is only the first chapter. While it is true that there was a committed group of neighbors who had many successes organizing for health equity, there were (and still are) many competing priorities that make it hard for us to sustain people's attention and commitment for the extended length of time necessary to transform our city into a healthier city. Although we worked on creating partnerships, maintaining them, creating new ones, and forging authentic relationships at all levels, this process takes a high level of skill, patience, collective sense of purpose, and many years of persistence and tenacity. The steps we have described so far – identifying a geographic area, conducting surveys to collect local data, sharing data with neighbors, identifying committed neighbors willing to help, building relationships with institutions, and getting funding to carry out projects – are necessary and foundational steps. But this is not a linear story at all! This is an iterative process that is re-invented every time we go into a neighborhood or into an apartment building.

The places: The anchor sites of Healthy Cities 92701

The people living in the zones where we were gathering information needed to have the opportunity to place their story in the context of the whole community. They needed the opportunity to see that their personal problems were also experienced by their neighbors, and the conditions fostering these problems were affecting entire neighborhoods.

Although the people coming together to listen to our report definitely shared common aspects of life and health conditions, we could not assume that they shared a sense of community belonging. The data collection had taken place in an area defined by the arbitrary boundaries of a ZIP code, not necessarily neighborhood-based boundaries. Furthermore, many immigrant families were relative newcomers, having been in the country for less than ten years at the time of our first ZIP code survey.

Instead of assuming that people felt a sense of community, our approach was to build a sense of community. We started building relationships with people directly where they lived – in their apartment buildings. We chose five large apartment buildings and a few nearby blocks with smaller apartment buildings. These five small neighborhoods within the ZIP code became the anchors of the Healthy Cities 92701 umbrella project where many other projects have since taken place.

Place 1: Roosevelt Elementary School and its surrounding community

The largest effort in our community work was devoted to community engagement, the second pillar of Healthy Cities. Without realizing it in 1996, the relationships we were building with and among neighbors, apartment managers, and some single-family homeowners would eventually move us closer to the sometimes elusive goal of creating a healthier city. Between 1996 and 2006, the main focus of the work in these neighborhoods was on weaving relationships by bringing in services. These services ranged from childhood immunizations to all types of health education classes, advocacy work, and leadership programs. (We will be discussing service-oriented programs throughout the book because they not only deliver much needed help to community members, but they also are critical in building relationships.)

One such service-oriented project was the Children and Youth Initiative, which we started with parents at the local Roosevelt Elementary School. The school is situated in a very dense, park-poor, low-income neighborhood with a high crime rate and lots of gang activity. LHA *promotores* had been working in the area for several years in different projects related to parenting and healthy living. Through these projects, many parents became involved.

LHA began the Children and Youth Initiative as a response to conditions identified by *promotores* in the area, namely, parents' concerns about the lack of after school opportunities for their children. (For a full description of this project and how it emerged, see chapter 3, page 77.) LHA assigned a civic engagement *promotora* who had once been a participating mom in our Children and Youth Initiative to work with the parents on envisioning alternatives. A breakthrough came when parents, accompanied by LHA, set out to establish a Community Access Agreement with the Santa

Ana Unified School District to allow public access to outdoor school facilities (such as playing fields and basketball courts) for park-like use. Immigrant, low-income, monolingual Spanish-speaking moms who were unfamiliar with the educational and political systems in the U.S., and were at first very shy at parent meetings, came together to advocate for their children's right to a space to play.

They stood before the district superintendent and school board to share data on the health of children in their neighborhoods and to make a case for why the schools should be open after school hours. This group of parents formed a committee and partnered with school police,

Before the work of the Children and Youth Initiative, this child had to "trespass" school property to play.

principals, and teachers to ensure that their "school-park" was a safe place for their children and families to come together and be active.

The parents solidified the committee by naming it "Comité PODER" *(Padres Organizados Defendiendo Espacios Recreativos − "poder"* is Spanish for "power"), which translates as "Parents Organized to Defend Recreational/Open Spaces." PODER members not only got access to a weekend school-park for a year-long pilot; their effort was so significant that the city of Santa Ana successfully applied for and was awarded five million dollars to build the first park and community center on school grounds and open to all Santa Ana residents. This concrete policy win for the neighborhood became an early win for the then new place-based initiative, Building Healthy Communities, whose sponsoring foundation, The California Endowment, had strongly supported LHA's efforts in this very neighborhood from the beginning. Furthermore, the work in this place reveals the ongoing commitment and civic participation of parents in strengthening bonds and networks among neighbors in the area, creating emergency response teams to organize fundraisers for families in financial need, and holding community vigils when neighborhood youth are gunned down. These parents no longer rely on LHA to activate them and their neighbors; they are now participating in larger-scale policy efforts, such as improving community–police relations, implementing restorative justice programs, and fighting for immigrant rights.

Place 2: Where there were no parks

In another neighborhood just a few blocks away from Roosevelt Elementary, youth between the ages of 14 and 21 were working as youth *promotores* in the Wellness Village 92701 project. Again with California Wellness Foundation support, these youth serenaded their mothers, conducted health education classes with peers, and mentored children in their own apartment buildings. Eventually the youth also engaged their parents in their efforts, and more neighborhood groups were formed.

During 2002, a group of women from this neighborhood who were participating in our Diabetes Self-Management Program approached LHA to ask for support in creating a safe space for their children to play. We had already received a similar request from the residents living in apartment buildings where we had been active and where we had created strong relationships with the apartment managers, the tenants, and businesses surrounding the buildings, especially the large grocery store across the street.

The idea was to transform a half-acre, trash-ridden, empty lot known for drug use and gang activity into a community center and park. In response to residents' request for a safe and open space to play and engage the community, *promotoras* convened residents to form the *Comité Familias Corazones Verdes* (Green Heart Families Committee) who began advocating at City Hall. The first win came when the city of Santa Ana agreed to lease three parcels in the lot to LHA for $2 per year. The second win came when Northgate Gonzalez Markets, owners of a parcel in the selected property, donated it to LHA. Ultimately, we received funds from the California Department of Parks and Recreation through the state's Proposition 84 and a great many in-kind services to develop the park. We received support from local businesses, professionals, and foundations, including St. Joseph Health, McCarthy Building

Beautiful smiles are one result of opening our park and community center.

The lot identified in 2002 as the space for the park and community center.

Companies, Inc., Taylor Design, Wells Fargo, the WWW Foundation, and Northgate Gonzalez Markets, among others.

The neighbors continued their work, cleaning the empty lot and holding small fundraisers to support the building of the park. After more than ten years of advocacy by the neighbors, the *Familias Corazones Verdes* Community Center and Park was inaugurated on June 1, 2013. The operation and programming at the park is now led by surrounding community residents, supported by LHA staff.

> *"When I think about what moves me, what gives me energy to do this work, I would say that number one is my commitment to creating communities where our families in vulnerable situations can have opportunities for health and success in life. I will not give up. My conviction was reaffirmed during our fight for our park. It took us 11 years to get a park and community center built in an area of town where we did not have any. I remember having meetings with the neighbors every week. We organized, advocated, studied, trained, found resources, completed the project, and opened the park in 2013. Now we are here doing programs and having a place where the community is invited to participate every day in the improvement of their own lives."*
>
> —Rosalia, promotora and coordinator of LHA Park and Community Center

The *Familias Corazones Verdes* Park and Community Center opened in 2013.

Place 3: Meanwhile, in the center of the city, the Wellness Corridor

In 2010, we had been working for 14 years in the 92701 ZIP code. Two of our strategic achievements – the construction of the *Familias Corazones Verdes* Community Center and Park and the relocation of LHA headquarters to our own building in downtown Santa Ana – led to a new concept: a Wellness Corridor. The corridor, about a mile long, would connect the two sites, crossing downtown from east to west, through the heart of the 92701 ZIP code. The first phase was to develop an urban trail that would create a vibrant and inviting corridor and encourage walking and biking in the heart of the city.

Recognizing that multiple stakeholder collaboration is the third pillar of Building Healthy Cities, LHA convened a multi-sector collaborative of 50 diverse stakeholders, which included the Santa Ana City Council, residents, business owners, arts groups, city staff representatives, the Orange County Health Care Agency (OCHCA), Santa Ana Community College, the Orange County Board of Supervisors, and other community-based organizations. The goal was to collectively create alternative open spaces, make the downtown more pedestrian- and bike-friendly, increase opportunities for physical activity, and increase access to healthful food options in Santa Ana.

This collaboration has become a community engagement structure in which community members of all ages, as young as 12 and as old as 80, have sat at decision-making tables with directors of Parks and Recreation, for example, as well as elected officials, to offer their input. As a result, the city has approved policies and allocated funding to improvements envisioned by the committee, such as adding benches to motivate more seniors to walk longer routes and engage in their downtown, and adding facilities to encourage biking.

The Wellness Corridor project has also provided a platform for residents and city staff to work together to create additional mechanisms for resident input. Through community workshops, forums, and town hall meetings in central Santa Ana neighborhoods, residents have participated in land-use decisions by working on the following city processes and plans:

• Update of the Circulation Element

• Development of a bike master plan

• Development of a pedestrian master plan

• Update of the housing plan

• Development of the city's five-year strategic plan

• Update of the Alcohol and Entertainment Ordinance

Each of these policies will have an impact on Santa Ana's land-use decisions over the next 10 to 20 years. Residents who had not previously participated in civic processes are now providing their input and recommendations so that the city will prioritize the interests of their under-served neighborhoods and improve access to open spaces, as well as provide a healthy and safe walking and biking infrastructure.

LHA and partner organizations make it a point to support residents to use "active transportation" methods to get to public meetings and activities. We organize people so together they can walk or ride bikes to events. This has increased the participation of low-income youth and families, particularly moms. Significantly, this increased participation has led to the creation of new advocacy groups, including a youth advocacy network and the first ever Santa Ana Bike Coalition. During 2013 and 2014, LHA engaged approximately 150 new community leaders in a multitude of

Santa Ana residents enjoy a bike ride through the Wellness Corridor.

leadership development activities, including information and skills education as well as hands-on advocacy in city planning processes and state-level legislation. We developed these trainings based on the needs identified by *promotores*, residents, and other steering committee members, and we focused on policy processes related to land use which could potentially support the vision and implementation of the Wellness Corridor.

By creating multi-sector collaborations and supporting community members with the skill-building training and information to effectively participate, LHA has invited residents to sit alongside the city's traditional decision makers and together develop a vision and plan for their community. This mechanism has allowed for collective planning, advocacy, and decision-making, providing opportunities for the community's ongoing input into and oversight of land-use decisions. Like many cities across the nation, we are challenging the idea that gentrification[2] will bring progress to everyone. In reality, the latest development efforts have left out the sectors in the most vulnerable situations in this city. The increasing presence of low-income residents in policy-making processes together with some changes in political leadership are creating the needed

---

2 Gentrification is the process of renewal and rebuilding that accompanies the influx of middle-class or affluent people into economically neglected areas, often displacing residents most affected by poverty.

power to make economic progress and a life with dignity a real possibility for residents of all economic sectors in Santa Ana.

We cannot do it alone

LHA has developed many projects throughout the years that show the strength of collaboration and the synergy of concerned, informed, and engaged neighbors working alongside grassroots organizations and institutions. In some projects, we have been the lead organization; in many other projects, we have been one of the members of a larger coalition. For instance, in 2009, leaders in the low-income communities east of downtown Santa Ana asked LHA to join forces with the Logan Neighborhood Association to identify other neighbors who could strengthen the leadership of their association. Through a series of town hall and neighborhood meetings, the *Barrio* Logan Empowerment Committee was created and went on to successfully advocate for the removal of a waste management facility in the neighborhood. The company had continuously violated its conditional use permit, operating its business in the Logan neighborhood. In 2010, the city finally enforced the permit, and waste management company trucks stopped entering the neighborhood. This major win for the residents was due mainly to the tenacity and perseverance of the community's leaders, and had been in the works long before LHA came onto the scene. Our role was supportive and built upon their many years of struggle.

In addition to this supportive role with grassroots groups, we have been part of citywide collaboratives. One of these is the Santa Ana Collaborative for Responsible Development known as SACReD. Our history with SACReD goes back to its creation and to the work of many residents and representatives from various city sectors who had been working together to create "a better Santa Ana" long before the formation of SACReD itself. This group of concerned citizens and organizations included Orange County Communities Organized for Responsible Development (OCCORD), Orange County Congregation Community Organization (OCCCO), Public Law Center, *Chicanos Unidos*, *El Centro Cultural de México*, the Kennedy Commission, Santa Ana Historic Preservation Society, LHA, and community lawyers, doctors, business owners, environmentalists, and neighborhood leaders, among others.

In 2010, LHA joined forces with the newly formed SACReD to advocate for a Community Benefits Agreement covering the Station District. A Community Benefits Agreement is a legally binding agreement committing the city, developers, and the community to achieve specific redevelopment goals. The Station District is an area located near the Logan neighborhood and is also in the 92701 ZIP code. As part of the effort, LHA organized and worked with SACReD members to educate and train residents to advocate for a Community Benefits Agreement comprising five priority areas:

1. Affordable housing

2. Secure open spaces and community centers

3. Cultural and historic preservation

4. Infrastructure improvements that enhance public safety

5. A redevelopment project to benefit local businesses

Although the Community Benefits Agreement did not pass, after more than a year of grassroots advocacy, the coalition was able to secure some benefits. Among the wins was the construction of a new community center at Garfield Elementary School, a council action to secure a 1.5-acre lot for a future park, as well as 28 units of affordable housing, five below-market-rate homes, and the building of a new community center and park in central Santa Ana. This effort solidified the formation of a new structure of collaboration between five community-based organizations: OCCORD, OCCCO, the Kennedy Commission, *El Centro Cultural de México*, and LHA, each with different missions (health, housing, arts and culture, community organizing) but all with priorities of community engagement and of including residents to reclaim their role in citywide decision-making. The collaborative became SACReD and is rooted in the principles of inclusion and of government transparency and accountability, and serves as a model for sustained, long-term community-leader engagement in policy advocacy efforts. Several years after the bid for the Community Benefits Agreement, SACReD successfully advocated for a local "sunshine" ordinance to open government meetings to public scrutiny and participation, and influenced priorities set in the city's first strategic plan.

Another important effort is the Santa Ana Building Healthy Communities project. This is a ten-year statewide initiative of The California Endowment, a foundation seeking to create healthier places in low-income communities across California by engaging and supporting community residents to improve their communities through policy and systems change (Preskill, Mack, Duffy, and Gutierrez, 2013).

LHA was the lead agency during the planning phase of the Building Healthy Communities project. During the first two years of implementation, LHA had the privilege of hosting the hub or coordinating team. Today, we are part of the local steering committee and active in all three major campaigns of the initiative. Throughout, LHA has been one of the organizations working on community engagement to advance the ten-year plan approved by the community. Bringing residents who may not be seen as conventional leaders into the decision-making process has been one of our greatest contributions. We are extremely thankful to be part of the Building Healthy Communities initiative, which we see as the natural continuation of our Healthy Cities work initiated in 1996. In fact, one of the *promotores* who, 18 years ago helped form Wellness Village 92701, became a coordinator of the initiative, and many residents and *promotoras* who have been active throughout the years became part of the local steering committee, providing continuity to the work.

We don't claim any individual organizational credit for the wins of these collaborations. Success is collective! We support but we don't necessarily lead these collaborations. The credit is collective and the gains and benefits are collective.

How do we work with other organizations?

As a community-based organization firmly rooted in the public health model of Healthy Cities, we believe collaboration is not optional, it is a necessity. We cooperate with a variety of organizations, some that focus exclusively on the provision of direct services and others that focus on activism and advocacy. Most organizations are easily categorized into one or the other side of that organizational spectrum. However, Latino Health Access is a hybrid. We do both: direct service and advocacy. And in both areas, collaboration is paramount.

At collaborative and coalition tables, our team often feels the uneasiness of having conversations that are mutually exclusive. The discussion tends to be either about services or about policy, or to focus exclusively on either short-term or long-term goals. *Promotoras* and other community members often feel uncomfortable at the meetings that do not address immediate needs when discussing long-term solutions, or vice versa.

In collaborations formed to discuss the need to provide short-term solutions or specific services only, we value the focused response, the immediate help, and the provision of resources. However, frustrations arise when we are called to support narrow interventions and Band-Aid approaches, and find a failure to understand and map the connections between problems and solutions. Our team often finds itself asking for deeper analysis to identify long-lasting policy changes.

On the other hand, in the policy/systems-only collaborations and coalitions, our team often advocates for short-term, pragmatic solutions in combination with long-term propositions. *Promotoras* and other community members see clear connections between low wages, lack of housing, stress, and a lack of ability to manage diabetes, for example. However, depending on their experience with the policy work, the *promotoras* and community members may not yet be able to visualize a path to solutions through larger policy/systems change. However, through exposure to and participation in these conversations, all of us – *promotoras*, community members, organizers, and direct service providers – learn the value of simultaneously addressing immediate needs as an entry to transforming our communities, and proposing policy/system change to attack the roots of inequity.

> *"Organizers from different groups had been meeting to strategize how to influence housing policies at the city level. Meanwhile, a woman from one of the neighborhoods where we had all been organizing arrived asking for help because she was being evicted that night. We were all caught off-guard. Some collaborative members said, 'We are so sorry, we wish we could help you but we don't do that in this group. We organize about housing policies for the long-term, but cannot really offer you anything to solve your immediate problem.' An LHA promotora who was*

there left with the woman in the eviction process, and by the next day had managed to find her emergency funds to pay a month of rent and temporarily avoid the eviction. I then received a call from one of the organizers asking me which was the program at LHA that helped people with emergency funds. My response was that there is not such a program; there are simply promotoras who have a lot of experience and knowledge about resources."

—Nancy, Director, Community Engagement and Advocacy Program

This hybrid approach we practice at LHA, focusing on direct service as well as on advocacy, is a necessity because we are already in the community, long before issues are raised and organized into campaigns. Problems are experienced and issues defined by community members. We help solve problems and we work on campaigns, but our objectives are not just to win new policies. We will pass a policy, stay on to celebrate, and then stay even longer to make sure the policy is implemented as the community wanted. We simply stay to work with community members on whatever else they would like to focus on and get ready for the next opportunity to make reforms. And the cycle continues, because *promotores* are already members of the communities in which we work.

When we collaborate with other organizations, we make a conscious effort to invite our partners at the table to work on both short-term and long-term strategies. We also try to increase awareness about the need to create spaces for collaboration in which community representatives feel welcomed and confident of their abilities and value.

The confident *promotora* who was able to help the woman facing eviction is the same *promotora* who used to hide inside herself at collaborative meetings. She did not speak, even though after the meeting she would approach the coordinator with all kinds of ideas and with her analysis of the meeting. Why does this happen? What does this have to do with the way we structure our collaborations?

Our responsibility as an Institute of Community Participation is to create spaces for those who are afraid to speak because they feel intimidated or inadequate. This is possibly one of our most important challenges, and addressing it directly has created some of the most valuable assets for our LHA team. Our *promotoras* are now more vocal at the collaboration tables. We invite to the table the very community that we are trying to organize. This is different. We don't bring the community leader who has overcome all of the trials and tribulations of poverty, of living in communities with high levels of conflict and youth violence, who underwent the pains of living in the margins but no longer does. We bring to the table people who are at this very moment being evicted due to ever-rising rents in the absence of rent control. We bring an aunt whose nephew was shot walking home from school. We bring a mother whose child is on probation and suffers from a mental health condition. These are not folks who made it despite the odds; these are people who are living and struggling with social inequities now. Not only do we bring them to the table, but we value their expertise and wisdom, we pay attention to their own understanding of the conditions in which they are living, and we ask them what types of solutions they see.

This way of collaborating is how we have learned to work inside of LHA. We make a conscious effort to listen to one another, to share our priorities and urgencies, to reach agreements, and to make decisions. We believe that we all — neighbors, organizers, program directors, and staff from agencies and institutions — need to improve the way we interact in coalition so we can achieve better results. We must honor the community's special place at the table and its various ways of understanding problems and solutions. Unfortunately, when *promotoras* step out of LHA into more traditional settings, their wisdom or way of communicating ideas may not be appreciated.

> "In our work, we interact with people who do not share or understand our philosophy. We find people who treat us as if our ideas, our ways of being and doing, are not the correct ones. When we leave LHA, there is another world out there, with many other ways of doing. It helps me to have conversations in LHA that allow me to learn and unlearn, to see what we are doing well, and to be reminded of why we do what we do. This gives me the strength to explain our way of seeing things to other people and other organizations out there."
>
> —Charis, promotora, Community Engagement and Advocacy Program

Gaining a deeper understanding of how to do community work and reflecting on and developing our Principles of Practice have been instrumental in improving the way we function in collaboratives. We are more aware than ever that we cannot do it alone, that partnerships are key to bringing services to the community and to changing the policies and systems that both create and maintain conditions of poverty, inequality, and violence. We believe that by making space for the community in these discussions, by democratizing the discussion, we are on a path to create common ground among different social sectors that will help the community and LHA to succeed.

We are at a pivotal time in Santa Ana's history. Santa Ana just passed its first ever five-year strategic plan, developed with community input gathered by a coalition of organizations. For the first time in the history of Santa Ana, resident input is being incorporated in a more transparent and intentional way. This is in large part due to city compliance with the Sunshine Ordinance adopted in October 2012 after a two-year campaign led by SACReD, demanding more government transparency and community participation. For the first time since 1998, the city has updated its Circulation Plan and will also be updating the rest of the General Plan. In order to ensure that the community participates in the update of transportation and circulation policies, LHA created a pathway for these recommendations to be gathered and voiced by community residents as the plan was being written, elevating the voices of residents living in divested and disenfranchised neighborhoods of Santa Ana. As a result, the residents from Santa Ana's low-income communities have added 23 policies into the city's five-year strategic plan.

The issues, politics and dynamics in every city, town, and community are different. Even so, many other areas are facing gentrification, exclusion, and lack of participation. We offer this story of our work in Santa Ana, California, in the hope that other communities can learn from our hard-earned experiences about potential avenues and processes to make change.

Confluence of streams and riding the current

Much has happened in the last 22 years that fills us with excitement and hope. We are proud of the advances of the communities in Orange County. In order to tell our story, we searched in our archive of treasures and re-read many of the documents that set the course of our organization. Among them is *Latinos in Orange County: Profile of Selected Demographic and Health Characteristics* of 1993, a document created by many of the individuals who eventually created LHA. In its executive summary, the following sentence foreshadowed what was to come:

> *"As we enter the 21st century, the question is 'how can we build upon the strengths of the Latino population – its high work ethic, youthfulness, and strong family support system – to prevent the problems we are faced with today?' The answer does not rest on one individual or organization, but rather on all who live in this county; more importantly, in the Latino community itself which must be and can be mobilized to create effective change."*
>
> —David Hayes-Bautista, for the Delhi Community Center, Bienestar Familiar Project, and HERR Coalition, 1993

The Latino community has indeed mobilized itself along with its allies and supporters. The coming of age of the children of immigrants in the county, the political maturity of leaders, the awareness of the power of one and the power of many, and the popularity of models that were born in academia, such as the socio-ecological model (Stokols, 1996) and the social determinants of health, have intersected much like rivers coming together. An international, national, and regional confluence of streams has resulted in a strong current that includes governmental agencies, community-based organizations, grassroots organizations, funders, academic institutions, and residents. Riding this current, LHA went from being an isolated project that embraced a place-based approach in our city to becoming part of several large place-based Healthy Cities initiatives throughout the state, and then becoming part of the national conversation about healthier communities. We are energized and humbled by the projects we have both initiated and collaborated on to achieve health equity through the genuine participation of ordinary people. The confluence of all these streams of work at every level is shaping a powerful current that propels us forward.

Our story

The story we tell shares the life of the people that make this work possible and the story of the organization. You will hear the story of a single mother raising her children in isolation and desperation who overcame so much to become a mother capable of mobilizing hundreds of fellow residents to win resources for their neighborhood. Intertwined with these individual stories, you will hear a parallel story of an organization that started with a staff of two and a grant of $25,000 and that currently employs more than 60 people and channels more than four million dollars annually into the local economy. The Healthy Cities model and the social determinants of health framework were embedded in the DNA of Latino Health Access from its inception and are evident in every story that emanates from our work. However, theoretical approaches and frameworks would continue to be lifeless and abstract if not applied in practice and confronted with the challenges of real life. At LHA, we are proud to bring theory and practice together in a space filled with the vibrancy created by passionate and deeply committed individuals who believe that they can change the world!

"We are different because we come from a culture that is rich. We know how to be a community. We come from communities where the children in the neighborhood are everybody's children, where 'your children are my children.' We bring this. I can remember when my own mother used to share our food, which sometimes was not even enough for us because we were too many, and I would ask, 'Why did you share the food with our neighbor?' But we knew that when we were short on food, our neighbor would help us. We were always helping each other; always in moments of crisis, like a community, like neighbors, like a family.

"There are many things that are different here. We don't know the system; we don't know how it works. The system starts to overpower us, and we feel vulnerable, and one day, because we

are vulnerable, we let the monster into our house, the monster known as alcoholism, depression, drug abuse. And because we are so vulnerable and lonely, we take in any companionship, even the monster himself.

"Here at LHA, I found a place where I felt companionship, where I could make my own decisions, and no one else was deciding for me. I found a place where I feel appreciated, loved, and protected — where I feel the warmth that I left in Mexico. I discovered I had a lot to offer. I discovered that I was part of a community and that my own pain was woven with my experiences of success. Today, I feel the responsibility to give back what I have gained throughout the time I have been here. A hidden or saved-up talent is of no use if it is not shared; a shared talent fuels more talent. I want to continue enriching our communities. We all hope to re-create the best of the communities that we come from and to ensure that none of us loses our humanity."

—*Soledad, promotora, Emotional Wellness Program*

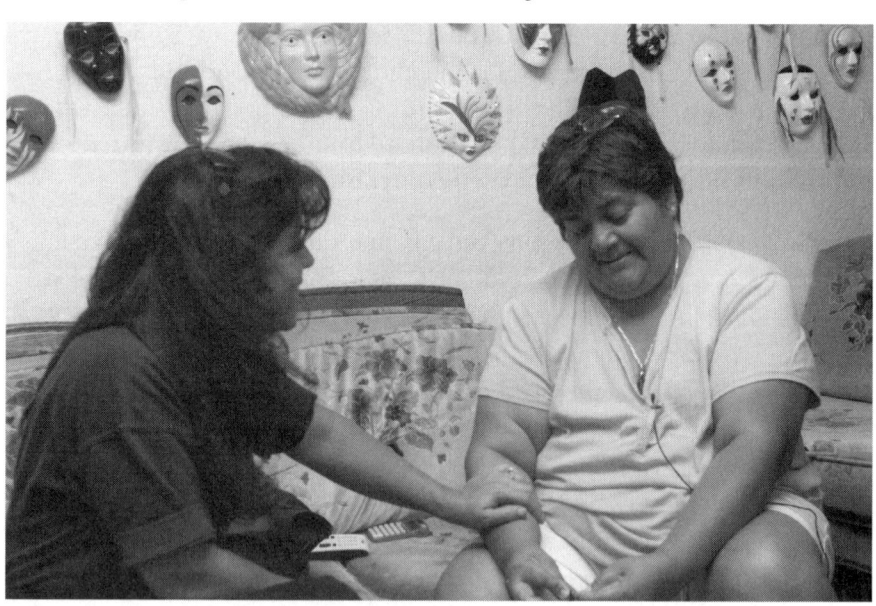

Soledad visits Teresa at her home.

Participation Makes the Difference

"There is a lot of poverty, obesity, diabetes, and other problems here, and none of it will be resolved if we do not get involved in the life of our city. For me, it is important that people participate. More heads think better than one. If we want to create change, we have to participate. I get involved more each time. I speak with our elected officials in Spanish; one way or another, we understand each other.

"Recently, we have been developing projects around gardening. This work connects me to my roots. We have created a microfarm project to plant vegetables. We hope to expand this project now that the city has approved allocating bigger lots for this purpose. We have a serious problem of obesity here. This project is important for people, so they can have a space to grow produce, to eat better, for children to learn about plants, and to generate income. This project has been possible because we are more organized as a community and we can be more effective in asking for what we need. We have a long way to go, but we are on the right track."

—Apolonio, community leader and volunteer

Apolonio, one of our community leaders,
caring for plants at a microfarm project.

Getting involved to generate solutions

Communities have reasons to get organized and involved. Many
people in our communities suffer from very low wages, over-
crowded housing, insufficient public services, lack of basic public
health infrastructure, drugs, violence, mediocre education, lack of
access to appropriate nutrition, lack of parks and open space, lack
of health services, harassment due to immigration status, racism,
classism, power abuses, and overall government negligence.

As we think about the many health problems affecting our
communities, our nation, and our planet, it can seem overwhelming.
Chronic diseases, cancer, HIV infection, mental illness, obesity,
malaria, lack of opportunity for prevention, and increasing health
costs – all of these disease-related problems co-exist with complex
socioeconomic and environmental challenges such as poverty,
climate change, and war. The worst effects of these global problems
are disproportionately harmful to people in our most vulnerable
communities.

Although the challenges are many, it is important to remember
that human beings have always confronted problems. Regular men
and women have always worked together in the course of their daily

lives and over the long term to be part of a process of generating solutions. Before everything was organized into distinct types of careers, professions, or institutions, human beings solved problems and helped each other. Before there were licensed midwives, there were women who gained expertise through experience, by learning from other women, and by receiving the wisdom passed down from many generations. Before there were highly trained lawyers and professionals, there were elders and councils that deliberated over problems. Now the helping professions are highly specialized. They require credentials and licenses. They are part of institutions that have certainly improved services in many ways. For example, today's midwives have more tools to save lives than the lay midwives of the past. However, the institutionalization of the helping professions has also had a detrimental effect. It is harder for regular people — for the whole community — to feel they are part of a process for generating solutions to issues that directly affect them.

Another way that people are cut off from participating in problem-solving is that corporations and governments often invest in a steady stream of new efforts focused on fragmented solutions to complex problems. For example, they develop new medications to fight diseases, with the underlying desire of finding a "magic bullet" that can alleviate problems at a minimal cost while generating high levels of profit. They do not ask community members what they need to be better equipped to prevent or manage disease. It is frequently the case that examining and addressing underlying community issues could prevent the disease from developing in the first place and could ultimately save money and produce better outcomes. But they continue the search for the magic bullet even when evidence indicates that there is no magic bullet and that we cannot fight diseases and inequities without involving the community in fighting the conditions that create, foster, and perpetuate them.

The institutionalization of problem-solving marginalizes participation and leaves people feeling they do not have a way to participate. Yet despite these challenges, people still get involved. Through churches, synagogues, and mosques, people create formal and informal volunteer networks that make big differences in the community. Setting up non-profits and community-based organizations, people take on problems and solve them.

Neighborhood groups of all sorts regularly improve people's everyday lives.

The difficult, ongoing work of increasing participation is critical to the health of our communities. No magic bullets can replace it. We must reclaim our right to help and be helped, and to do so on our own terms. We must remember that humans created the institutions in the first place. These institutions may feel inaccessible at times, but we have noticed that regular people often fight against all odds to have their voices heard. We know that by participating in our communities, by joining together to solve problems, we can re-shape our institutions to make them work better for all of us.

If participation is so important, why is it not the norm?

Our observations through our community experience at the local, national, and international levels indicate that civic participation is not what it should be. People tend to defer the role of seeking solutions to institutions despite the fact that people with college educations inside those institutions will generally approach solutions from the point of view of their prescribed roles. The results tend to be limited in analysis and scope. Solutions tend to be imposed on communities. Surely, this is not the best process for addressing complex problems that require complex solutions.

Generally, when we observe how government functions, how cities are designed in ways that contribute (or not) to the wellness, safety, and prosperity of its inhabitants, how the medical system relates to patients and its surroundings, how educational systems relate to families and their neighborhoods, we notice that our institutions have limited understanding of the role of communities in improving services and systems and even less understanding about how to include them. Very often institutions see themselves as providers and the community as receptors of services. In this paradigm, only people who are engaged, vocal, and aware of their rights proactively attempt to influence institutions and hold them accountable. The rest of the people, the great majority, either use the services or not without making their opinions or ideas heard. When people have low incomes and live in vulnerable conditions, they tend to be less aware of their power. They may be working several jobs and therefore have no time, or they might be undocumented and therefore understandably nervous about raising their voices. This results in a low level of participation and subsequent difficulty in producing the changes that are needed in their communities.

Governments and other public institutions, and their representatives and employees, have been trained to create solutions that come from the top. The process of generating solutions usually includes the formation of an elite group of "Problem Solvers" that have been selected because of their political or administrative positions or their academic knowledge. On many occasions, solutions are influenced by their political and life views or by the special interests of powerful wealthy groups that have the privilege of political power. Their solutions tend to reinforce their own power and at the same time reinforce the marginalization of low-income families, immigrants, and people of color. Mainstream institutions and "Problem Solvers" don't just benignly ignore community members; their practices are often designed to marginalize them and the contributions they could make to the analysis or solution of problems.

Much of the data used to formulate solutions offered by government and academia result from surveys and consultations with families in neighborhoods to "learn what they think." Frequently, the inquiry is followed by reports with explanations of why these communities have so many problems and what should be done. However, community members that live the data and experience the problems are not considered to be among the problem solvers. They are only considered passive receptors of programs given to them as a result of data about their own communities and lives, organized in charts, graphs, and other forms that they can no longer recognize.

Are we missing opportunities to make our communities healthier?

Let's look at the example of physicians. They are trained to recommend, prescribe, and inform. In the majority of transactions between the physician and the patient, the doctor treats the patient like a passive entity, an empty receptor waiting to be filled with a fix or a cure. Obviously, an informed physician may have good advice, information, and treatment ideas for the patient. There is no doubt that is often true. But the advice is better formulated when the physician understands that the "patient" is a person seeking advice and has a lot to offer in terms of the explanation of the problem and the potential solutions. This patient is a person showing an active role in the pursuit of better health. The reality is that the person seeking medical advice and his/her family make the majority of the decisions about personal health management. People who go for medical consultations and their families are health and wellness providers to each other. If a physician actually believed that the person in his or her office had more to offer in the transaction, the conversation would be more equally balanced; it would flow both ways and include input from the person seeking advice. The patient would be invited to reflect, think, explain, and offer possible solutions. It is not just the doctor's training that is at fault. Many health institutions are driven by profit or by insurance reimbursement requirements, so they have reduced interaction time to the minimum amount it takes for the provider to deliver recommendations. There is no time for discussion.

Most hospitals, health centers, and clinics tend to have little involvement with the communities and neighborhoods surrounding their facilities. The lives of the people in these communities might not find a place on their agendas except as markets for their services or targets for selected charities. Health institutions and health professionals generally are highly respected by common citizens. The institution's lack of involvment in community life reduces its "health" activities to the interaction with diseases without addressing the root causes of those diseases. Why not see health as something that requires interacting with the whole person and indeed with the whole community? Such an approach would allow health care providers to help address the root causes of diseases and collaborate with residents to create healthier communities. For example, health care providers could go into schools, athletic clubs, support groups, religious institutions, and even nightclubs – both to share expertise and to listen to what people are saying about their health. Health centers and hospitals need to evaluate on an ongoing basis how to increase important opportunities to interact with the community.

Technical expertise is not enough

Everything seems to indicate that the technical experts who have been officially in charge of providing solutions can't do it alone. Consider these health problems:

- Chronic diseases such as diabetes and heart conditions are increasing. No evidence indicates that racial/ethnic disparities in prevalence and incidence of diagnosed diabetes decreased from 2004 to 2008; however, socioeconomic disparities worsened during the same interval (CDC, 2011).

- Prediabetes is a serious health condition that increases the risk of developing type 2 diabetes, heart disease, and stroke. 79 million Americans — 35% of adults aged 20 years and older — have prediabetes. Half of all Americans aged 65 years and older have prediabetes (CDC, 2014). Without lifestyle changes to improve their health, 15% to 30% of people with prediabetes will develop type 2 diabetes within five years (National Diabetes Prevention Program).

- Obesity is an epidemic, and it is worse in communities of color and low-income communities (CDC, 2011).

These are not just individual health problems. They are community health problems, and we need the communities most affected by them to take part in finding solutions. Many of the conditions that give rise to high rates of diabetes, teen pregnancy, and gun violence are rooted in the way our society works. Yes, individuals need to change their behaviors, but as the Committee on Assuring the Health of the Public in the 21st Century wrote in 2002, "It is unreasonable to expect that people will change their behavior easily when so many forces in the social, cultural, and physical environment conspire against such change." To address these forces, we need to re-learn how to include the community and how to engage institutions, business leaders, and other groups in a process of reflection and action that will improve everybody's life. In the same way, the community, including each of us, needs to re-learn how to be part of the solution and how to initiate transformation that can allow us to regain faith in ourselves. In the end, the questions are not only whether we are willing to include the community, but also whether we are willing to improve the current systems in ways that represent the interests of populations gravely affected by inequities in health, education, criminal justice, housing, jobs, and other areas.

How do we re-learn to participate?

This was the question we asked ourselves, and the question that takes us back to the beginning of our story. Since our inception, LHA has made participation central to our work. Through myriad strategies we engage and encourage others to participate. In the following pages we share some reflections about participation and about our framework to increase participation at the community level.

Activating the participation and leadership of everyone

"I became involved with LHA at age 15 as a volunteer. Back then, I was easily tangled up in trouble. You find yourself accused of many things when you're a teenager and growing up as a Latino male in America. I did not like going to LHA, but I felt safe there. They supported me and helped me to discover my talents. They included me in activities when I said I liked something and I showed them what I could do. I always enjoyed music. I play guitar. Then I became the official musician of LHA. I played my guitar at retreats, meetings, parties, and fundraising activities with others in the community. Here, I grew up protected and my skills flourished. My talents can be used, be shared, and serve as a model. They defended my voice and trained me. By doing, I saw how my community improved. The strengths come out when you have a design that allows them to come out and to be recognized. I just finished college. I studied music. I was a volunteer promotor for several years. I have been a paid promotor with LHA for 16 years. I work with youth and with a project to use the arts to create healthier communities. We are constantly inviting participation and the sharing of talents."

—*Moises, promotor, Community Engagement and Advocacy Program*

Moises with participants of Youth Initiative at Roosevelt School

Community participation is necessary and it is a challenge. We need to better understand, redefine, and encourage participation so that we can exercise our rights and our duties and pursue our human vocation of service.

Assumption:
All people are leaders.

We define leadership

Leadership is the ability to make decisions and carry out actions that influence yourself or others.

We define participation

Participation is combining our individual leadership in an active way, and being committed to a purpose for a common benefit.

What are the benefits of participating with others?

A key benefit of participation is that it fosters leadership. Look how Moises grew. He describes in the quote above how he came to LHA reluctantly at first. But being in a place where his talents were noticed encouraged him to participate more and develop even more as a leader. Similarly, when someone takes charge of their health by coming to LHA to enroll in a Diabetes Self-Management Program class, or when a person comes to a support group to deal with depression, she is a leader of her own life. From that step, she might easily become a leader in the community, spreading her knowledge to others. Communities are filled with leaders. We just need to find them, invite them in, and encourage them.

Assumption:
People understand the advantage of participating with others.

In our discussions and trainings with local and international communities, together we answer the questions: What do we gain by joining with others? What are the benefits of participating with others?

We can:

- Think with others
- Feel like part of something
- Generate strength and power to achieve what we want
- Protect each other
- Work, advance, achieve
- Divide up the work
- Make sense of life in connection with others. Discover one's self, and discover one's self in others.
- Defend our dreams
- Witness personal change and change in others
- Love and reconnect with others
- Turn into a better, more complete, less selfish, more patient person
- Learn
- Be active, be part of the solution
- Enjoy the benefits of being informed and have access to services
- Defend cultures and traditions
- Give our talents
- Improve our strategies and organize ourselves better
- Overcome fears and sadness

- Help to build change
- Have the opportunity to play
- Use our privilege
- Find ways to manage and channel our outrage, our rage about so much injustice and discrimination

We gain:

- Strength to fight
- New ideas and inspiration
- Independence and autonomy
- Loyalty and commitment
- Respect
- Influence and opening to the influence of others
- A sense of community
- A sense of purpose
- The opportunity to practice compassion and solidarity
- Space to listen and be heard

We can create:

- Solutions
- Opportunities for the expression of ideas with words, with the body, with art
- Relationships
- Common + Unity = Community
- Structure to make accomplishments
- Spaces for bravery
- A legacy that others can inherit

If people see the value of participating, what are their reasons for not participating?

"You have to have patience with people. Give them their time and give them your time. You must support, search for options, be there. When the time is right, it's going to happen. I was very insecure. I had a lot of pain. I thought I did nothing right. I learned we are not separate from each other. You have to believe you can change. You need to believe this internally so it can be achieved externally. For that, you need to work on yourself and be supported by others. You need to have opportunities to feel your changes.

—Araceli, promotora, *Community Engagement and Advocacy Program*

Adults are independent. They don't have to do anything they do not want to do unless they live in an authoritarian regime, they are in the judicial system, or they are dependent. It is out of respect for adults that we invest effort in thinking about the reasons people do not participate. We recognize that we are not entitled to anything and people do not have to open their doors or respond to our invitations. We know that individuals have different realities. We are not looking for cookie-cutter or one-size-fits-all types of answers. We are looking for ideas and strategies that respect the unique situation of individuals and that can remove barriers in ways that can motivate or convince them to participate.

When we talk about participation, it is common to hear that "people don't like to participate." People often say this after they have been unsuccessful in reaching others or engaging them in activities. We often blame each other for not getting involved.

At LHA, exploring the question of why people don't participate is an important part of our training for neighbors, *promotores*, and supervisors. When we invite people to reflect on this question, here is some of what we've learned:

People do not participate because they:

- Are embarrassed
- Are tired
- Are used to having others solving their problems
- Fear the consequences of participating
- Have had bad experiences when participating
- Work too much and fear that participation will take time and decrease their income
- Believe that nothing is going to change
- Have opposing views – they disagree
- Have not been invited
- Feel intimidated by the place, the people, or the level of discussion
- Feel they have nothing to offer
- Believe it is other's responsibility to solve their problems
- Think it is a waste of time

People do not participate because they don't:

- Believe in the organization that is asking them to participate
- Have information
- Have a place to leave the kids
- Have time
- Understand the need to participate in this issue
- Speak the language
- Feel motivated

People do not participate because the issue:

- Is not a priority
- Does not affect them or they think it does not affect them

Understanding where participants are: The Participation Continuum

"In 1996, I was at home suffering from depression and not wanting to interact with anyone. All of a sudden I heard a knock at the door. I opened it and there she was: Adela, a promotora from LHA, inviting me to some activities. I said I could not go. She came back several times and insisted. One day she asked for my help. She said that we were not going to be able to have a better community without the help of all neighbors. I started helping her. Helping others helped me. I have been involved ever since."

—Manuela, *LHA volunteer and community leader*

In 1996, Manuela started helping LHA by doing outreach. She was a founding member of our Children and Youth Initiative and remained involved for many years. She participated in numerous trainings and community forums where she became more aware of the situations affecting her community. A few years later, she became a member of the *Comité Familias de Corazones Verdes*, which was instrumental in creating a park and community center in a very park-poor area of our community. Simultaneously, she joined several resident committees to change policies and participated in the creation of the Strategic Plan for the city of Santa Ana. Manuela served as a member of the Board of Directors of Latino Health Access.

Levels of Participation

At LHA, we try to understand that not everybody is ready to participate at the same level. We talk to people, offer services, invite them to events, treat them with respect, try to create interest in the activities we offer, and talk about the benefits of getting involved. Then, with patience, we try to recognize where the person is regarding her ability and willingness to participate. We start where the individual is, and respectfully accompany our participants along the path of readiness.

Based on the pattern we have seen repeating over the years, we have identified four levels of participation along a continuum.

Levels of Participation Continuum			
Level 1 ➡	Level 2 ➡	Level 3 ➡	Level 4
Residents engage in direct service	Participants show awareness of disparities	Participants take action	Participants catalyze change

Level 1 — Engage in Direct Service

Residents ask for help, use the programs, and only offer ideas if asked.

Level 2 — Show Awareness of Disparities

The participants want to help others with specific projects. They begin volunteering time and accept certain responsibilities. They come to trainings and meetings that are not related to the program they are participating in. They participate by organizing short-term projects and offering ideas. *Promotores* help participants see how problems are related to social conditions and opportunities or lack of opportunities.

Level 3 — Take Action

Participants are interested in improving the community. They want the community to have more opportunities and to be better off. You can count on them as volunteers. They have scheduled a time for volunteering, and they may be in charge of a group, a project, or a class. Their presence is consistent in meetings and community events. They accept invitations to represent the community in committees, meetings, and site visits. They share opinions, concerns, and points of view with neighbors and outsiders. They participate in the creation or implementation of projects, know how to gain access to resources, and ask for help when needed for themselves or their families. They help the community utilize programs and connect people to additional resources.

Level 4 — Catalyze Change

The participation becomes more mature. The participants understand how problems and solutions are connected to larger systems. They understand the importance of having power in order to influence decision-making. They understand how community engagement, mobilization, and awareness increase power. They understand that their participation makes a difference and has an impact on well-being. They understand government structures better. They are more strategic in the use of leadership and organizational skills. They understand and participate in activities related to public policy. They understand the importance of expressing their ideas, and they do it every time they have an opportunity. They represent the community on committees, boards, and even in elected positions.

Charis, *promotora*, Community Engagement and Advocacy Program, gives a presentation.

LHA sponsors a community event.

Here is an example of the levels of participation as they apply to increasing active living and healthy eating.

Levels of Participation Continuum			
Level 1 ➡	Level 2 ➡	Level 3 ➡	Level 4
Residents engage in direct service: • Children's Initiative • Youth groups • Exercise classes • Cooking classes • Diabetes classes • Healthy Weight Program classes • Other health and wellness activities and direct services as needed	Participants show awareness of disparities: • Begin volunteering • Begin surveying neighbors • Engage in analysis of what is needed in built environment to sustain health • Explore and reflect on social inequities • Articulate how social determinants of health affect their families and community	Participants take action: • Initiate Hope-Energy-Action projects to influence the built environment such as building vegetable garden beds for the neighbors • Join committees at schools and in neighborhoods to influence the built environment	Participants catalyze change: • Engage in larger policy change movements for the entire city or county • Participate in monitoring implementation of Santa Ana's Strategic Plan. • Participate in shaping Santa Ana's new General Plan to influence the built environment • Join city-wide or county-wide committees, such as health department, public safety, housing, school board, etc. in order to influence the built environment

How do we assess whether we are supporting the participation of others?

We challenge our team to build capacity in our community. We are constantly reminding ourselves that we don't do things for people; we work with them to build capacity. The team at LHA often discusses that no single organization can make change alone. We know that we got involved because we found those opportunities to participate. That's why we are obligated to create these opportunities for participation in our community on an ongoing basis.

Numerical indicators of participation at all levels include the numbers of:

- outreach contacts (indicator of our effort to involve others)
- people attending programs and activities
- people reciprocating in any form
- people who return from the classes, groups, or services to volunteer
- participants receiving training as leaders
- people offering/using talents in the project
- ideas from the participants that have been implemented
- people who take action without you
- people taking responsibilities in projects
- number of people in committees
- people advocating community concerns to public or private institutions
- people accepting appointments by their community to serve in specific projects, coalitions, or committees

Supporting individuals to make progress along the Levels of Participation

Not everyone moves through all four Levels of Participation. Many more people simply come for services than are ready to volunteer. The number of participants decreases at each level. For those that do progress from Level 1 to Level 4, this progression can take years. It is very gratifying to see participants grow in their commitment and understanding, and increase their level of participation.

To accompany someone in the process of participation and change requires patience, empathy, and understanding. We have to be persistent in our efforts to include them. We have to invite them over and over again. We must be willing to enter into relationships where we can learn from the person we are accompanying. It can take a long time to gain confidence in our own capacity and the capacity of others to grow and change.

Nancy, from LHA's Community Engagement and Advocacy Program, invites a community member to participate.

The worker for the job

We have to find out why people don't participate without blaming or judging them, and we must be proactive in removing barriers and dealing with the reasons people don't participate. For example, if the problem is that they had bad experiences in previous attempts at community involvement, offering them child care will not get them to participate. Instead, how do we make sure they have good experiences? Sometimes the answer is more technical in nature. If the issue is transportation, for example, we can offer a ride.

However, this may not be as simple as it looks. Multiple barriers to involvement can co-exist. Before helping others deal with barriers, people must know each other, trust each other, and have the opportunity to work together. The workers for this endeavor must be humble and smart, with a great sense of solidarity, and with a high degree of emotional intelligence. They must care about their communities and be invested in the results. They must be part of the culture and speak the language of their neighbors.

Who are these workers and where can we find them? These are people in whose very nature it is to help others. They are people who suffer when they see others suffering and take it upon themselves to defend them. These are individuals that earn the trust of others and then become more influential in helping them make decisions and act. These people exist in every community: the person who knows how to read and teaches others, the person who has diabetes and helps others manage their condition, and the woman who survived domestic violence and now is leading support groups for other women trying to leave violent situations. These are the ones who help others harvest the crops or take care of the children. These special individuals are able to develop relationships that are egalitarian, deep, and long-lasting. We call them *Promotores* or Community Health Workers. They don't call themselves *promotores*. They call themselves friends, *compadres*, *compañeras*, sisters, aunties, brothers, buddies, friends, and neighbors. Once they start working on specific health strategies with health institutions and community organizations, we know them as health promoters, or in Spanish, *promotores*.

Promotores are community members and community experts. As we write this book there are thousands of them working with low-income communities in urban and remote areas throughout the world. They work with dedication. From the grandmothers in Nepal to the *promotoras de salud* in Mexico, or the community health workers in Africa, Asia, and the U.S., they are all over the planet helping their communities or waiting for the invitation to share their wisdom (United Nations Children's Fund, 2003; Hilts, 2005).

In the next chapter we will take a look at these workers, their role as change agents, what it takes to do their job, and how they are so successful.

We invite you to think...

If you are a community member:

- In what ways do you interact with your neighbors? In what ways do you take responsibility for what happens to your family and your community? (For example, do you look out for neighborhood children? Do you bring food to sick neighbors?)

- Do you feel comfortable talking to your doctor or other health professionals? Why or why not? How could you start that conversation? What are some of the barriers you face when talking to members of the medical establishment?

- In what ways are you involved in the civic life of your city? What makes you feel motivated to vote? What gets in the way of you wanting to vote?

- Did you participate in the approval of the school budget? How many parents work or volunteer in the school?

- What could be different if more parents got involved in school meetings and activities?

- Are low-income community members involved in the advisory board of the local hospital?

- What do you think could be a small step to begin increasing community involvement?

- How many community members work in city projects and receive a salary?

- How many renters participate in generating the city plans? What changes could be possible if more renters participated in city plans and projects?

If you are with an organization:

- In what meaningful way is your organization engaging communities? What institutional barriers do you face? What are some initiatives you have implemented to engage communities?

Community Experts:
Involving the Promotores of LHA

"It is extremely valuable to have these services for better
management of diabetes, free, in Spanish, in the community,
in a place where people feel comfortable. I have seen people
who had gone years without visiting a doctor, who had no
money for medication. I have had participants with diabetes
who are extremely poor and also suffer from bipolar disorder or
schizophrenia. These participants need home visits and close
companionship for themselves and for their families. I have
had participants who are blind, without legs, or with damaged
kidneys. It is not easy. It hurts me to see their suffering. It has
given me hope to see them learn, improve, and gather strength to
keep fighting for their lives. I am committed to share what I know
so people can manage their diabetes and not develop complications.
Here, we care about people, not about money. We look for our
community, walk the extra mile with our participants, and do not
give up so they will not give up."

—Luzy, promotora, Diabetes Self-Management Program

Assumption:
Community members are experts in their lives and their communities.

Promotores are community experts

Community members are experts in their lives and their communities. They have accumulated wisdom in many arenas of life and have a practical ability to problem-solve. They are leaders in their own right. They have their fingers on the pulse of their communities and are the first to learn about what is affecting individuals, families, and neighborhoods, including issues, barriers, threats, recommendations, possibilities, opportunities, disasters, and more.

At any point in LHA's history, more than half of LHA's paid workforce has been comprised of *promotores* and the majority of them live in the communities they serve. They promote health, but they do more than that. They create relationships in the community. They educate, serve, and advocate. They are trusted because they understand what it is to be a recipient of the local institutions' services. They speak the language and have similar cultural understandings and practices as their neighbors.

They have great ownership of LHA and remind us constantly that we exist first and foremost to serve the community, and that funding restrictions or the lack of funding cannot stop us. They live in the community and return there every day. We see our *promotores* as the "Accountability Department" for the mission of LHA. They are the eyes and ears of their communities. They care deeply about reaching and helping as many people as possible. They are willing to challenge rules or procedures that make our work ineffective. They have great common sense, are experienced problem-solvers, know how to find help, and are very creative in supporting programs that have lost funding.

When *promotores* participate, they are more effective in encouraging others to participate. As they gain more experience, knowledge, and power, they become better advocates for their own children and their own communities. The *promotor* is directly accountable to the organization, but also to the community. At the same time, the organization and the community are accountable to the *promotor*. The community is accountable to itself. When community work is not paternalistic, everybody is accountable to everybody else. We all are accountable for the results or the lack of results. The paradigm of mutual responsibility obligates all of us to achieve a high level of inclusion from conceiving ideas to carrying out projects. This way of working commits all the players, both LHA's staff and members of the community, to ongoing learning, reflection, action, and evaluation.

The presence of an organization like ours inside the community, and the reliable presence of the *promotores*, gives structure, quality, stability, and continuity to community work. This approach does not remove leaders from the community; rather it assures that their commitment, experience, and credibility stay in the community.

Promotores engage community strengths to address community needs

> "I arrived at LHA because I had diabetes. I consumed alcohol and drugs for a long time. My diabetes was out of control. At LHA they treated me well. They supported me and taught me without judging me. I learned from other promotores that you are important no matter who you are or what you bring. For them, the important thing was that I went to class. All they saw was my desire to regain my health. I learned to manage my diabetes. I have been a promotor at LHA for 13 years. I help all I can in the same way that they helped me. I do not judge. The fact that participants come shows their desire to improve. Later they learn how to do it."
>
> —Mario, promotor, Community Engagement and Advocacy Program

Assumption:
Women, men, adults, and youth in our communities want the best for themselves and their families.

The dominant paradigm says the patients have the problems; the professionals have the answers. Patients have weaknesses; providers have strengths. One is empty, while the other is filled with knowledge.

LHA sees the relationship differently. In our practice, *promotores* relate to participants as equals. They help people think. They help participants strengthen their voices and engage in action and self-advocacy. *Promotores* are companions for our community, supporting neighbors in their quests for change. This change could be at an individual level, such as eating better, taking medications, being active, or talking to your health care provider. It could be a change at the family level, such as reducing violence, finding healthier eating options, or participating in the schools. It could be a community change, such as creating parks or advocating for safer neighborhoods.

Bienvenida, *promotora* in the Diabetes Self-Management Program, talks about nutrition and cooks with participants.

Needs do not change people

For our *promotores*, the point of engagement is not the need. It is
not the diabetes, the lack of parks, or the violence. The point of
engagement is the strength. Focusing on needs puts the emphasis
on what people do not have. From our point of view, it is absurd
to create a relationship with someone based on something that is
missing. It's not that *promotores* don't see the needs and problems.
Indeed, because they are members of the community, they often live
the needs and the problems. But *promotores* start the engagement with
people's strengths – what is good about them, their love for others,
their loyalties, their aspirations and talents. *Promotores* see, in each
mother in the neighborhood, a caring mom who may already be a
leader in her family or her community. *Promotores* see each young
person as a survivor – perhaps of difficult schools, unfair policing
practices, or other challenges. *Promotores* see older adults as excellent
problem-solvers, experienced navigators of various kinds of jobs and
government bureaucracies.

Promotores help others find their voices and recognize and use
their strengths. In this process, *promotores* recognize their own voices
and find their own strengths. When they work with a participant
on a problem, they are not outside the story, looking in. They see
themselves in the stories, and as they work with participants to solve
problems, they get hope and courage to improve their own health
and their own lives as well. They help to transform and heal, and
they are transformed and healed in the process.

The person is separate from the problem

We are re-learning how we see people. Instead of an "alcoholic," we
see a man who is battling alcohol addiction. Instead of a domestic
violence "victim," we see a woman resisting violence. The person is
not the sum total of the problem he or she is facing.

> "When a man living with an addiction mistreats his partner or
> kids, it moves me. I feel connected because I remember my dad
> drinking alcohol. I said I was not going to be like my dad, but
> then I used drugs. It wasn't until I stopped using drugs that
> I started to make changes. I worked with the guilt of having
> done things I should not have done, and I faced the hate, the
> resentment, the frustration, and all those dark feelings within me.

"I think when you've been through that experience, you have compassion for that person, you believe in him and his strength to behave differently. I will not judge or criticize anyone because it would be criticizing and judging myself. If I do not think he can change, it's like believing that I did not change. That's one of the things that has value for me; I have a conviction that a change can be made. I say, 'Hello! I understand that you have been working very hard to get clean and it's not enough. Yeah, that happens when you are struggling with an addiction. But do not give up. I also had battles with addictions. And now I have 20 years of not using drugs. Yes, it is possible! You can do it too. I invite you to come to our men's group where you can share with trust and without being judged.'"

—Oscar, promotor, Emotional Wellness Program

Focusing on what people are good at is not an easy task, particularly in a society that constantly disqualifies people judged as "unsuccessful" because they do not fit the model of good wives, capable providers, honorable citizens, well-behaved children, and other "normal" people.

We are committed to focusing on strengths at all levels of the organization. This practice of consciously focusing on strengths allows us to recognize our skills, efforts, successes, kindness, and acts of resistance. We join with those we serve. We strengthen and support ourselves with the things we already have, and then we fight for the things that we want but don't have yet. Two good examples of how we focus on strength to generate solutions are the Children and Youth Initiative, described later in this chapter, and our annual *Tamalada*, described in chapter 9.

What do *promotores* do?

Our programs are facilitated by the *promotores* who teach and engage residents on a peer level. Programs and services at LHA are customized to be culturally appropriate and to assist participants in taking control of their health and encouraging others to do the same. These *promotores* are community experts who are supported by a team of technical experts, including some with doctoral and masters' degrees in public health, health policy, evaluation, and mental health.

Our *promotores* are often the first point of contact in cases of crisis within the families we serve. *Promotores* organize the community to rally for peace in our homes and neighborhoods, advocate for parks and safety, and create healthier environments for our families. *Promotores* build capacity among participants so they can learn to navigate systems and be independent, yet the *promotores* always remain a reliable part of the social fabric of participants' personal networks. Moreover, *promotores* organize the community for civic participation and political actions that can help to create or change policy at the local, state, or national levels.

By using a variety of methods, *promotores* have demonstrated repeatedly the important impact they have in identifying isolated individuals, connecting them with services, assisting with service navigation, providing direct services, advocating alongside them, and providing ongoing support for them and their families.

People in our communities have come to believe in the *promotores*, have witnessed *promotores* improving their own lives in deliberate and successful ways, and view them as role models and teachers. Our *promotores* visit families and are available and accessible. Families reciprocate with volunteer work in activities such as cooking snacks for the Children and Youth Initiative, doing outreach with us, advocating for others, and more. LHA is known for its advocacy on behalf of low-income families and immigrants. People in the community know and respect that. After meeting people, building relationships with them, helping them, and creating trust, then and only then do *promotores* go deeper and talk about new possibilities, such as developing different behaviors, exploring opportunities, and remembering the dreams that brought us here. By then, many neighbors are ready to listen.

We are often asked what community workers do. At LHA, because our programs are comprehensive and based on the Healthy Cities model (see chapter 1), our *promotores* are integral to nearly all functions of the agency, produce nearly all of the outcomes, and are engaged in a variety of activities to reach those outcomes. With proper recruitment, training, and support, *promotores* can do just about anything.

LHA promotores

- Promote health and wellness
- Support behavior and lifestyle changes
- Initiate and support ongoing community environmental change
- Support, organize, and advocate for policy change
- Identify issues, trends, concerns, resources, and opportunities
- Represent LHA and the community to the rest of the city
- Represent their community inside LHA
- Inform LHA's strategy
- Assist with research design and research implementation
- Help develop evaluation plans and tools
- Help with program design and implementation
- Assist with dissemination of LHA's model
- Help with funding development

We invite you to think...

If you are a community member:

- Do you care about being consulted by your health care provider about your treatment options? Do you care about being consulted by your city about city plans and use of the budget?
- What could be different about your involvement and responsibility if you were consulted?
- Do you see yourself as having something to offer in making your community a better place? Have you ever participated in something, even if it was small project, to improve your neighborhood?
- Do you offer your time as part of advisory boards, parent organizations, or similar groups?
- Do you attend and offer your opinion in meetings with the city where you live, the school in your community, your local hospital? What do you think about yourself when you are participating?

• What can you do to improve your participation in community organizations and share your point of view with others?

If you are with an organization:

• What is the role of the community you serve or represent in your organization?

• Who are the community experts in your team? Are they hired from the community?

• Do they have a role informing the organizational strategy? In delivering services?

• Are they on your Board? Do they have an advisory role? How could you improve the participation of community members in your organization?

LHA's mission, strategic objectives, and program outcomes by Areas

Promotores are central to accomplishing LHA's mission, strategic objectives, and program outcomes. Our mission is to assist in improving the quality of life and health of low-income, uninsured, under-served people through quality preventive services and educational programs, emphasizing everyone's full participation in decisions affecting their health.

Latino Health Access forges partnerships, engages and elevates the community's voice, and advocates alongside the community and partners to achieve health equity for all.

We do this by: 1) delivering culturally appropriate health-related services and programming to address urgent health concerns; and 2) engaging individuals in transforming their environments and creating positive, concrete changes in their homes and communities by providing tools, training, and mechanisms for civic engagement and participation.

We strive to: 1) reduce the burden of chronic disease; 2) strengthen family mental and emotional health; and 3) create healthier communities through a culturally competent and collaborative approach.

In the long term, we are working toward a system where health care and access to opportunities to better develop one's potential and enjoy a healthy, active life is viewed as a right and not a privilege.

LHA's *promotores* operate within four main areas of action listed briefly here and described in more detail below.

Area 1: Outreach	We look for our community members in order to invite them to exercise their leadership and to actively participate in decisions that affect physical, mental, and social health.
Area 2: Creating spaces	We create spaces where we can constantly strengthen relationships, and we invite others to participate.
Area 3: Services	We provide direct, relevant, quality services.
Area 4: Mechanisms	We create mechanisms for increasing hope, inclusion, and participation.

Area 1: Outreach

We look for our community members in order to invite them to exercise their leadership and to actively participate in decisions that affect physical, mental, and social health.

> *"We reach thousands of women every year. We go everywhere so they can learn about early detection of breast cancer. Success for me is when they get their mammogram and they learn that they are healthy. It is also important, if cancer is detected, to connect them with services and make sure they know they have the chance to do something about it."*
>
> — *Mary and Espi, promotoras, Breast Health Program*

Through outreach, we get to know our community so we can disseminate information, collect information, and invite participation.

At LHA we see ourselves as a team of people that offers something of high value: the possibility of a healthier community, with everybody's participation. In taking the message to our neighbors, we insist and persist, and we are tireless. We don't wait for people to come to us. We have been able to engage many people. In 2011, LHA conducted 32,423 outreach contacts throughout Orange County. In 2013, the contacts increased to 174,781 with the objective of mobilizing for action, sharing critical messages, and connecting residents with services.

However, there are even more people that we haven't met yet. The change we want to see is not going to happen without those that we still have not met. We need them; we want to involve them. We look for them. We find them, and we offer them our messages and services. Some individuals accept the invitation to come, and others ignore us. As with every good sales force, we keep working without blaming the person for not wanting what we offer.

> *"There is a person participating with us who I made contact with in a church. At that time she was not ready, but then she came and told me, 'I was given a flyer in a church.' That woman was ready for change; we gave her the information. She wanted to stay with us. 'You are not going to leave,' I said. She did not know how to take the bus or buy stuff because someone had always bought things for her. Now she was alone, without a partner, and did not know how to do things. And I said, 'You do not have to stay alone. You must come. Stay here and we will figure out how you can start doing things by yourself.' And now she's here volunteering; she's babysitting to help other women. That's one thing that I find very beautiful about her. She was ready and just needed someone to listen and say, 'You are not alone.'"*
>
> — *Tere, promotora, Emotional Wellness Program*

We are constantly looking for creative ideas to promote participation. We offer programs, activities, ideas, discussions, possibilities, dreams, and very real mechanisms for individual, family, and community involvement. From an invitation to come

Lupita, Tere, and Alex, *promotores*, with Francisca, Director,
Emotional Wellness Program

and learn to manage their diabetes, to an invitation to become
a citizen and vote, the outreach is done by phone, in person, on
the streets, and in homes, laundromats, supermarkets, anywhere
possible. The most important ingredients we bring to our outreach
are our effort and our creativity.

> *"We go to the streets every day to find women like us. Women
> who are suffering violence in secret like I was. We offer tortillas.
> When women come to get free tortillas we tell them, 'Tortillas
> are part of our culture but violence is not.' Women receive a free
> package with six tortillas and a business card with my name and
> contact information on it. My objective is for any woman in need
> to know that she does not have to take the violence, and that I
> will be there for her when she is ready."*

> —Norma, promotora, Emotional Wellness Program

How can we invite you to participate if we don't know you?

To be more effective with our outreach, we get to know people. We
think about who they are and what they do. Teams of *promotoras* and
their supervisors decide on what type of outreach to conduct and

Alex, *promotor* in the Older Adult
Program, conducts door-to-door
outreach.

Rosa Elena and Antonio, *promotores*
for the Diabetes Self-Management
Program, staff a table at a health fair.

where and when to conduct it, depending on the audience they want
to reach. If we want to reach mothers with school-age children,
then our teams will be at the entrances of schools during drop-off
and pick-up times. Other outreach locations may be laundromats
and supermarkets after 10:00 a.m. For door-to-door visits, we
start at 10:00 a.m. and make sure we alternate with evening visits
before 8:00 p.m.

We also do a variety of outreach activities during weekends,
such as attending health fairs, door-to-door canvassing, and sharing
information at supermarkets. From time to time, we do outreach
inside places of worship where religious leaders of different faiths
allow us to pass out information or directly address the members
during the service.

> *"I believe that when you find someone in a particular condition of need
> or when you go to do outreach, it is because you want that person to
> feel she has someone. She is not alone. You want to tell her a story
> that she hasn't heard yet. I feel that instead of saying, 'Come to our*

program,' you are saying, 'Come; you are not alone. Bring the fears you've grown up with, the ideas that make you feel so afraid. Come out from where you are now and we will walk together.'"

—Noraima, promotora, Emotional Wellness Program

We invite you to think...

If you are a community member:

- Do you engage in any special effort to reach out to others so they can be involved in an issue important to you?
- Do you talk to others about issues affecting you or your family that are also affecting others, your community, or the nation?
- Do you invite others to talk as a group? Do you act as a convener? If not, what do you think is keeping you from doing so?
- Could you improve your efforts to connect with others with the purpose of improving a situation affecting you and/or them? What would you do? Who can help you think? Who can go with you? How can you start? When?

Area 2: Creating spaces

"I started volunteering with LHA in the Children and Youth Initiative, which is based at Roosevelt Elementary in my neighborhood. This was the space where I learned to participate. I was given the responsibility of recruiting more moms to volunteer. I suffered. I spent one year with only three mothers in the group. I thought, 'What can I teach them? What example can I give them?' I myself was trying to leave an abusive relationship. I was desperate. I had no patience with my children. I needed to be alone. I used to leave my children in the Children and Youth Initiative just so I could get some time to myself. Throughout the process, the space was always there, with other women and children, developing friendships and supporting each other.

"Hiromi, the program coordinator, visited me. The promotoras at LHA helped me take control of my life. This is like an institute of growth for parents and children. Here they do not only train

us and invite us to teach our community, we are also taught to think. For me, it was a school that helped me to be a better mom.

"To sustain itself, a program depends not only on funds. If you have money, you can give that. We invite you to give something: some beans for the children's snack, some tortillas, some salsa. We gather to meet anywhere, even under trees. The promotoras taught me to be more independent, to become more flexible. They convinced me that I am useful.

"When fear comes to me, I take a few steps back. Then I talk to others in my community and stop being afraid. I think I have to tell the story of LHA as the story of the place where, when I arrived, I did not know that I can do the things that now I know I can. What happens and what we achieve in our community work depends on the quality of the relationship. We belong to each other. Every day we work to create and invite people to safe, protected spaces where they can be themselves, feel stronger, overcome their fears, and be part of the solutions."

—*Sarai, promotora,* Community Engagement and Advocacy Program

We create spaces where we constantly strengthen our relationships, and we invite others to participate. Our *promotoras* define space where we invite as that place, environment, or process that enables the creation and strengthening of relationships, which in turn leads to activities, projects, and actions.

Our relationships are the most important ingredients of our organizing. Without the relationship, we do not know each other and we cannot create community, we don't have trust, we cannot help each other, we cannot count on each other. If I don't know you, I don't have to listen to you or believe you or accept your invitation. With good relationships, we have conversations and deepen our understanding of each other. We can reflect and take actions that make us more effective in all areas of our lives.

Having money for projects is important, but without people there are no projects or changes. Our people are our main asset. We take care of our relationships by continually nurturing each other. Thus, we are able to stay active, engaged, and motivated for the countless conversations, agreements, actions, and transactions that are required for the work we do. When we don't work on relationships, or if the environment of the relationship is negative, we lose the will to participate and the energy we need to persevere is diminished. We risk abandoning the process and we risk demoralizing each other. The quality of relationships is fundamental to sustaining the will to work for change over the long term.

One of the most important roles of *promotores* is to create spaces that build and deepen relationships. The expectation is that the relationship is reciprocal and enduring, helping to transform us into better people, and eventually allowing us to come together in order to improve our families and communities.

Area 3: Services

We provide direct, relevant, quality services. Services are fundamental to maintaining or improving the quality of life in the present and are one of the most important entryways for participation and building relationships in the community. When we provide services, we are also disseminating information, promoting health and wellness, contributing to the prevention of diseases, managing existing diseases and other problems, promoting recovery, and offering social support and reintegration into communities. By communicating in a language that neighbors understand and providing them with immediate access to tangible, concrete services, we make ourselves relevant to the community. By providing direct, relevant, quality services, people see that we are there for them and that we are ready to help them deal with the problems they face today. *Promotores* provided a total of 71,135 direct services in 2014 alone.

Gina, *promotora*,
Healthy Weight Program

How do we decide what to offer?

The health issues that our participants face every day combined with LHA's resources and staff capacity determine the creation and implementation of services and programs. As front line staff and community experts, *promotoras* are key in identifying what is needed.

Program coordinators, supervisors, and our Evaluation Department team also identify trends in requests from participants, which allow us to either respond ourselves or refer people to other groups.

Here are the programs and direct services *promotores* offer:

1. Chronic Disease Self-Management Program
2. Health Promotion and Education Program
3. Emotional Wellness Program
4. Worksite Wellness Program
5. Health Care Access and Navigation
6. Community Engagement and Advocacy Program
7. Youth and Children Leadership Initiative
8. Provision of Technical Assistance to Non-profits and Governmental Agencies

Promotores provide services by:

- Taking time to listen
- Engaging others
- Organizing community members
- Training others to become leaders
- Visiting homes
- Supporting their neighbors and each other
- Conducting one-on-one wellness and problem-solving coaching sessions
- Facilitating educational sessions and meetings
- Facilitating support groups
- Supporting, representing, and advocating with and on behalf of participants
- Referring and connecting participants with resources and services
- Educating and supporting participants to gain access to health services
- Helping neighbors connect with one another

- Defending their neighbors
- Advocating for their neighbors
- Conducting civic engagement activities
- Incorporating culture and tradition through the arts
- Using and training others in Freirian popular education methods
- Utilizing Narrative Practices[1]

In addition to program-related activities, the *promotores* devote several hours per week to completing administrative forms, documenting their work, and participating in internal committees, staff meetings, and trainings.

Area 4: Mechanisms

We create mechanisms for increasing hope, inclusion, and participation. Hope moves us to the world of possibilities. Participation moves us from the place of possibilities to the place of opportunities and concrete gains. Therefore, participation is the best strategy to keep hope strong. So we create mechanisms for increasing hope, inclusion, and participation.

Sometimes we get tired. We think that nothing will change and we stop believing. Pessimism and hopelessness paralyze us and leave us without energy. Sometimes our sadness is personal; other times, tragedy is felt by the whole family. We wonder if we can ever improve our lives or our communities. The idea that we could be respected and heard seems like something out of fiction.

Yet, every day in our lives and our work, we witness how we are transformed when we get involved. People increase their faith in their own capacity to influence change at the individual, family, community, national, or global levels when they participate. The result of this participation could be that we have a group where we can get support to contemplate leaving a violent relationship,

---

1 Narrative practices are an evidence-based approach for emotional wellness work with individuals and groups that has been used by community workers all over the world, especially in communities where people live in vulnerable situations. See: http://narrativepractices.com.au/; http://www.colectivo.org.mx/; http://dulwichcentre.com.au/

build a support network to fight domestic violence, develop a more egalitarian relationship with our doctor, or create a network of friends to exercise with. It could result in having a quality afterschool program, a different political representative, a change in immigration laws, or social and economic changes to decrease global warming.

Achieving results during the process of participation creates the conviction that "participation makes a difference." If the experience is a positive one, if people have good outcomes, then the possibility that they participate more and at a deeper level increases. The process of reflection and action described by Paulo Freire (page 102) is constant during participation. People think, take action at various levels, reflect on the results, and then take action again. It's a process that feeds our self-confidence, self-efficacy, awareness, and hope.

The work of LHA creates mechanisms for people to participate, so together we can create changes at all the multiple levels where they are needed in order for communities to become healthier. We partner with the community and provide various ways for volunteers to get involved, including: 1) at all levels of the organization and across all programs and activities, and 2) in special projects where volunteers have responsibilities for all or part of the project or those that require a community-based committee to take a leadership role.

Volunteer participation

Providing mechanisms for volunteer work increases participation and helps to create a workforce that strengthens the organization and helps sustain the programs.

Volunteer opportunities are available for community residents, students, businesspeople, and professionals. Children, youth, and adults donate thousands of hours per year to help with a variety of projects. Examples of volunteer work include babysitting children while women attend a self-help group on domestic violence, teaching kids how to dance Mexican ballet *folklórico*, supporting the *promotores* as they teach classes for overweight children or for people with diabetes, helping to organize a march for peace, calling people to get out the vote, serving on our Board of Directors, or driving someone to a medical appointment.

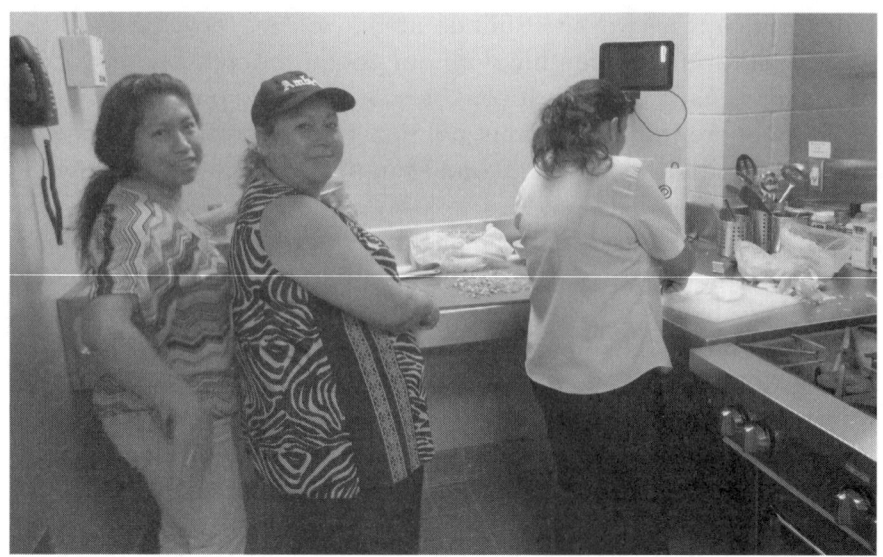

Gloria, Antonia, and Lidia, LHA volunteers, help with cooking.

When people participate as volunteers, they are deciding to use their personal leadership for the collective good. They move on to Level 2 of the Participation Continuum (page 45). They interact frequently with a *promotor* and other staff members. In this way, they become familiar with the organization and our philosophy. The relationship with volunteers strengthens during the daily work and creates ties of trust. Often, at this level, participants offer their specific talents and have the expectation that those talents, such as dancing, cross-stitching, or cooking, will be noted and appreciated.

Volunteers are invited to *promotores'* and leadership training. From there, many people offer more time and talents to a specific program. They participate in a project of their own initiative, such as organizing a children's dance group, leading an exercise program, or joining a collective project such as the creation of a park. These projects are called Hope-Energy-Action Projects.

Hope-Energy-Action Projects

We define Hope-Energy-Action Projects

Hope-Energy-Action Projects are projects that increase hope through positive action and tangible results that benefit the individual or the group. The projects offer opportunities for us to gain individual experiences that help to increase participation. The projects have structure and are fully or partially supported through the fundraising efforts of project participants.

Hope-Energy-Action Projects provide an opportunity for volunteers to take their participation to a new level. Some are practicing reciprocity. They have engagement with LHA and have had important needs met, so they want to give back. Often there is no clear distinction between the giving and receiving. By joining a volunteer effort, we receive many gifts. We develop or strengthen skills, support our communities in recognizing their power, and enjoy new relationships and friendships.

Assumption:
We all give; we all receive.

Remember Moises, the reluctant youth who got involved with LHA because he felt safe there and because LHA members noticed his talent for music (page 38)? Part of what made Moises feel safe was that people noticed his gifts and created a pathway for him to share his gifts. It is hard to distinguish where the receiving ends and the giving begins. As a youth, Moises started his own Hope-Energy-Action Projects. He continued the intertwined actions of giving and receiving. He led a project with youth in a collaborative effort with LHA and another non-profit to bring art and

Microfarms and small edible gardens are examples of Hope-Energy-Action Projects.

music to the community. Moises continues as a *promotor*, investing his energy in youth and policy change.

> "When in the neighborhood where you live, like it was for me here in Santa Ana, there are no role models other than gang members, addicts, and teenage parents, you see that as normal. Some people take for granted that a young man becomes part of a gang and no longer does anything else with his life. If instead you are exposed to a different way of living, where it is not normal to have violence in the streets of your city, where it's not normal to be without pleasant spaces to play or spend time with your family, where it's not normal for the young people to drop out of high school, or for the youth to become parents at an early age, or to get involved in gangs, then you learn that everything you used to see in your streets or community is not normal.

> "It is very difficult to take so much and give nothing in return. It is very difficult. It is very difficult not to return the support they have given you, what they have discovered in you that you never saw. Like your parents have been telling you, that you're very talented and sometimes you yourself do not believe them. But when people trust you and let you share those talents you have and let them flourish, everything changes and you find a way, you find the path to return that talent, to share."

> —Moises, promotor, Community Engagement and Advocacy Program

Oscar, *promotor*, Emotional Wellness Program, with Moises

Elements of Hope-Energy-Action Projects

Hope-Energy-Action Projects can be large or small. They might involve building a bike trail or planting flowers. Regardless of the size and scope of the project, they all have common elements.

1. **An entry point.** Any activity that involves interacting with our neighbors is an entry point. The entry point could be a diabetes class, a support group, or an aerobics class.

2. **A place where we invite each other.** All Hope-Energy-Action Projects have an identified place and activities that offer opportunities to interact, and to establish and cultivate trust. Having a place where we can strengthen relationships gives us an opportunity to invite people to be more deeply involved. Hope-Energy-Action Projects often generate multiple projects within the same space to address the multiple ideas, interests, and talents of the group. A good example of this was the various projects required to create a park, such as hosting a fundraiser, communicating with the media, increasing awareness among neighbors, and organizing cultural events on the vacant lot to engage others. However, the creation of the park in itself was also a project.

3. **Pre-established relationships.** In order to trust each other, a basic relationship needs to exist. It is difficult to invite someone to join a project when we know nothing about each other.

4. **An idea of what we want to solve, do, or have.** This idea or wish is the initial motivation for community members to approach the LHA team or vice versa. The initial idea may be about creating an exercise club to improve health, a cross-stitching group to learn a craft and meet neighbors, a reading project for kids to improve their school readiness, or a support group for parents of children with disabilities.

5. **A preliminary idea of what it would take to happen.** We usually require multiple conversations to think through how to make a project happen, what we need, what we already have, what the risks are, and so on.

6. **Identification of talents and other assets.** Whatever the project is, we need to identify assets. The main asset is the

personal willingness to share talents and time. Therefore, we conduct an assessment with the group. The questions to ask are: What can you offer to make the project a reality? What do you know that you are willing to share? How much time can you commit? Talents may include knowing how to cross-stitch or being willing to share your love of reading. Perhaps you could prepare snacks or make phone calls. Other assets may include: a patio where people can exercise, a living room where people can meet, books, supplies for classes, etc.

7. **Clear responsibilities and inclusion of talents.** We need to have clarity on who is responsible for the different tasks, making sure the entire group feels included with their ideas, time, and talents.

8. **Accountability.** As group members, we need to decide where, when, and how we will meet and report back to participants to make sure they are moving in the right direction and everyone is honoring their commitments.

9. **High level of community leadership.** Participants make suggestions, have input, and influence decisions about the project design and activities. The number of volunteer community members involved in the project is larger than the number of LHA staff.

10. **Structure.** There is a committee or recognized community group leading and following up on commitments. There is a clear way of making decisions. There are specific days and times when the group meets or there is a process for arranging when to meet. A staff member assigned to the project keeps records and supports the project.

11. **Opportunities to improve the project.** There are ongoing opportunities to assess our progress, giving ourselves a chance to reflect, correct, and improve.

12. **Opportunities to increase participation to Levels 3 and 4.** Take the example of a Hope-Energy-Action Project that starts out as a support group for parents whose children have disabilities. On the Participation Continuum (see page 45), participants may be at Level 1 (using direct services) or Level 2 (gaining an awareness of disparities). For our

parents' group, this might mean they are sharing the benefit of supporting each other. They might also be asking questions about what resources are available to them and why there are disparities in how resources are distributed. Over time, participants are likely to move to Level 3 (taking action). They might visit schools to learn more about resources and programs, and they might advocate for more of these. Moving on to Level 4 (catalyzing change), they might spin off a Hope-Energy-Action Project that lobbies for changes in state laws, helps elect school board members who are more sympathetic to their cause, and develops alliances with other groups working for educational and health justice.

A model Hope-Energy-Action Project: The Children and Youth Initiative at Roosevelt Elementary School in Santa Ana, California

Song to start activities:

> *Roosevelt's little sun*
> *Roosevelt's little sun*
> *We are promotores in the community*
> *We are promotores in the community*
> *And leaders forever ready to help*
> *And leaders forever ready to help*

Background

The Children and Youth Initiative is a program for child and youth *promotores* that began in 2003. The children start as *promotores* at age six, although children ages three to five also come to the Children and Youth Initiative with older siblings. A group of community women created it with LHA in response to several situations:

- Afterschool activities for our children were minimal.

- Many children ages 8 to 14 were looking after younger children without sufficient preparation or support from adults.

- We had learned through our work on the streets that children under age 12 were excited to participate. They wanted to learn and go out with us to do organizing.

- Parents of children under 12 were easier to attract to programs.
- We didn't need to start from scratch. There were plenty of effective models available to us for teaching children about health.

The place

We decided to start the project in our 92701 ZIP code in Santa Ana, California, an area highly affected by poverty, where our Healthy Cities work had involved young adults and *promotores* since 1996. Our *promotores*, adults, and youth from the project in 92701 already had relationships in the community and knew many moms, aunts, and grandmas who could help us. Several of our *promotores* were

A child *promotor* explains to an adult how to prevent poisonings.

A Children and Youth Initiative neighborhood activity

former residents. The project began in Roosevelt Elementary School where the school director was an ally.

We chose a school because in many parts of the world, schools are centers for social cohesion and social life. People see schools as a safe place to gather. They view teachers with respect. We felt that by locating our project in a school, we would be developing children's leadership, strengthening families, supporting parents to take part in the life of the school, and building ties between teachers and communities that would also lead to academic success.

Mothers and children participate in a peace march following several murders in the city.

Our theory of change

Our theory was that if children were involved as health *promotores* in their community, they would learn how to take better care of themselves and their siblings, carry messages to their families, and invite their families to participate and to improve their health. If children, youth, and adults were all involved, then we could create a great community team that could work to improve their neighborhood. And so it was!

Inviting the community

To attract children, we put together a play "starring" LHA workers and their sons and daughters. In the play, the bad character tried to convince the children that if you're really good and loving, you will run out of love. The good fairy then appeared and helped the audience find the truth.

For several weeks, we went door to door inviting children from the community to come for a pajama night to watch the play. We announced that the play would be performed at the neighborhood school and we would serve milk and cookies. The children were excited.

Welcoming the community

The day of the play arrived. Between children and adults, about 400 people attended. The play was a success. Children screamed, laughed, asked questions, and answered them. At the end of the play, thanks to the fairy, we had all come to the conclusion that love never runs out and that it grows and replicates when we help our neighbors and our community.

The initial invitation to participate

At the end of the play, before we served cookies and milk, we talked to our excited audience about a beautiful opportunity for our children to strengthen their hearts and their respect for others. We invited them to come on the following Monday to participate in the Children and Youth Initiative. Then we ate a lot of cookies.

The team

The team was made up of *promotores*, including three young adults who were previously youth *promotores* and were now working as LHA employees. On the technical side, we had people with formal training in education and psychology, which allowed us to develop materials and effective educational strategies. This team also made it possible for us to respond to children's and parents' immense need for emotional support.

Welcoming our leaders

The next Monday, the *promotores* welcomed 70 children, ages 3 to 16. About 20 arrived without their parents. We gave them their registration forms, which had to be signed by their parents or guardians. Days passed. Our 70 children kept coming back, most without permission slips. More children gathered. *Promotores* went to homes to ask the parents to sign the permission slips. The mothers started to prepare afterschool snacks, and they invited other mothers to participate. More children came. More mothers came.

Children's activities

A local school allowed us to use its multipurpose room to meet on Mondays through Fridays, from 4:00 p.m. to 7:00 p.m. Community children could come even if they did not attend that school. Monday through Thursday they learned different topics with the adult *promotores*. Friday was the day to share the information they had learned that week with the community. When we had enough

Children *promotores* and an adult volunteer knock on doors.

resources, we took field trips. One of the favorites was a trip to the beach. Many of the children and youth had never seen the ocean, even though it was only about 20 minutes away.

Children as leaders and *promotores*

Children were able to come up with new ideas, implement a variety of activities, and recruit new participants. The community outreach efforts were ongoing.

Working with parents

The parents, mostly women, met weekly to discuss topics of interest and give each other support. In the process, they deepened their relationships with each other and developed their abilities to participate. Active and experienced parents in the program welcomed the new parents. Together, they offered tangible support to the children by accompanying them in activities in the community,

Mothers offer support by providing snacks during children's monthly birthday celebrations.

Soledad discusses educational skills with mothers of the Children and Youth Initiative.

helping to celebrate birthdays, and supporting fundraising efforts. Parents were also invited to participate in other LHA programs.

> *"That space at the Children and Youth Initiative was my salvation, my relief. I had been affected by a great depression. But the Children and Youth Initiative was a place where I could learn and feel useful, and my children could benefit. I was part of something. I took care of the children's snacks. I always invited other moms to help. We became friends, and we still are to this day.*
>
> *"Everyone can contribute. What happens is that the women sometimes feel ashamed and they think, 'What if they do not like the soup I made?' We must tell them that their soup was so delicious. We must encourage them and support them. We all need someone to lead us, to pull us into the group. You can do things to make the community better. It's not complicated. Someone asked me why I was involved. I said, 'I live here; my kids are there. I am interested in making sure your child is good because I don't know if he will end up being my daughter's boyfriend. Maybe we will end up being mothers-in-law.' She said, 'You are right,' and she relaxed."*
>
> —Tere Baltazar, mother and promotora

Tere, *promotora*, participates in a staff activity.

The Children and Youth Initiative has become one of LHA's best examples of a "space where we invite each other to participate."

In the past 11 years, three volunteer mothers from the Children and Youth Initiative have become full-time *promotoras* at LHA and one became a part-time employee at our Park. Two of them represent their community in citywide initiatives. Many more are participating in different advocacy activities. The mothers and a few fathers created a committee called "PODER," which means "power" in Spanish, and stands for *Padres Organizados Defendiendo Espacios Recreativos*, or in English, "Parents Organized to Defend Recreational/Open Spaces." Many of the committee members have received numerous trainings in leadership and have been very vocal expressing their ideas and concerns to local elected officials.

The new generation of moms has revamped the Children and Youth Initiative to fit what they believe are currently the most important activities. They are also involved in fundraising efforts so they can have more flexibility planning their activities.

LHA's work with children and youth today

The Children and Youth Initiative continues with activities that help youth learn about the Healthy Cities model and how to mobilize the community. Additionally, LHA has created a youth leadership component within our Community Engagement and Advocacy Program and Emotional Wellness Program.

Moises and Charis, *promotores*, prepare an activity with families.

Youth who join our current youth programs are sometimes the children of community members or they find us through cultural activities or friends. They find a home in our youth groups. They also join efforts with other youth groups in the city to assure their voices are heard, and they advocate for policy changes. Youth are, more than ever, a great dynamic force in our organization. Many of the former youth *promotores* now serve as program coordinators and data specialists within LHA, and even serve as program officers in local foundations.

The Children and
Youth Initiative
in action

The Children and Youth Initiative is a good example of a project that started as a Hope-Energy-Action Project and quickly became an active incubator and generator of more Hope-Energy-Action Projects. These have been projects started by children and youth on behalf of their neighbors, and also by parents on behalf of their children. Throughout this project and all of our programs, nurturing participation is at the heart of what we do.

How We Work with Promotores:

Recruiting the Heart and Training the Brain

*"Where did the promotor concept originate? At LHA, we like
to think that the first promotora was a woman. She was a cave
woman and she discovered fire. After discovering the many
benefits of fire, the next thing she did was to share her fire with
other members of her community. Since then, promotores, men
and women, young and old, have been sharing their fire with
communities around the planet. The concept of the promotores,
individuals who help each other, comes from the people and
belongs to the people. It is a concept filled with logic, common
sense, passion, and endless effort to accomplish those things that
you dream of, with a lot of creativity and few resources."*

—America, CEO, Latino Health Access

Recruitment, co-learning/co-teaching, and supportive supervision

In all communities in the world, we find wonderful, talented people who are concerned about what is occurring in their surroundings. These individuals willingly offer their ideas or labor when invited to do so. They have a deep sense of solidarity, fairness, and commitment to justice and the well-being of others. At LHA, we call these individuals *promotores*. We invite them to join a project or strategy, or we invite them to conceive of and develop their own project or strategy. When we provide infrastructure, training, and support, *promotores* can channel their willingness to help in a more deliberate and organized manner. Using the *promotor* model, we create a collective effort that is effective and far-reaching in helping and supporting others and ultimately transforming our communities into places where all families have opportunities to be healthy and prosperous.

At LHA we do not dictate to people what they should do, but instead we accompany them in their process of change, of becoming more of who they want to be. We try to be consistent with this whether we are facilitating a training for diabetes self-management or organizing the neighbors to advocate for safer streets. We believe that we transform our communities by participating alongside the people of our communities.

LHA works to create healthier communities by working directly with and through trained community members, using the *promotor* model. This model is sometimes called the "community health worker" model or the "peer-led" model. Much of the degree of success of a *promotor* program can be attributed to the initial selection and recruitment of the *promotor*, or community health worker. At LHA, we are convinced that in order to do the type of community work we espouse, individuals must have the heart to help others discover and use their strengths, lead their own lives, and transform their circumstances. It is this heart that fuels the passion, energy, self-motivation, desire, and inner drive that helps us to be persistent and to invest the immense effort required to do this work day in and day out. We then provide the space and opportunities for co-learning/co-teaching in which *promotores* and the rest of the team can share their knowledge and wisdom, participate in specific skill-building training, grow in their abilities, help others in the team better understand the community work, and inform the organizational strategy. At LHA we do our best to "recruit the heart and train the brain." If the heart for this type of job is not there upon recruitment, it will very difficult for the person to become a *promotor* with the competencies needed to be effective. Everything starts with recruiting the right individual.

Characteristics of effective *promotores*

Promotores are community experts and front-line community workers. In addition to a caring heart, one of the *promotores'* most important qualities is the ability to create and maintain relationships in which they feel equal to those they are accompanying. They have to believe that people want the best for themselves and their families, and they must also have the humility and discipline to learn and improve. Therefore, we must recruit people who already possess the human, philosophical, and cultural characteristics needed to be an effective *promotor*.

The main characteristics of a *promotor* cannot be acquired in school and are hard to measure in an interview. We recruit candidates after they have demonstrated their commitment to the community, an open communication style, the ability to empathize, their good judgment and common sense, and their respect for others. We assess these qualities by examining their track record in community work or by allowing them to volunteer for the program for a while before hiring them. You can't train people to have these qualities, so we observe people and select individuals who are strong in these areas to be *promotores*.

With input from thousands of community workers who have participated in our trainings over the last 21 years, we have compiled a list of characteristics of an effective *promotor*. Some of these are "natural" to a person, some are learned, and some reflect engagement with community realities. For more on characteristics of effective *promotores*, see *Helping Health Workers Learn* (Werner and Bower, 1982).

The natural qualities of an effective promotor:

- Has a pleasant personality
- Enjoys people
- Cares about the people being served
- Has compassion and empathy
- Is respectful
- Is trustworthy and responsible
- Is willing to put time into serving others
- Is creative
- Speaks the community's language and belongs to its culture
- Is eager to learn and open to new ideas
- Identifies with and defends the interest of those in greatest need
- Is kind, honest, and patient
- Shows good judgment and a mature personality
- Is humble and feels equal to others
- Understands and respects people's beliefs and traditional practices
- Has integrity, is the same person when nobody is looking
- Generally does not have more than a high school education

The learned qualities of an effective promotor:

- Knows how to read and write
- Is a good leader
- Is organized
- Models healthy habits
- Is able to communicate ideas clearly

The community engagement of an effective promotor:

- Has demonstrated a long-term commitment to the community being served
- Has a personal interest in and will benefit from improving our communities and lives
- Is willing to and capable of representing the community
- Is respected by and in turn respects the neighbors/participants
- Lives in and will stay in the area, is not likely to move
- Is a past or present consumer of similar services to the ones that will be offered
- Has volunteered for community programs
- Is accepted and respected by all, or at least by the families with less power, money, and influence

After creating this long list of ideal characteristics during our conversations and trainings with communities, we humorously ask participants to raise their hand if they have all of these characteristics 24 hours a day, 7 days a week. We all agree that nobody has these characteristics 24/7. So, if nobody is like this every minute of every day, how can we recruit workers with these characteristics?

Recruitment and selection in practice

"I came to LHA to accompany a friend who had diabetes. I was working as a dental technician. The classes seemed interesting. I remember the promotor who was teaching the class asked who had diabetes. I did not raise my hand because I thought I didn't have diabetes. Two weeks later I found out that I also had diabetes. I felt very bad and sad with that diagnosis. I kept going to the classes to support my friend. I began to help serve snacks for the class participants, babysit for parents taking the class, and help the promotor with setting up the chairs and tables. All of this while struggling internally to accept my diagnosis. I was very worried but when I went to the classes to help and listen to other people

with diabetes, I relaxed and I felt strong. That class ended and I signed up to participate in the next one, this time as a person with diabetes. I continued volunteering. I like to sing and play guitar so I composed a song for people with diabetes. I also went to the mountains for a retreat with families participating in LHA's Emotional Wellness Program. I was in charge of the music, which entailed inviting people to sing at campfires in the evenings. I began to control my diabetes by losing weight and having more balance in my emotional life. After a year of being involved in LHA, I was invited to join the team as a promotor. They did not pay what I made at my other job, but I was very happy. At LHA, I discovered my passion for people. I love helping my community and I have a strong commitment to help in the same way that they helped me."

—*Antonio, promotor, Diabetes Self-Management Program*

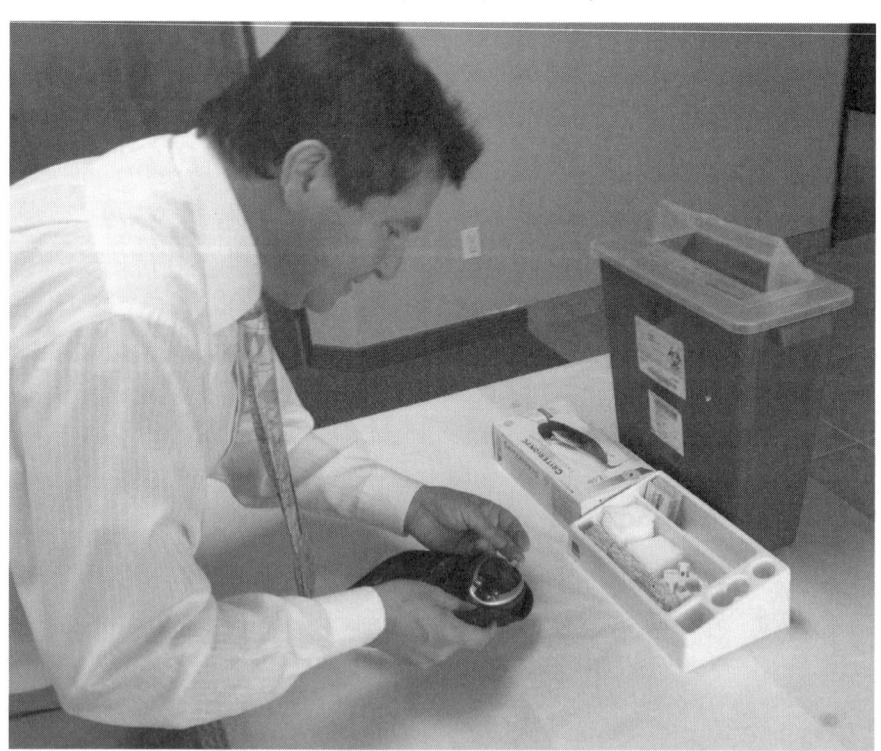

Antonio demonstrates how he measures his blood sugar.

At LHA we look for individuals with the characteristics on the list, but we don't expect them to have all those characteristics upon recruitment. Instead, we seek individuals who have the potential to grow and develop. Throughout the years, we have seen a continuous transformation in our team. By doing the work, we grow. By taking action and participating, we deepen our relationships with each other, increase our commitment, and improve our understanding of what needs to be done. In this process, we reinforce or discover our passions. When we want to recruit a *promotor*, we watch for volunteers in our programs. If by connecting to LHA's community work, they demonstrate they have the heart and commitment, we may invite them to become part of the paid staff if we have an opening.

Consider the example of Noraima. She was LHA's first volunteer 21 years ago. At first, her volunteer work helped her find her voice and affirm her experiences. Over time, she emerged as a powerful leader. Now she has been employed full-time for 17 years. She has been part of both the Diabetes Self-Management Program and of the Emotional Wellness Program teams. She has been a *promotora*, a Program Assistant/*Promotora* and a Program Coordinator/*Promotora*.

> "*Convinced by the outside voices that dictated for years what I should think, believe, and be, I had deeply internalized the ideas that the verbal and sexual abuse I experienced was not abuse, but was my life. Then I had the crisis of being raped in a public nursing school. That pushed me to find an answer, to fight for my essence as a human being, as a woman. I had been looking for the courage to cross that fine line that separated my inner voice from the outside voices, which I ended up calling 'the voices of social schizophrenia.' I was basically lost in this noise when I received the call to fulfill a great mission...an invitation to share my deepest feelings in a place where my voice could be heard even by myself and could be shared with all due respect for the noblest causes, helping others.*
>
> "*LHA has influenced my life by giving me the opportunity to grow and improve as a human being. They have given me the maximum reward of being able to touch the souls of others and be*

their partners as they go through their own processes of getting in touch with their own souls and achieving their own well-being.

—Noraima, promotora, Emotional Wellness Program

When we are ready to recruit for a paid position in a specific program or initiative, we look for the specific characteristics listed on page 90. LHA's currently employed *promotores* are vital players in recommending and recruiting new *promotores* because they are working directly with the community members who are participating in the projects and directly observing their capabilities and eagerness to lead. However, over and over, our practice reaffirms and reminds us that the most important characteristic of an effective *promotor* is a caring heart for the most vulnerable.

"I work in the Older Adults Program, and when I do outreach, my invitation is for people to live healthy and learn how to take care of themselves, that they don't suffer from diseases that can be prevented or managed with so many free programs that can help them. I go to them so I can let them know about the programs. It saddens me to see older people saying, 'I am alone. I don't have anyone to take me to the market, anywhere. I have no children and no one.' I went to visit a lady. She can only afford to rent a hallway in a crowded apartment and that is where she sleeps. It is very sad that she cannot move to a better place. We visit her from time to time. I just took her a few bottles of shampoo and some food. It is very sad and hard and I am talking to other promotores to see what else can be done."

—Espi, promotora, Older Adults Program

Educational level

Our *promotores* do not usually have more than a high school education and several have less than a fourth-grade education. Often there are individuals with higher levels of education who are interested in working as paid *promotores*. They may appear to be "easy recruits" because of their readiness to work inside an institution or because they are bilingual and have a driver's license. However, it may be a mistake to sacrifice the many critical characteristics of a successful *promotor* in order to recruit a person with a higher level of education.

Advantages of hiring those with college education:

- May have more technical and theoretical knowledge in health and social areas
- May have connections with other organizations at the time of hiring and know how to mobilize outside services
- May have more experience in teaching, public speaking, writing, computers, etc.
- May be more familiar with theoretical models, reports, and evaluation
- May be able to relate to others without easily being intimidated

Those with college education may be able to work as as *promotores*; however, they must have other characteristics such as feeling equal to those they serve, humility, commitment, similar experiences as the community to be served, personal investment in that community, and the other factors we have outlined in previous pages, or they will not be effective *promotores* and team members at LHA.

The training received in institutions of higher of education usually favors dominant paradigms of hierarchical relationships and values technical knowledge exclusively. It may be a mistake to prioritize hiring individuals who have had higher education.

Disadvantages of hiring those with college education:

- May assume the role of traditional teachers and treat the community as pupils in a top-down relationship
- May think they know it all and have little to learn from the community
- May think that the work is about their views and forget that the community has the starring role

- May have difficulty building teams with *promotores* and community members who have less formal education
- May have difficulty engaging the participant's wisdom and experience
- They may over-value theory about community work and under-value experience
- May treat others as inferiors
- May use complicated words and have difficulty simplifying messages
- May have difficulty with those parts of the job that may be less glamorous, such as door-to-door outreach on hot summer days, setting up and tearing down for community events, and going into apartments with substandard housing conditions

We do not recommend hiring individuals with college education to serve as *promotores*. Instead, we recommend hiring local people from the communities we partner with, those we serve and with whom we work – many of whom may have less formal education. We believe they better represent the hopes and needs of those whose voices are needed at the table to create healthier communities for all.

Building healthier communities takes time, and it takes a commitment from those living within the communities themselves. These committed individuals are the ones best suited to lead their own communities toward wellness. By creating opportunities for invested community members to serve others, we are supporting them in their growth and development as leaders. It is in action, in the field, where we can better observe and recruit those who will, given the proper training and support, succeed as *promotores*. When we are deciding whom to recruit as *promotores*, we take direction from other *promotores* and community members; their opinions are highly influential in the recruiting process.

Promotores as employees vs. *promotores* as volunteers

During the evolution of the *promotor* movement in the United States, several groups have grappled with the question of whether to pay *promotores* for their time or instead to ask them to volunteer in service to their communities.

Since its establishment in 1993, Latino Health Access has been leading community change by training and mobilizing thousands of community members in Southern California. LHA has also trained and supported several other organizations in the U.S. and abroad in the use of the *promotor* model. We hope that our positions on this topic might help deepen this conversation. Our goal is to promote employment practices that are aligned with equality and justice.

The continuum from volunteer to paid employee

"Adela, who was a promotora for LHA, taught in the building where I lived. She knocked on my door every week to invite me to learn about a variety of topics. I told her I didn't need it. I was living in a violent situation at home; it was very painful. I knew that I needed help, but… One day she approached me and asked, 'What are you good at?' Then she invited me to prepare snacks for children. I volunteered with LHA doing a variety of things for three years. One fine day, Adela told me there was an opportunity to work part-time at LHA, and I took it.

"During my time as a volunteer and now as an employee, I have come to realize that I could and I wanted to discover my capacity to serve others. Many things came together for me to not be afraid to grow. They trained me and gave me support. I understood that God is not an accomplice in violence and I do not have to put up with abuse. Now I had a job, my own money to move with my children, and also the support of my neighbors and colleagues. Then I let that abusive relationship go and my life greatly improved. I have been working with groups for 16 years and creating spaces for other women to feel protected like I felt, and to

learn that they can take steps to defend their dignity, their lives, and their families."

—*Soledad, promotora, Emotional Wellness Program*

LHA's workforce includes *promotores*, among other employees. We write our proposals with the *promotores* in mind so their funding is included in every budget. Compensating *promotores* with full salary and job benefits is not an afterthought. Simultaneously, LHA has hundreds of volunteer community members who could become *promotores* in the future or remain as volunteers, depending on their qualifications and our programmatic opportunities. We oppose having programs in which the positions for university-trained personnel are compensated and the ones for community members are not. However, we want to make it clear that we support the inclusion of volunteers in community teams. Voluntarism is important because it creates a mechanism for participation in the creation of a healthier community, helping one's neighbors, supporting activities, advocating and leading. It reduces isolation and creates community. Voluntarism is critical because

Adriana, Soledad, and Verenice, LHA employees, cook for our volunteers.

organizations around the planet will never have all the funding needed to hire all the hands required to build healthier communities. We will always depend on volunteers. Voluntarism can also lead to employment. In fact, we are convinced that the path to become a *promotor* or to do other work in the community is best initiated through volunteer work.

Community members in particular have multiple opportunities to participate in creating change in their neighborhoods and cities. Paid *promotores*, along with community members, create these opportunities by engaging neighbors in meaningful projects. Frequently, ideas for projects and for volunteer opportunities come directly from non-paid community members. For example, they might want to hold a workshop with the community about how to create a cooperative to make and sell crafts. If they move forward with the idea, the neighbors who proposed it might become involved in bringing it to fruition. At other times, neighbors offer their talents, such as teaching weaving or dance. These classes or gatherings become safe spaces for conversations about issues such as domestic violence, or for brainstorming action steps needed to make the community more supportive of health and safety. In this way, one person volunteering a talent serves to invite others to volunteer and to participate.

Community participation is especially essential in areas where the social conditions that determine health are working against the community members. These are the areas where the need for change is the greatest and where community members need support to see their role in the change process. Once connected, a volunteer can begin to engage in a series of trainings and opportunities for mentoring with a paid *promotor*. This experience raises the knowledge level and political awareness of the volunteer.

Community members participate at different levels. Latino Health Access has identified four levels of community participation, which are described on page 45. Once engaged as volunteers, many individuals show natural leadership capabilities and a hunger to learn more. As explained before, if they also possess the other characteristics of successful *promotores*, and if the financial resources are available, then they may be considered for employment by Latino Health Access.

The majority of the paid *promotores* at LHA started as volunteers and were able to demonstrate initiative, common sense, depth of analysis, a strong social commitment, the capacity to organize, leadership abilities, and other characteristics that made them highly desirable as recruits for paid positions.

Why we pay *promotores*

At LHA we work hard to pay our *promotores* a fair salary with benefits such as health insurance, vacation, and sick days. We realize that not all organizations have the ability to compensate their *promotor* teams, and we don't mean to pass judgment on organizations that work with a volunteer-based model. However, not all arguments against compensation are based on funding issues. We have participated in countless conversations in which some people argue that *promotores* do not have the same commitment to community work when they get paid, or that if there is compensation, people may join the project just for the money.

We see it as our obligation to challenge those beliefs in this book, the same way we do with colleagues when we hear those comments. It is true that many people join projects where there is money, even if they are not committed to the cause. It is also true that most people get paid for their work in any field (academic, non-profit, or governmental), and for the great majority of positions there is no question about commitment. It seems condescending to presume that community members' commitment may be so shaky that the presence of money will compromise it. In addition, the effort to assess candidates' commitment to the project needs to be completed before selecting and recruiting them (see page 88).

When we hire and pay *promotores*, we are helping remove barriers to participation. Now, they have the time, money, information, training, and opportunities to develop their vision, to reflect, plan, experiment, organize, act, and receive coaching and support. An individual in this position now has more power and resources to change her/his own community.

When we work with *promotores* in this way, we are working with the community at two levels: 1) inside the organization, where *promotores* represent the community in which they live and return home every day; and 2) outside the organization, where *promotores* bring their energy, resources, and knowledge to help neighbors change their surroundings and their lives, and where *promotoras* as neighbors can improve their own lives

The *promotor* assumes a pivotal position in what is nonetheless a multi-directional structure of accountability, an interdependent web of relationships making the *promotor*, the organization, and the community accountable to each other for results or the lack thereof. The natural rules of this organic structure force us to aim for and achieve a high level of inclusion from the initial brainstorming phase of a project through the ongoing trainings, reflections, actions, and evaluations that occur as the project evolves. The stability lent by an organization such as LHA that has the resources to hire and train *promotores* provides support and continuity to the community's organizing, and preserves and extends the human and social capital of the community over time. Long-term employment of *promotores* helps them to participate more fully in creating change. They learn how to be more strategic and more effective, and they teach others how to participate as well.

Our *promotores* make sure our services are appropriate for reaching out to low-income communities. They have an important voice inside the organization and help shape our strategies and programs. At LHA we try to create the space that allows *promotores* to increase their analytical capacity, their political awareness, their courage to propose and fight for changes, their ability to help others recognize their own power, and their skills to organize and teach, to document and report, to evaluate successes and failures, and to connect programs and processes to create more comprehensive approaches. In other words, we try to model internally what *promotores* in turn will create outside the agency. All of this is possible because a salary gives them the financial security to focus on the transformation of their communities and the acquisition of resources and skills to make it happen.

Why talk about equity, solidarity, and the need for opportunities if our own organizations and projects do not exemplify these values through our labor practices and our commitment to support the economic well-being of our own teams and communities?

We want to invite those organizations working with community workers and *promotores*, organizations that without second thoughts compensate directors, coordinators, evaluators, and researchers, to consider the fact that the *promotores* making important contributions to the projects have many financial needs that, if met, could give these leaders the opportunity to get further involved in the transformation of their own communities.

Training and learning with *promotores* at LHA

The best way to conceive and design trainings for and with *promotores* is to ask ourselves, "What type of *promotor* does our community need?" The assumption in the design of the Latino Health Access training is that we are partnering with leaders so they can become even better leaders. We go into the training knowing we are working with experts. If our *promotores* are experts in their communities, the question follows, "How are experts trained?" In the type of trainings produced by LHA, the *promotores* are also trainers. We use critical listening and reasoning skills to draw out participants' experiences so they can learn from each other. Our activities become models for the *promotores* to take back to their communities where they then treat community members as experts in the issues that are important to them. As *promotores* and community members use trainings to share expertise and learn from each other, we transform the health and wellness of our communities.

Becoming protagonists in our own stories

Our activities are inspired by the teachings of Paulo Freire (Freire, 1986). Paulo Freire was a Brazilian educator who is famous for his work in developing popular education methods to address widespread illiteracy, poverty, and oppression. Our activities are designed to increase consciousness through what Freire called problem-posing. We question the world with the purpose of redefining and re-creating our realities.

There is not one group that knows and one group that does not

The LHA trainings increase awareness and teach skills to encourage thinking, planning, problem-solving, and engaging in actions and behaviors that can bring about the desired change. Activities are designed to improve the ability to promote human relations in ways that enable people to realize their individual and community power to improve their lives and their communities in solidarity with others. Trainings are not limited to disease-related information. Our experienced team members, some of whom have worked more than 35 years in community health, design trainings that are informed by the life experiences and realities of the participants. The training plan provides structure and flexibility in an atmosphere that acknowledges that we all teach (co-teaching) and learn (co-learning). We are very clear that there is not a group that knows and one that does not.

It is essential that *promotores* acquire the skills and self-confidence they need to motivate and engage people in their communities to get involved in their own health at the individual, family, and community levels. The competencies needed to promote this philosophy are not developed in one session, which is why LHA offers ongoing co-learning and co-teaching opportunities with our *promotores*.

LHA's trainings use questions and situations to create conversations among participants. In these conversations, participants share their experiences, points of view, and ideas. Sometimes, participants will research topics and share what they learn. We use questions, real-life testimonials, music, poems, games, drawings, case studies, and many other methods that can help us start a conversation and move into a deeper analysis of the topic. In addition, we read and discuss books in groups and share information that can enrich the dialogue and our understanding of an issue. LHA trainings are very down-to-earth and practical. They are

A typical training with LHA staff

completely grounded in the needs and strengths of the community we partner with and serve. *Promotores* start working with their community the first week of training because the interaction with residents helps create the relationships with individuals, families, and community, the understanding about their reality, the firsthand knowledge about potential barriers and solutions, and the day-to-day opportunity to problem-solve and become better leaders, supporters, educators, and organizers.

A different way of teaching and learning

The LHA trainings are designed for the benefit of all staff, including *promotores*, to improve their competencies to do their work. The trainings are described more specifically in chapter 8. Topics might be suggested by anyone in the team. The training delivery may be more traditional for those topics requiring a specific technical discussion: for example, a demonstration of a procedure or the presentation of regulations and norms. However, for those topics involving more reflection and requiring the generation of ideas for action, the facilitator will use dialogues, popular education, theme generation, and other non-traditional methodologies. The content and activity design is in the hands of the team or department putting together the training. However, in this approach it is the participants' involvement that will determine the quality and depth of the activity. The person facilitating the training may have multiple roles such as co-teaching and co-learning with the participants, facilitating, and motivating. For many participants, this type of training may challenge their beliefs about education. It is important to clarify expectations from the beginning about who will do the teaching and the learning, the need for active participation, how the activity will flow, and how it may differ from traditional school type models of training. In this training, there is no hierarchy among participants. We are all experts, we bring our wisdom and points of view, and we are all committed to learning as much as possible from the experience. Training topics are identified based on participants' experience of what is needed to do this type of work and updated as new skills are needed in a changing landscape. A trainer or training team is identified to research the topic and prepare an interactive learning session. It is our training. We need to make it work. It must be relevant, fun, and interesting. We are all smart and we can all learn.

Our daily work and training of all staff – this culture of collective learning – changes pre-conceptions about the way we teach and the way we learn. This investment is made so LHA staff, including the *promotores*, will co-learn and co-teach with the community, within a paradigm of respect and inclusion.

Learning by questioning

Questioning is fundamental to our work in the community and with each other. In order to have an effect on the root causes of disease and despair, we must teach ourselves and others to question dominant discourses. Critical thinking happens when we allow time and space for people to think about questions that might seem to have obvious answers. It requires us to be curious. For example, asking the question, "Why does this neighborhood have no parks when the other neighborhood has several parks?" yields a different course of action than simply observing there are no parks and accepting that as the reality. The question may lead to other questions and then to the realization that there is an unjust distribution of resources, which may lead to an investigation of how resource distribution occurs in a city, and what it would take to change that resource allocation going forward.

When we begin this work of questioning, we have to ask, "Who owns the right to question?" In a physician's office, for example, the provider is the one asking the questions. "When did you begin to feel this way?" "Does it hurt here? There?" For the most part, the person consulting the physician is expected to answer what is asked and then take the prescribed action dispensed from the wise one who is holding the pen. The health care provider is the one writing the story. How do we get the other story, if the one with the concern is never the one holding the pen? How do we become the writers and protagonists of our own lives, and how do we help others reclaim this right?

When people consulting physicians are invited to ask questions and think with their providers, they become part of the health care team and are much better able to manage their conditions or to prevent them in the first place. When people question why their children are obese, they might learn about the unhealthy ingredients the food industry adds to packaged foods, and they could end up joining a campaign to address that. Maybe they will see the trash-filled vacant lots in their neighborhoods and join with others to transform them into parks.

We know as trainers and facilitators that to encourage and prompt questioning will mean we will not be able to control the answers. However, we remind ourselves of some basic truths:

- No one has all the answers.
- No one has all the questions.
- A deeper understanding of issues becomes evident as questions are formulated and answered.
- The answers lead to more questions.
- This process of questioning and answering generates ideas and solutions that lead people to take action or even to resurrect effective solutions they tried in the past.
- Asking questions with authentic curiosity is also a way of honoring the experience, knowledge, and wisdom of others.

No exams

Just as no one person has all the answers, no test can truly measure a person's ability to lead their community. For this reason, and because tests for people who have not had much formal education can be intimidating, there are no exams or tests in our *promotor* training. *Promotores* may be required to take exams by other institutions working with us when becoming certified as an HIV Counselor or Passenger Safety Instructor, for example, but not for a *promotor* skill-building training. In order for the facilitator to assess understanding, we role-play or we ask participants to present their ideas and conclusions. When the *promotores* are in action, they receive support and supervision. When *promotores* need to facilitate a training themselves, they use the same model. Depending on the topic they will receive a specific curriculum to guide the educational sessions and frequent updates.

Basic Training with *promotores*

Once *promotores* are recruited as volunteers or employees, they participate in the Basic Training. In this training we share the fundamental principles of our community work. The purpose of the LHA *promotores* training is to increase community leaders' understanding of the principles and values that guide our work and to increase their skills to assist, educate, and inform their community in a way that stimulates creativity, inclusion, participation, commitment, reciprocity, reflection, and action among participants.

The activities draw on people's own experiences so that they may reflect on, analyze, critique, and increase their understanding on a variety of issues that affect health and well-being. Training emphasizes respect for the fact that each of us "owns" his or her own life and is the main protagonist for the changes that occur within it. The Basic Training content is designed to help leaders help other leaders. Because of this, the training provides an opportunity for participants to reflect upon and discuss in depth issues of style, prejudice, world view, power, and control.

Basic Training content

The initial Basic Training consists of 15 foundational modules. They are:

1. Getting to know each other. The importance of relationships in community work.
2. Training expectations and group norms. The importance of reaching and respecting agreements.
3. Characteristics and scope of the work of a health promoter. Why community work helps you become a better you.
4. Defining our community. Discovering the dominant discourses inside our head. How do we identify and confront internalized oppression, racism, and classism? How do we recognize and work with our prejudices?
5. Popular education. Creating conversation for change.
6. Engaging adults. Learning the principles of adult education.
7. Working with groups. Learning facilitation and team-building skills.
8. Communication 101. Getting the intended message across.

9. Reflecting about perceptions and assumptions. Barriers to communication.

10. Taking co-learning and co-teaching to the community. Developing and delivering a presentation.

11. Participation makes a difference. Understanding participation, leadership, and representation.

12. Finding our neighbors. How to organize and conduct outreach in the community.

13. About Latino Health Access. LHA's history, philosophy, principles, and program.

14. The Healthy City framework. How to create healthier communities and how to move from services to policies.

15. Social determinants of health: Understanding how the places where we live, play, learn, and work, together with the circumstances of our lives, influence our health.

Learning from experience

Promotores need to start working on their projects from day one. For this reason, activities in the classroom are combined with experience in the field as much as possible. For example, we may have a discussion about how to conduct outreach followed by real outreach to real families that are going to be in the program. *Promotores* also learn from experience about services available to the community by having conversations about quality and access and by visiting these services and making actual referrals.

Team-building from day one

LHA trainings are designed with a high level of human and social interaction so that we can start to learn about each other's styles, talents, motivations, and passions. Participants naturally share personal stories and problems, creating an intimate space that unites them. We all take responsibility for the success of our learning experience; we set up the table together, eat together, clean together. We take advantage of every opportunity to create a relationship among *promotores*, supervisors, and the rest of the team for effective teamwork from day one.

Who are the trainers?

Our own teams are responsible for implementing internal trainings in our organization. Everyone at LHA trains and gets trained. For example, our Evaluation Department team trains on how to reduce errors in data, maintain our database, and design surveys. Our Community Engagement and Advocacy Department team trains on how to advocate for better laws and regulations and how to effectively work with our political representatives. *Promotores* train on community outreach and engagement, and on strategies for promoting health. Our Emotional Wellness Program team trains on mental health in the community, addictions, and family strengthening. The Executive Director trains on models of Healthy Cities, leadership, and principles of adult education.

In addition to internal trainings, *promotores* also enhance their skills and knowledge by visiting other organizations and going to conferences. Universities and colleges, hospitals, non-profit organizations, and other less obvious organizations such as unions and political groups are all important sources of trainers and coaches. Many of the outside trainers have more traditional styles, but their contribution to the knowledge of selected issues is significant. All *promotores* participate in trainings in multiple subjects. However, once *promotores* are assigned to a program, they receive additional content-specific training in their focus areas.

Promotores as trainers

> "For me, Latino Health Access has been a university. During internal trainings, we listen to each other's points of view on various themes. It's wonderful how your mind opens. I have grown as a person and I have been trained to do my job better each time.

> "I've lived with diabetes for 25 years. For a year and a half, I thought I could manage it with natural medicine and did not go to any clinic. After that, I learned about LHA, where I learned to manage my diabetes instead of letting it manage me. When I facilitate Diabetes Self-Management Program classes, I remember that I, too, have diabetes and that it is hard to accept

this condition. I have learned to work with adults in a manner that respects their opinions and independence. In each class I share our curriculum and experience. At the same time, people with diabetes who come to our classes are my teachers, and they help me to remember that I, too, have diabetes and that it is important to manage my condition. I am very happy to see the difference between the time they arrive and when they leave. The majority of them leave with more hope that they can manage their diabetes, with tools to do so, and with more stable glucose."

—Bienvenida, promotora, Diabetes Self-Management Program

Bienvenida celebrates graduation with program participants.

Promotores train the community and teach classes on topics such as diabetes self-management, mental health, breast cancer, how to organize neighborhood councils, and more. They also lead support groups and develop activities with families in the community, including weekend retreats. They participate in trainings internally, helping to train each other and their supervisors. Those with higher levels of experience train new ones, helping them become familiar with the programs and the organization, and serving as mentors to new *promotores* who shadow them in the community. They inform the data collection process, fund development activities, and all strategies.

The *promotores* are also involved in training people in other organizations that want to replicate our disease management programs or request trainings about our community work. For example, Latino Health Access *promotores* are trainers for Family Medicine residents who complete a community rotation at our organization, as well as for other groups that are learning to implement the *promotor* model. They also participate in local and national conferences where they present their experiences.

Commitment to ongoing learning

Trainings are designed to respect where every participant is in her or his development and style. We all explore themes, we all learn in different ways, we reach different conclusions, and then we all are ready for the next level. At LHA, supervisors must ensure that *promotores* participate in ongoing training and are qualified to do the job. When a project is new, the coordinator has to ensure that the *promotores* have a good understanding of the objectives and have opportunities to contribute ideas on how to achieve them.

Ongoing training will ensure that *promotores* have a comprehensive knowledge base and that their skills are developing. At LHA, we repeat trainings on different topics every so often and we try approaching the topic from different angles and with different levels of complexity. We reiterate during the training that this is just the beginning of an unlimited learning journey. Ongoing training is built into the workday. Monthly, half-day staff meetings are mandatory and always include trainings and updates. In addition, *promotores* participate in retreats, one-on-one coaching, peer learning opportunities, and trainings outside LHA. Additional discussions of how we learn at LHA and of the competencies for our various positions can be found in chapters 5 and 8.

What have trainees taught us?

Since our first training, Latino Health Access has adapted, modified, and expanded the concepts and the design of learning sessions based on our experience conducting trainings with thousands of *promotores*. Through this process, we have learned a great deal.

What makes a training successful?

- Trainings need to be designed to include the views of the *promotores* regarding the community's problems and solutions.
- Use of jargon and specialized vocabulary is not helpful and does not create common understanding.
- Training based on lectures does not provide *promotores* with the space to interact effectively and offer their wisdom.
- Trainers need to be carefully selected to ensure the right learning environment.
- *Promotores* enjoy hands-on activities where they can talk, share ideas, and come up with solutions.
- Conversations need to be relevant and connected to the personal and professional lives of *promotores*.
- Learning for *promotores* occurs mainly when interacting with other *promotores* and community participants.
- Popular education methodologies that invite critical thinking through the use of songs, poems, stories, role playing, skits, questions, and the like are very effective and tend to help *promotores* remain engaged. Trainers need to be familiar with this type of education.
- The different situations in the community, the way the *promotores* seek solutions and the results of their actions are key ingredients for continuous learning. Space needs to be created to dialogue about these experiences.
- Training must include not only health-related information but also the information and opportunity to practice all competencies needed for the job, particularly those that help create long-lasting relationships with the community.
- Many of the skills and much of the knowledge needed to be effective at community work are developed over time, together with personal growth and self-confidence. Ongoing training and nurturing are essential to support such growth.
- The themes generated during conversations with *promotores* and communities, the topics they would like to further explore, and the skills needed to advance the resolution of their problems should be determinants in the design of the training plan.

Should community experts be certified?

Over the years there has been debate about whether there should be certifying bodies that affirm *promotor* competencies.[1] As more people in health and social service institutions become aware of the power of the *promotor* model, the debate is intensifying. A movement toward certification seems to be underway.

Context of the debate about certification

In 1978, the World Health Organization in Alma Ata recommended the adoption of Primary Health Care as a way of improving access to health services. The WHO suggested the inclusion of community health workers into multi-disciplinary teams to carry out this agenda of primary care with the majority of the world's population to support local champions in making their communities healthier places (World Health Organization, 1978).

The idea was not new. For centuries, community members have been helping each other as the only guarantee of survival, support, and progress. In Latin America, these helpers have come to be called *promotores*, a name that has been adopted in many communities in the U.S. *Promotores* are also called lay workers, lay advisors, primary care workers, navigators, community health workers, and other such titles.

In many places, *promotores* or community health workers are not aware of titles given to them. They only know each other by name. Neighbors know that if they have a problem they go to Tere's house, or that Marcela is always there for them no matter what. They rely on Oscar to organize and represent them in cases where they have been abused or suffered a lack of justice. People in our local community who have diabetes learn to manage their condition with Luzy and love the feeling of being in charge of their diabetes.

---

1 Several authors have documented competencies and skills that community health workers or *promotores* should have in order to be effective. These documents include: California Department of Public Health Office of Binational Border Health, 2011; California Health Workforce Alliance, December, 2013; and Centers for Disease Control and Prevention, *Community Health Workers*, 2011. See chapter 8 for a discussion of LHA's "competencies" for *promotores*.

Some of our *promotores* in training: (clockwise) Vicky, Anthony, Socorro, and Oscar

In other parts of the world, Elizabeth goes out for days and walks miles to let everybody know that the doctor will be in town. Carmen organizes women to sell goods or to help someone with a family crisis. More than 40,000 grandmothers in Nepal became community health workers and led a successful health crusade to decrease malnutrition and eliminate night blindness among children (UNICEF, 2003). These special individuals are experts in many things, but they do not stop to analyze their own expertise. They do not write books about themselves with tables of competencies needed to make them good helpers. However, they have the trust of their communities and are a key resource for any strategy designed to improve the health and well-being of populations around the world, particularly those with fewer resources and less power.

The effectiveness of these neighbors has attracted the attention of institutions and individuals from all walks of life, particularly those in need of credible intermediaries to convey a message. That is why community members are recruited by marketers to sell products to their own people or to conduct surveys in their communities – because they deliver results.

In the health and human services field, the work and effectiveness of *promotores* is a source of hope for continued improvement in health and living conditions of those in need, particularly in low-income communities of color (CDC, 2011). Other health institutions are looking for workers who can increase profits by assuring access to and utilization of services, increasing compliance, and decreasing costs.

Public health officials, policy makers, and health justice advocates are focusing more and more on community health workers/*promotores* in the United States, and discussing their role as part of the health workforce. The health care reform movement and the Affordable Care Act of 2010 have heightened interest in community health workers/*promotores* for their role as cultural brokers and guides in health service navigation, which, as is widely known, is a major barrier to health care service utilization.

The increased interest in community health workers/*promotores* raises important questions about certification, including: What are the reasons some advocate for certification? Is there an institution or organization that is truly able to certify that someone is a community expert? Who really owns and controls the right to help others? What are some alternatives to certification that can preserve the spirit and efficacy of the *promotor* model?

> *"I am involved also in our work in Food Justice with some of the edible gardening happening now at the park. In order to see the changes we want to see, we have to persevere. It also gives me energy to do my work when I think about the many families I interact with. I remember their faces, their difficulties, their dreams. I feel one with them. I feel a high sense of responsibility towards them. I believe in relationships with solidarity. I do not think that what makes me a promotora can be certified. How do you certify commitment, compassion, sensitivity, and responsibility? I think people need to bring those characteristics to this work. Once here, we learn and improve. To become a better promotora, a commitment to ongoing learning must exist in the personal and professional areas, on the part of the person and on the part of the agency we work with. We have to be supported. LHA has given me the support I need for my work as a promotora. I am delighted*

with the work I do in my community because together we are accomplishing the positive changes we are seeking."

—*Rosalia, promotora and Coordinator of Familias Corazones Verdes Park and LHA Community Center*

What are we hearing in the national conversation that supports certifying *promotores?*

- It is easier for institutions to hire community health workers who are already certified as such. Institutions that are potential employers can assume that workers have a defined set of competencies and are ready to perform a specific job.
- Reimbursement can be easier to obtain if workers are certified.
- A certification process assures standard training and skills of workers.
- Performance measures can be established against a defined set of competencies and roles.
- Institutions will maintain their quality of services and will not increase their liability.
- *Promotores* will be received with a higher level of respect by other professionals in institutions because they are certified.
- It increases the possibility of a salary or higher salary for *promotores.*
- It starts *promotores* on a "career path" to becoming "professionals."

LHA's position on certification

While the reasons above may be good reasons, we are not convinced certification will accomplish what its proponents desire. A community member who demonstrates commitment and concern for the community served, belongs to that community, speaks its language, understands its cultural beliefs and practices, has the respect and trust of the community, is kind, open-minded, and likes to learn is a community member who is ready to be recruited as a *promotor.* We do not believe it is possible to certify that a person is committed, caring, respectful, credible, trusted, and concerned with social justice, which are critical characteristics of a *promotor.* It is our position that the characteristics and competencies that make a *promotor* effective cannot be certified. They are developed by the individual in daily interaction with and service to his or her community.

Is it better to recruit *promotores* because they have completed a certification program or because they have the attributes to be effective? The qualities that make a good *promotor* are either present or not before the person is trained. The critical component in determining whether a *promotor* will be able to lead her community toward wellness comes at the time of recruitment. To assume that a person who has become a "Certified Community Health Worker" will have these critical characteristics would be a grave mistake.

Promotores' most important competencies are those they already had before they joined the organization. Once they are recruited, they may need to develop additional skills, and for some of these skills, certification makes sense. Examples include HIV counseling, cardio-pulmonary resuscitation (CPR), health system navigation, insurance enrollment, and phlebotomy, among others. It is the prerogative of the hiring institution to certify or find a certification program for the *promotor* in particular areas of work where this is recommended or required. However, health care institutions hiring *promotores* should remember that to reduce the role of a *promotor* to a prescribed set of certifiable skills is to lose the power of the model, which was the driving force for adding *promotores* to the team in the first place. Traditional medical training risks changing the role of the *promotores* into reduced-scope medical assistants, when in reality, we need *promotores* to be leaders of wellness agendas and change in their communities.

Training community workers as part of the health care team

Community health workers, though not always called so, have been part of the health care team around the globe since the beginning of time. They are extremely effective in providing services and helping their neighbors gain access to the services they need. In today's health care environment, where time is money and providers are pushed to their limits to see more patients in less time, and where health plans are beginning to be incentivized based on outcomes, the idea of adding a community health worker to the team is very attractive indeed.

Many hospitals and health departments in the U.S., such as the Inland Empire Health Plan's Health Navigator Program, with which we have worked, have successfully integrated community health workers into their team. How have they done this? Those that are successful generally partner with a community-based organization for help with recruitment and training. They invest in training the rest of the health care team about the role of the *promotor*, they create an environment where the *promotor* can use her full range of competencies to do what she needs to do to improve health, and they select a supervisor that knows how to work with *promotores*. And the institution assures support for the uninterrupted work of *promotores* with families, both in clinics and offices, and in the natural community setting.

Who should train *promotores*?

An institution that wishes to work with *promotores* for the first time can engage a credible, community-based organization already working with the *promotor* model to train them. There are several organizations with track records in recruiting and training well-rounded, effective community health workers. In our opinion, an institution or organization that wants to hire *promotores* would be wise to consult with one of these experienced organizations to receive advice about recruitment and training. It is better when *promotores* are part of the training team.

Institutional commitment and readiness

These experienced community-based organizations also place value on helping the institution get ready to have a *promotor* program that is successful. Many programs fail because academic approaches to training and heavy-handed, hierarchical supervision styles undermine the *promotores'* abilities to take initiative and be effective in their communities.

When *promotor* programs fail, there can be a tendency to blame the *promotores*. If the institution or organization has a commitment to community transformation, to the community having a voice and a role in service delivery, then the carefully selected and trained *promotor* will likely succeed. As institutions, we have to be ready to give over some power of decision-making and vision-setting to the community, to invite its members to lead, and not just tell them what to do so we can meet our goals.

It is important that individuals in charge of supervising *promotores* undergo training on this model preferably by a community-based organization with a track record. Following initial training, supervisors working with *promotores* should monitor, train, and support their staff on an ongoing basis to assure that the desired competencies are further developed.

The institution and the *promotores* can discuss the program and the realistic expectations together. A job description, listing skills, competencies, and performance measures, could then be created based on the specific institutional program or needs.

A certification process may be useful to develop skills for special medical or administrative training; this may apply particularly for primary care workers in many parts of the world who are part of the medical team and perform medical duties. But it must be remembered that a certification process can only assure the validation of a set of skills that can be readily measured at one time. Follow-up and continued opportunities to learn are also necessary. All trainings should be given using the principles of adult education, that is, relevant, simple, and applicable in the *promotor*'s community.

If *promotores* are community experts, who will certify them?

One of the main problems with *promotor* certification is the risk of giving too much authority to the government or college or whatever entity is doing the certifying.

To deem an institution as the "certifier" would mean that we have given over the role of recruitment to that certifying body. As we've discussed, those that register and graduate from the certification training do not necessarily have the characteristics and attributes that will make them effective *promotores* even if they now have a diploma. In reality, this "certificate" might misguide those who are looking to recruit *promotores*. They might think that the certificate assures the *promotor*'s effectiveness, when in fact the *promotor* could be lacking many of the characteristics mentioned in the recruitment section on pages 89–91.

Who would certify the certifying body? How could a university or a government entity possibly certify that someone has the competencies needed to be persuasive with their neighbors in increasing community health when these are the very institutions that the community tends not to trust, based on their historical track record of entering the community for their own purposes, such as conducting research, co-opting organizing, carrying out deportation raids, and the like?

The concept of *promotor* belongs to the people and the people need to protect it. Many of the most effective *promotores* are recognized and validated by their own communities. What would happen with those *promotores* who have been working in their communities for many years? Would they be now practicing the art of being *promotores* illegally? Will they need to go to college to be recognized? Certification may create two classes of *promotores*: those recognized by the certifying institution and those who are non-credentialed despite the fact that they are recognized by their communities.

Does certification help ensure that *promotores* will be treated with respect?

This all depends on what moves health care professionals and employees inside institutions to respect or disrespect others. *Promotores* are individuals with a profound wisdom about their lives and communities. They generally come from and work with low-income communities. If those employees in institutions do not respect community members, we suspect that they will not respect the *promotores* just because they now have a certificate. If an institution does not share the values of community inclusion and input, community representation and guidance, then they will never respect and embrace the *promotores*, even if they have a certificate.

For those who are not familiar with *promotores*, it is our experience that the issue is related to their credibility and that will not be solved by a certificate. *Promotores* achieve credibility when they are given the opportunity to show the impact they have in many areas of their work, such as finding the community members, connecting them with services and the health system, helping others with health decisions for themselves or their families, assisting participants with disease management, helping them achieve desired health outcomes, improving their communities, and so on.

Does certification ensure that *promotores* will have a decent salary and a career path?

We believe *promotores* should be paid, should have health insurance, and should receive other benefits. Certification will not change whether an institution values their contribution enough to provide good salaries and benefits. Likewise, we believe that *promotores* already are professionals in their work and that they are experts in what they do. There is nothing keeping *promotores* from choosing a career outside their role of *promotores*. However, to design a *promotor* program that is intended to discourage them from being *promotores* by insinuating that being a *promotor* is just a step on the path to another job that is more "professional" is another way of blatantly saying that to be a *promotor* is not important in itself. It implies that *promotores* should not be satisfied with being *promotores* because they are not real professionals, and that *promotor* positions are only entry-level steps to a better career. We do not believe this to be true.

The strength of a *promotor* program is in part assured by the long-term commitment of its team of *promotores*. At the same time, this long-term commitment is influenced by the opportunity to have a salary and/or relevant incentives, opportunities for learning, leadership, action, and the *promotores'* commitment to the transformation of their own lives and communities.

In the workplace, *promotores* appreciate supportive supervision and respectful work environments. At LHA, *promotores* can have different roles and different levels of influence in the program and the institution, such as Lead *Promotor*, *Promotor* Coordinator, *Promotor* Assistant, etc. These different roles and responsibilities that *promotores* fill are compensated accordingly.

A career track for *promotores* should be developed by themselves and their organizations. *Promotores* could become trainers, team leaders, or program coordinators. They could move into other careers to become nurses, social workers, or physicians. A worker's experience as a *promotor*, regardless of the certificate, may help to create a compelling case for why he or she deserves to be accepted into an institution of higher education. In addition, a *promotor's* training and experience in community work may prove to be of great value when studying and practicing a career in health and human services. The main barrier for *promotores* who desire to obtain higher education as preparation for professional careers is not the lack of a certificate but the academic, administrative, and financial requirements imposed by the educational system. When possible, and if it fits the plans of the organization, *promotores* who want to pursue higher education could be supported by the institution.

Promotores are community experts in their own right

Community health workers are vital to the health improvement of our communities. They know their communities and care deeply about their well-being. They should be carefully selected, paid, and well-trained both initially and on an ongoing basis. They should be supervised, supported, and nurtured. Respect for their role rests with all of us, including community health workers, and with our ability to document the impact of our work as teams. No certification can take the place of these elements.

We invite you to think...

- Who does the *promotor* model belong to?
- When is an institution ready to work with *promotores*?
- Is it possible that those who would best be recruited as *promotores* in some institutions are already there seeking services, and their potential is not seen? If so, what are some of the reasons this is happening?
- Is it possible to certify a *promotora*'s heart? Does it matter? Why or why not?

Supervision, coaching and support of *promotores*, and the selection and recruitment of supervisors

"If we take community health workers and place them in traditional settings with traditional supervision and give them the same restrictions that have made our work ineffective, how can we expect different results?"

—*America, CEO, Latino Health Access*

LHA's mission is accomplished every day through the work of *promotoras*. Embracing and supporting the role of *promotoras* so they can better inform our strategies and effectively work with the community is a collective responsibility. *Promotoras* work in different strategic areas, in different programs and departments. Every department has a director, and programs have coordinators who have a direct supervisory role with *promotoras*. Our organization also has departments of Human Resources, Accounting, Information Technology, Facilities Management, and Evaluation that support our programs and activities so *promotoras* can carry out their work.

Supervisors play a crucial role in supporting *promotoras* not only in their daily work but also in the ongoing development of competencies. Supervisors also are in charge of assuring completion of contracts and compliance with regulations, procedures, and laws. As explained in other parts of this book, LHA is a community-based organization in which the institution and the community co-exist in a very productive environment with many healthy tensions.

In this setting, it is important that supervisors are able to co-lead teams with *promotores* and deal with the inevitable tensions and conflicts in ways that reflect LHA's principles and general philosophy. In order to be effective leaders and managers, supervisors need to gain the trust of *promotores* by investing in a relationship with them, and having a great deal of flexibility, common sense, sensitivity, and emotional intelligence. It is extremely important that supervisors include *promotores* in the design and content of program and activities, and that they understand why and how *promotores* do what they do. *Promotores* need to feel that supervisors include them and their ideas, and that they are supported to do their jobs and are treated with respect and fairness.

Supervisors are considered LHA's team of technical experts. They come to our agency with formal training in various areas of health and human services and with different levels of direct field experience. Some supervisors are *promotores* who do not have formal college training but have had many years of community work with LHA. Supervisors have much knowledge, skill, and experience to offer, and they must do so in ways that include the knowledge and wisdom of *promotoras*, our community experts. Our paradigm is not one in which the boss or supervisor knows how to do the job and tells an obedient team what needs to be done.

Supervisors support *promotoras* in three main dimensions: Human, technical, and financial/administrative

> *"At LHA we are united by an invisible link that we know but do not see: the story of our experience, internal life, labor in our work, and even in the endearment we feel toward the participants in our support groups. There is an invisible contact that becomes visible when we have conversations with the coordinator. The coordinator and I do not only talk about the problems of the participants, but also about the good things that are happening, about our environment, even about my own problems. In these discussions, invisible connections become visible and we all contribute to make our community more united. All this helps LHA to grow. It helps me grow."*
>
> —*Alex, promotor, Older Adult Program*

The **Human Dimension** of supervision refers to supporting *promotores'* personal aspirations and growth, providing opportunities for self-development, offering recognition, and providing the time and space for the *promotora* to express and manage frustrations, problems, or conflicts.

Supervisors support human growth when they:

- Develop a relationship with the *promotor* in which he/she feels accepted and respected.
- Get to know the aspirations and visions of the *promotor*.
- Coach one-on-one and/or seek help with coaching the *promotor* on how to accomplish what they envision or in dealing with problems affecting their performance.
- Offer and request timely and regular feedback.
- Identify and offer opportunities for individual self-development, beyond the realm of program content.
- Identify and offer opportunities to protect their physical, mental, social, and spiritual balance.
- Create opportunities for team-building within the program and the organization at large.
- Recognize their good work in private and in public.
- Follow up on requests and communications with the team.
- Assure the inclusion of the *promotor* in the resolution of any concerns and difficulties.
- Handle conflicts and frustrations as soon as they arise.

The **Technical Dimension** refers to the support of *promotores* so their practice can be aligned with the principles and philosophy of the organization, and their work can be of the highest quality.

Supervisors support technical growth when they:

- Share and maintain ongoing conversations with *promotores* about the vision, mission, strategies, Principles of Practice, and overall philosophy of the organization, and assure the team is aligned with them.
- Assure the collective creation of a vision for the direct program under their supervision.

- Assure that learning happens in an atmosphere of critical and creative thinking, in which *promotores'* expertise is valued by all in the organization and their points of view inform the program and the organization's overall strategy.
- Assure that *promotores* participate in ongoing, appropriate, timely training and that the training plan facilitates the development of core competencies.
- Offer and request timely and regular feedback, and offer opportunities for improvement.
- Assure that *promotores* become familiar with program expectations, outcomes, objectives, proposed activities, and evaluation.
- Assure flexibility in program design and the action plan to accommodate the changes recommended by *promotores* from the lessons learned in the field.
- Assure that *promotores* allocate time to participate in meetings, committees, retreats, and trainings.
- Plan activities with *promotores* to assure that they make sense and are doable based on the *promotor* experience and their knowledge of the community.
- Meet with *promotores* on a weekly basis to jointly assess what is working and what is not, to plan activities, and to troubleshoot.
- Discuss with *promotores* what reports are required to funders and stakeholders, why they are required, how to document their work, how this documentation links back to the objectives, and the importance of ensuring timely data collection and reporting.
- Assure through training, coaching, and additional help, if needed, that all forms for program documentation are completed and submitted on a timely basis. The supervisor needs to be aware that competencies around program documentation and data-related activities might need to be developed. However, it is important to make sure *promotores* avoid spending too much time dealing with data instead of working with participants and being in the community.

- Train *promotores* on how to use technology, including computers, projectors, and other technical resources that are offered.
- Assure that *promotores* create and/or engage in activities to share and disseminate the goals and accomplishments of the program to community, partners, co-workers, visitors, funders, and other groups as requested.
- Provide opportunities for the *promotores* to learn from others through conferences and trainings outside of the agency.
- Ensure the *promotores* have opportunities to share and highlight their work and their learnings internally and externally as trainers, committee members, and in meetings.

The **Financial and Administrative Dimension** refers to the support needed by *promotores* to be aware of their rights, duties, and benefits, and to become familiar with the procedures to obtain resources for program activities, complete administrative requests and forms, comply with regulations and laws, and assure worker and public safety. Orientations and trainings in these aspects of the job are primarily the responsibility of other departments such as Human Resources, Accounting, Facilities Management, or Information Technology.

Supervisors support Finance and Administration when they:

- Assure *promotores* receive orientation on personnel policies, rights, duties, and benefits, and that they sign related documentation.
- Assure *promotores* comply with regulations and laws governing our organization and line of work.
- Assure *promotores* are familiar and comply with internal policies and procedures.
- Assure through training, coaching, and additional help, if needed, that *promotores* complete and turn in forms such as time sheets, mileage reimbursement requests, and requests for time off.

- Inform *promotores* about how the organization gets funding. Explain the program budget so *promotores* know how to plan and when to look for more resources.
- Encourage and allow *promotores* to participate in the overall sustainability plan of the program and agency. Encourage *promotores* to find additional resources within the community through small fundraising activities.
- Assure *promotores* are trained on safety protocols and disaster preparedness inside the agency, in the community, and for program participants.
- Conduct performance evaluation as requested by the Human Resources Department.
- Maintain records of trainings.

Hiromi, coordinator, and Marcela, *promotora*, of the Children and Youth Initiative

How can we recruit the right supervisors?

To recruit the right supervisors for programs at LHA is not a simple task. The recruitment process starts when we open a position and advertise internally to our staff and volunteers, and externally through appropriate media, at colleges, universities, professional associations, and through our network. Each candidate is interviewed by several staff members.

We assure that the person has the right qualifications as listed in the job description. Candidates must have prior experience in a type of job where they were able to show commitment and concern to vulnerable families such as the ones in our partner communities. In this type of program, supervisors lead together with *promotores* and communities. We are aware that candidates' resumes do not offer enough information to make a decision. The interview process needs to be such that it allows for the discussion of case scenarios where values, logic, and common sense can be assessed. It is critical to understand the leadership and supervising style of the candidates to assess if they can supervise and train leaders without becoming defensive, and if they can provide work structure without being oppressive.

Candidates for supervisory positions worry us when they give voice to:

- Paradigms with traditional models of authority, power, and hierarchy that go against LHA's more inclusive and egalitarian approach.
- Rigid views of organizational functions based on vertical, hierarchical, authoritarian models.
- Expectations that a supervisor's work happens only in the office.
- Much theory and little practice.
- Difficulties articulating how to engage *promotores* as equal partners in program planning, implementation, and evaluation.
- Too much value placed on formal education and too little on *promotor*/community wisdom and experience.
- Difficulties working flexibly.
- Feeling challenged when *promotoras* assert their leadership.
- Lack of humility.
- Inexperience working with people of color or people in poverty.

To be faithful to the model of community engagement that the *promotor* model represents, we need to protect the leadership of the *promotores* to guide the work. Individuals hired as supervisors will need to interact with leaders and community experts. These are outside-of-the-box, forward-thinking, inclusive models that require outside-of-the-box, forward-thinking supervision.

LHA is privileged to have a highly competent and committed group of supervisors who believe in the mission of our organization. Like the *promotores*, supervisors have a crucial role in supporting the team, informing our strategies, accomplishing our goals and protecting the organization. They work long hours and, for the most part, report a great deal of satisfaction with their jobs. However, there is no doubt that there is much to do in nurturing, supporting, and developing our supervisors. As in every aspect of LHA, we all are committed to ongoing improvement.

What Have You Unlearned Lately?
Paradigms for Learning and Unlearning at LHA

Today, between 9:00 and 10:00 a.m. we are having an audit. The Accounting Department shows the auditor our employee timesheets and receipts for all expenses. During the same time, one of our promotoras is picking up Ms. Lopez at a place near her home to take her to a domestic violence shelter. Ms. Lopez's husband has a drug problem. Another of our promotoras is having a conversation with colleagues about her child who is suffering from discrimination at school because he has a mental health condition. Her colleagues are indignant upon hearing the story and offer advice. They all seek resources to advocate for the child. In the reception area, there is a man who is experiencing homelessness. He has a toothache and is asking for help. LHA is not a clinic nor do we offer dental services, but people know that we can guide them toward help. A team is preparing to do outreach for our Breast Health Program. At the same time, our Evaluation Department is preparing a training on how to improve data collection. Our

Human Resources Department is preparing to explain our health insurance renewal options to staff. A colleague is telling us that he was diagnosed with cancer. Another promoter is asking for donations for a drawing to win a woven blanket to raise money to help a neighbor meet her monthly house payment. Meanwhile someone sends an email that says, "We will be celebrating Alejandra's birthday at 12:00 in the kitchen."

LHA is a non-governmental, non-profit institution. As such, LHA must comply with legal requirements such as labor laws, financial regulations, participant protection, and so on. We also have different contractual requirements from multiple entities. We are constantly navigating relationships with multiple sectors including religious, governmental, business, educational, and grant-making institutions. Our most consistent relationship is among ourselves and the communities we serve, those with whom we participate in the struggle for improved health.

As an institution, we have a vision and mission of what we want to achieve, and strategies, programs, and activities to achieve them. Even though an institution has a physical location, material resources, methodologies, procedures, operational rules, and more, at LHA, we believe that people make the institution.

LHA has 67 employees organized into four groups: 1) the *promotores* or community experts; 2) the program directors or technical experts; 3) the administrative support and data entry workers; and 4) the operations team.

The *promotores*, also known as community health workers (CHWs), are salaried employees of the organization, dedicated on a full- or part-time basis to improving their communities. These *promotores* share the culture, language, history, and reality of the communities they serve. They live in the communities where they work. From the founding of our organization, the *promotores* have informed our strategy and programs, ensuring that our work is dedicated to promoting successful, healthier lives for our families. *promotores* keep our work relevant to and inclusive of people's needs and ideas.

Program Directors and Coordinators include individuals with bachelors, masters, doctoral, and specialty training in health, education, psychology, social work, research, and public policy.

This team also includes experienced *promotoras* with management skills who have been promoted internally. The directors and coordinators are in charge of administering and providing oversight to the different programs. They play a key role in informing and improving LHA's strategy, coordinating efforts across the agency, and assuring contract compliance, program evaluation, and appropriate supervision and support to *promotores* and other staff.

The administrative support and data entry team is in charge of supporting directors, coordinators, and *promotores* in all programs with administrative tasks, including data entry. This team includes individuals with bachelor's degrees, college students, and a few *promotoras* who play a dual role.

The operations team provides the infrastructure to sustain programs and is in charge of daily office operations. It is led by a Chief of Operations and includes Departments of Accounting, Human Resources, Facilities Management, Information Technology, Grants and Contracts, and Fund Development.

More than half of the technical, operational, and administrative groups are comprised of people who were born and grew up in the communities where we concentrate our work. All the rest came to love our communities from different corners and countries of the world.

LHA staff retreat

In addition to staff, the work of Latino Health Access is supported by a volunteer Board of Directors.

The Board of Directors of Latino Health Access

"This agency definitely has a personality. Being a board member at LHA, I am much closer to the community and to the individuals the agency serves. It seems much more personal

than sitting on some other larger boards. We have to have an understanding of our community and place, and of the fact that we have a responsibility to contribute in any way we can to help our neighbors. Board members should be compassionate and caring. We should be concerned about the future of this city and the youth of this city."

—*Modesto, Board Member and former Board Chair*

Latino Health Access created its first Board of Directors from among the people who conducted the study that led to LHA's formation. And so, from our inception, we have placed great care in the recruitment and engagement of board members who bring needed expertise, as well as passion for building community capacity, to the governance body that guides and guards the organization. The concepts of engagement, community voice, and partnerships are well embodied in our Board of Directors. The board has representation from the business, health care, education, and legal sectors, as well as community members and youth. Members bring expertise and influence to the organization and also commit passionately to the mission of the organization and the community it serves.

LHA's Board of Directors and its relationship to the CEO might be different than in other organizations. Our CEO is our founder and is also a member of the Board of Directors. "Recruiting the heart and training the brain" also holds true when we think about adding a new board member. In the same way that we work hard with the community and staff to reduce hierarchical thinking, we work to select board members who will do the same.

LHA Board members:

- Have a heart for community work
- See themselves as contributing to a larger goal
- Set aside personal agendas
- Understand that the CEO leads the creative and collective effort for the development and dissemination of the organization's vision

- See themselves in partnership with the CEO, in support of the CEO, and not so much as the CEO's boss
- Believe that we can come together to improve health in partnership with the community, going beyond traditional concepts of health care
- Honor community wisdom
- Bring additional resources to the agency
- Protect the agency
- Promote the agency

We get to know prospective board members before inviting them to serve on the board to ensure, as much as possible, that we are recruiting someone who shares the heart for this work and will work in a collaborative way.

Monthly board meetings devote a great deal of time to issues of philosophical alignment and realignment. Each regular board meeting is structured to include time for members to learn something new, and to allow sufficient time to discuss policy issues and fiduciary matters. At each board meeting, one of the 20 Principles of Practice that guide LHA (see chapter 6) is discussed to encourage board members to reflect personally and collectively about the organization's core beliefs. Board meetings are also an opportunity to learn about the details and outcomes of LHA's programs. Program staff are often invited to bring participants and share results of their work. This educational aspect of board meetings allows for directors to engage with the work and membership of the organization to which they are accountable, and to achieve a deeper understanding of the important and unique role they play in governance.

In addition to regular meetings, the board holds an annual two-day board retreat to review, revise, and update the mission and strategic plan with the goals of maintaining our relevance, re-evaluating our direction to meet the needs of an ever-changing community environment, confirming our policies and practices, and providing guidance to our organization's advocacy work.

LHA's staff and board members at a retreat

This balance between learning and action is central to the beliefs of LHA. The framework of building knowledge, allowing for informed dialogue and personal and collective reflection, reaching consensus, taking appropriate and positive action, and celebrating the outcomes of that action, is key to the functioning of the Board of Directors. It is an application to governance of the same framework that guides the organization's work.

How do we learn and unlearn at LHA?

All that we are able to do at LHA, all our successes and failures, are connected to our ability to work as a team, to understand each other, and to appreciate and use our experience and collective knowledge. We have the ability to plan, implement, learn, incorporate lessons, create better strategies, develop better projects, involve more people, disseminate what we are doing, stay motivated, keep imagining, and continue re-inventing. We constantly improve ourselves, always developing and strengthening ourselves and our communities.

It is a challenge to develop and maintain a team capable of all this and at the same time create mechanisms to become more competent. In addition, it is difficult to align all members of the organization including those just entering so that we are on the same page in all areas. We are people who come from different places. We have different ways of seeing life and we have diverse educational levels, religions, ages, sexual orientations, and so on.

How can we work together if we have different ways of seeing life and of reacting to events? It is not an easy task. We are constantly trying to work out tensions and to reach agreements. Sometimes we disagree. We focus on what we have achieved or want to achieve together, and from there we work continuously to create an environment where we can learn, unlearn, understand, and align. At the same time, we strive to create and follow rules and our Principles of Practice. The principles that guide LHA's community work also guide us in our internal teamwork.

If there is one thing we all agree on at LHA, it is that we love our community. We feel part of it. We admire our work. We believe that we all contribute. We enjoy harmony, respect, and learning opportunities. We value everyone. We appreciate being treated fairly. We like to be included in plans and decision-making. We enjoy the success of our organization, and we feel a responsibility to discuss difficulties and solve problems.

At LHA, we share our lives every day. We interact with the community in their homes, on the streets, and during community events. Similarly, we interact with foundations, the government, the media, political representatives, educational institutions, religious institutions, and visitors interested in learning about our work. Every interaction tests who we are, what we know, our social skills, our consistency with LHA's principles and values, the quality of our services, our organizational skills, how well we have prepared, our common sense, and especially our ability to learn, unlearn, change, and improve. Every interaction tests how competent we are.

What is unlearning?

Some people say that learning is the process of acquiring knowledge. In popular education, we say that to learn is to change. If we are committed to learning, then we must commit not just to acquire knowledge, but also to look for opportunities for change and growth, for learning and unlearning.

We define unlearning

Unlearning is the process of abandoning concepts and practices in our personal, group, institutional, or community thinking and behavior. We reject some of these concepts and practices because they are ineffective or unscientific, because they are unethical, or because they are in conflict with the principles and values that currently guide us.

Here are some of the things we seek to unlearn and to learn:

We want to unlearn	We want to learn
Homophobia Racism Judgments about the ways people dress	To celebrate differences and to respect each other because everyone has the right to express what they value
Our tendency to generalize	To see people in their particularities
Ineffective ways of dealing with issues	To find better ways to deal with problems and issues together as a group
Holding grudges	To talk things through, resolve conflicts, forgive, and refocus on our mission
Sayings, jokes, and expressions that make fun of indigenous people, women, people of color, and so on	To stop perpetuating discrimination
That only certain people have the right to have knowledge	To open learning spaces for everyone because we think that everyone can learn
That youth and children are immature and can only lead in the future	To create opportunities for children's and youth leadership because we think they are marvelous and strong forces for change right now
Ways of supervision that oppress	To engage in supportive and collaborative supervision
Our internalized oppression and pessimism	To create more opportunities for hope and justice to grow

We invite you to think...

- What have you unlearned lately?
- What is the meaning of learning?
- How do you demonstrate that you have learned something?
- Is learning a process of knowing more about something or is it also related to change? If so, how? If not, why not?

Re-cognizing and Re-naming

To paraphrase Paulo Freire: When we dare to analyze and name our world through critical thinking, when we speak about our aspirations and rights, when we use language to name our realities and hopes, we are in fact re-making and re-naming the world in our imagination as a prelude to what is to come. Through this process, the world's dominant discourse begins to crack.

"Imagination and conjecture about a different world than the one of oppression are as necessary in the process of transforming reality as it necessarily belongs to human toil that the worker or artisan first have in his or her head a design, a conjecture of what he or she is about to make" (Freire and Araujo, 1994).

Like artisans, we at LHA seek to create the spaces inside LHA and in our communities that will allow us to engage in an analysis of our world and imagine a new one. We re-think and re-name our practices, and re-tell our stories and aspirations, thus sketching out the design that informs what we will create through our collective work.

There are many things that we do, that we know, or that we believe in that we must change. How do we re-cognize them? How do we correct and improve? The first steps are to observe others' behaviors and observe our feelings and the resulting impact of our own behaviors. At LHA we find that one-on-one feedback sessions and group conversations help us to become more insightful and to challenge assumptions. When we re-cognize it is like "knowing again." It is a process that helps us reconsider, with a critical view, who we are, what we have, and what we do and compare it with who we want to become, what we would like to have or to do. It is through this process of reflection that we enter the world of possibilities to create, adapt, improve, and change. Re-cognizing is a fundamental step in the process of unlearning and learning, and it helps us to find and commit to new and better ways of being and doing.

Language is critically important, not only so that we can anticipate the new world but also so that we can communicate in ways that reflect our new understanding of affairs. The evolution of our language, as we name our world, represents an important example of our learning and unlearning. Here are some examples of re-naming:

Old name/phrase	New name/phrase
· Community workers and professionals	· Community and technical experts who act in a professional manner
· Diabetics	· People with diabetes
· Depressed	· People with depression
· Target population	· The people with whom we participate
· Patients	· Participants
· Clients	· Participants
· Going down to the level of the community	· Doing things in an appropriate way. We are actually on the same level.
· They are ignorant	· They lack information
· Everything in male gendered words	· Gender neutral language such as spokesperson, chairperson, or alternating feminine and masculine forms of words

Words have meaning and power. Being conscious about our choice of words and the power of language allows us to engage as a collective in the creation of a different narrative, where equity and justice have a central place. This cannot be accomplished by just substituting words, but by embracing a way of thinking. So the process of learning and unlearning goes beyond language to the realms of paradigms, stories, and behaviors.

Individuals make up our teams and teams make up our organization. Individuals have a way of seeing the world, have stories, emotions, and personal behaviors as well as skills and work-related experiences. At the same time, our organization has an overarching philosophy; has teams whose personal stories, emotions, and behaviors have an impact on our work and on our ability to function as a collective; and has established expected competencies. The individual affects the team and the team affects the individual in ways that are often positive, sometimes not so positive, but seldom neutral.

We are aware that the personal and professional are inextricably connected, but for the purposes of learning and unlearning, we find it helpful to separately examine three realms in which the individual and the organization interface:

1. Our ways of seeing and doing things, the paradigms we favor

2. Our stories, emotions, and behaviors

3. Our work performance

Individual	Organizational
1. Paradigm: My personal world view and ways of thinking	1. Philosophy: Our assumptions and Principles of Practice
2. The personal: Recognizing my stories, emotions, and work ethic	2. The intersection of the personal with the professional: The impact of our personal stories, emotions, and behaviors on our work and our ability to work as a team
3. Job skills and training: The quality, quantity, and management of my individual work	3. Work: Required competencies and expected performance as outlined by the organization

Only if we take a critical look at these three realms at both levels, the personal and the organizational, and then try to understand how they connect, can we honestly identify what we need to learn and unlearn, to improve or change.

Paradigms analyzed and recreated

To know what we need to change, we must recognize our ways of seeing and doing things – our paradigms.

We define paradigm

A paradigm is a way of seeing and explaining things that informs what we think, what we aspire to, what we assume, and ultimately acts as a compass guiding our values, principles, and practices in relation to work, community, and personal life.

Paradigms are like air: they surround us. We breathe them in and speak them out. We subscribe to paradigms even when they are imperceptible to us. However, their messages are broadcast all around us. Dominant discourse is the mouthpiece of the dominant paradigm. Several disciplines define "dominant discourse" as the most prevalent way of speaking or behaving on any given topic. These ideas and behaviors most often reflect the ideologies of those who have the most power in society.

We create our ways of seeing things from what we learn from family, media, and other institutions that repeatedly transmit messages of the dominant discourse. We all have been subjected to these messages. Everyone grows up in a society where we are taught what is valuable, what is important, what power is, and how power is achieved. We learn the rules of the workplace: how to dress and act, who determines the rules, the consequences of breaking the rules, and how and when to apply the rules. We learn who the decision-makers are, who is a professional and who is not, and what defines a respectable institution. At LHA, we realize that whether we studied at the elementary level or the university level, the dominant discourse is present in all of us. And the dominant discourse wants us to believe that the explanation and answers to problems such as illness or poverty belong only to those who are trained as "specialists" in the matter and not to those affected by illness or poverty.

Who creates the dominant discourse? Who defines what is acceptable, desirable, reprehensible, appropriate, and beautiful? At our trainings and internal discussions over the years, we often generate a list of those who have the most say in creating the dominant discourse and the institutions that help transmit it.

Who creates the dominant discourse?

- People with power
- Men
- People with light skin
- People with money
- People with weapons
- Religious institutions
- Government officials

What institutions help transmit the dominant discourse?

- Schools
- The mainstream, political, corporate, and social media
- Advertising and marketing agencies
- Churches and other places of worship
- Health clinics
- Welfare and assistance programs
- Our networks of friends and social clubs
- Our families

During discussions about the dominant discourse, we recognize that society often equates poverty with lack of intelligence, being indigenous with being inferior, being beautiful with having light skin, being successful with having trendy cars, being experts with formal education, and being powerful with being rich. The question of whether we have equity in our lives does not even enter into the conversation. The assumption is that we live in a society where equal opportunities are offered to all, when in reality they are not. During our discussions and reflections, we feel shame and pain when we realize that we are not immune from allowing the dominant discourse to seep into our thinking. Many of us even end up devaluing ourselves, as well as immigrants, people of African descent, indigenous people, and the disenfranchised. Often we doubt the skills of those who have no formal education, have low incomes, or who do not speak the dominant language. We tend to question the intelligence, wisdom, and capacity for success of someone living in a garage, cleaning houses for a living, or selling tamales. And sometimes we end up blaming individuals for what we see as an inability to take responsibility for their own success or failure.

It soon becomes evident that there are multiple dominant discourses. One of the potential dangers of dominant discourses is that they become so pervasive. Often, we cannot even imagine an alternative to the overpowering messages we have received our entire lives. For example, some dominant discourses on organizational structures suggest that the only functional model is vertical, where respect for hierarchy is absolute, and where the experts give the orders and define the strategy, while lower-ranking workers – the non-experts – unquestioningly receive the orders and implement the strategy. These hierarchical models often have strict rules and rigid consequences for those who do not follow them. This dominant discourse says there should be a set schedule for everything, a dress code, and formal agendas for every meeting; in the meetings, people have been trained to be brief and concise, and "being productive" is solely defined by quantifiable and financial terms. Community members are often viewed as clients or patients, the consumers of products or the recipients of services, as only having needs without the capacity to give anything back. It is often considered a lawsuit risk to create an organization that opens doors to greater community participation from less-privileged people. The dominant organizational paradigm tends to see the leaders of the organization as people who are trained to know the needs of the community so they can carry out successful agendas without community input. When community members do work in these institutions, the dominant paradigm often denies their humanity by requiring that they do their jobs without taking into account their potential, their personal barriers, their ideas, or their wisdom. Frequently, it is expected that the personal and the emotional be left out of the workplace, as if they have no influence on the individual or on team performance.

Principles of Practice:
Guiding LHA's Community Work

"Our communities are being assaulted. There are many accomplices
of alcoholism that aggravate the problem in a culture that
normalizes excessive drinking. In Santa Ana, we see that the
rules are broken and the legal distances between liquor stores are
not respected. Our Latino community is attacked and is very
vulnerable. Some of the programs that exist to prevent alcoholism
and violence put more weight on the problems than on people
skills, increasing our pain rather than helping our families. Men
and women need to think there is a different way of living. We
are not entirely good or bad. It's all about choices. I think people
eventually learn how to use their skills, and acquire new ones
when the old ones no longer work for them. I spoke with a lady
about how Hispanics are frequently labeled as dirty or as gang
members, among other despicable labels. I don't believe that we
left our lives in our home countries to allow our children to be
drunks or gang members. We left to have a better life. But this
environment needs to be changed. The culture of violence and
liquor stores is growing. I do not think there is just one factor, but
many we need to address that make our problems grow worse."

— Soledad, promotora, Emotional Wellness Program

For 22 years, LHA has been offering an alternative discourse, which is evident in our principles and in our practice of community participation. We believe that those most affected by a problem are key to solving the problem, so we let those voices guide our work.

Our ability to generate an alternative discourse lies in our capacity to continually question the dominant discourses inside and outside of each of us and within LHA, challenging what does not work and daring to create alternative practices to guide us in our organization and community work.

We have distilled some of our learning into what we call our Principles of Practice. We measure ourselves and our decisions against these principles in meetings, at retreats, and in our daily work. They serve as guides, help to orient new people, help us correct our course when necessary, and help us stay aligned with our values. These principles are integral to our work.

These principles help us stay grounded in what we aspire to be. They are reflected in every aspect of the organization, from the way we knock on doors, to our approach to developing activities for and with the community, to the way we treat each other. We often falter, but then we have a chance to correct ourselves.

1. We work for health, not for the absence of disease.

LHA agrees with the World Health Organization, which says that health "is a complete state of physical, mental, and social well-being, and not merely the absence of disease or infirmity" (WHO, 1946).

America, Robert Ross, and community members inaugurate LHA's new building.

We work hard to offer initiatives and programs that help people have better health physically, mentally, and emotionally, as well as in relationships with others and as a community.

2. Health is a right and a responsibility.

The constitution of the World Health Organization says, "We, the Member States of the World Health Organization (WHO), reaffirm our commitment to the principle enunciated in its Constitution that the enjoyment of the highest attainable standard of health is one of the fundamental rights of every human being; in doing so, we affirm the dignity and worth of every person, and the equal rights, equal duties and shared responsibilities of all for health"[1] (WHO, 1999).

Because we share the beliefs in this first postulate of the WHO, we propose initiatives and programs that promote access to information, prevention, and health care that honor the dignity of the person. Lack of health interferes with our ability to enjoy life, to be partners and parents, and to be productive. It can put us at risk of losing our homes, our ability to work, and even our lives. What is on the line when health declines is not only health itself, but human dignity.

3. Without equity and justice, we cannot have health.

Because people with less opportunity suffer worse health outcomes, LHA works with low-income communities. While we do cooperate with other sectors, our priority is to improve the social and economic lives of vulnerable families. They are the ones that have fewer opportunities. These vulnerable families are the first to be forgotten and the last to be consulted about allocations in public budgets. One can clearly see the impact of chronic lack of opportunities in the lives of low-income populations. These include myriad diseases that have many of their roots in poverty, as well as in a lack of safety, quality education, good jobs, adequate housing, citizen protection and services, civic engagement, and political power. All of these elements create conditions that are unfavorable to our communities. Without equal opportunities and justice, we cannot have health.

---

1 Preamble to the Constitution of the World Health Organization as adopted by the International Health Conference, New York, 19-22 June, 1946; signed on 22 July 1946 by the representatives of 61 States and entered into force on 7 April 1948.

If one compares these communities with other social groups with more privilege, one can see radical differences in health outcomes, life expectancy, academic success, and representation in the criminal justice system (WHO, 2008; Iton, 2006). This is why we subscribe to the 1998 WHO Declaration, which says:

> *"We recognize that the improvement of the health and well-being of people is the ultimate aim of social and economic development. We are committed to the ethical concepts of equity, solidarity and social justice and to the incorporation of a gender perspective into our strategies. We emphasize the importance of reducing social and economic inequities in improving the health of the whole population. Therefore, it is imperative to pay the greatest attention to those most in need, burdened by ill-health, receiving inadequate services for health or affected by poverty. We reaffirm our will to promote health by addressing the basic determinants and prerequisites for health."*
>
> —*51st World Health Assembly, 1998*

4. The places where we live, work, play, and learn affect our health.

Our programs are designed to confront the immediate issues of disease and other health problems at the same time that they address the multiple root causes of these problems. Working within this philosophy, it becomes clear that the struggle for better salaries is a struggle for better health. Helping youth graduate is a health strategy. Offering literacy classes to women leads to improved health in the whole community.

Health is determined by social conditions, and the place where one lives is a major factor in limiting, determining, enhancing, or inhibiting health. We have been working within a place-based approach since our inception. We see this principle grounded in the larger international, national, and regional bodies of work that continue to build the evidence for the soundness and relevance of this approach, such as the WHO Commission on Social Determinants of Health (WHO, *Closing the Gap*, 2008) and the entities that set national and regional agendas, such as the U.S. Department of Health and Human Services' *Healthy People 2020*, which says:

"The Social Determinants of Health topic area within Healthy People 2020 is designed to identify ways to create social and physical environments that promote good health for all. All Americans deserve an equal opportunity to make the choices that lead to good health. But to ensure that all Americans have that opportunity, advances are needed not only in health care but also in fields such as education, child care, housing, business, law, media, community planning, transportation, and agriculture."

5. We analyze problems in their historical, social, and political context.

Because we believe that the problems in a community are the consequence of multiple factors, we work hard to understand the historical, social, political, and psychological contexts and trajectories of our realities. Social problems and individual responses to them did not appear overnight. We try to learn and understand the current circumstances of individuals in these vulnerable communities connected to histories of oppression, colonization, racism, forced or volunteer immigration, discrimination, chronic disinvestment, individual and collective trauma, poverty among families for multiple generations, and contexts of violence, political corruption, and drug and sex trafficking economies in Latin America, the U.S., and the world. We are conscious of the cumulative effect of historic injustice and the lack of restorative practices in our society. It is extremely important for our team to understand these socio-historical contexts, to analyze why things happen and the elements that influence people's points of view, behaviors, and decision-making. We are always encouraged to deepen this analysis and not settle by saying, "If they wanted change, they would have done it," or "They should stay in their countries," or "That's how Latinos are," or "People are just like that," or "They deserve those living conditions." It is our duty to challenge these myopic and simple explanations and engage in deeper analyses.

6. Participation makes the difference.

Without participation, we are passive witnesses to the decisions of others and we suffer the consequences of others' actions and our own inaction. Therefore, at LHA, we continuously work to activate mechanisms of participation.

Of all the behaviors that people can practice to improve their lives and communities, participation is the most important. When we decide to take part in something, we add our voices and our energies, and the chances of achieving what we want increase. It is easy to take advantage of communities that do not participate because they do not use their power and instead endure in silence. On both a micro and a macro scale, unequal participation creates unequal power dynamics. Whether it is talking to our doctors, advocating for street improvements, or fighting for changes in immigration laws, when we participate, we are stronger, we have more power, and we achieve more.

7. We strive for unity with purpose.

Because we believe that unity makes a community more powerful, we strive to create a common purpose. We assume that we have two things in common: that every individual wants the best for him/herself and their families, and that everyone has something to contribute. From there, we think about how to improve our community and how to act in unity. So we work for unity, for the common unity, for community.

Unity of a community does not occur naturally, whether among Latinos, whites, blacks and indigenous people, the LGBT community, or other groups. Unity needs a purpose. It requires effort and an intentional process to achieve and maintain unity. Even geographical, religious, cultural, or family unity requires common goals, sacrifice, and a level of selflessness to focus on the most important things for the group.

We need to be united to achieve healthier communities and stronger families. We want unity that helps drive us toward developing strategies and taking actions that will improve our communities.

8. We create healthier communities by engaging each other's strengths.

We understand that people have needs, but as organizers, we do not focus on needs. Instead, we mobilize people's strengths and capabilities. By engaging people's strengths, we create possibilities. When we see possibilities, we become hopeful. We celebrate that every person has knowledge, skills, strengths, and talents that can be mobilized to build healthier communities. In the same way that unity does not occur in the absence of purpose, people don't contribute skills unless they think it is worth it, and they trust that their contributions are needed and welcomed. We approach our work with the assumption that we all value having a healthy, prosperous life for ourselves and our children. It is our responsibility to provide the mechanisms and opportunities for people to use their strengths, wisdom, and desires to make their dreams come true and contribute to a better community.

9. We all can reflect and take action.

We invite all members of the community, young and old, with or without formal education, to be included in the process of reflection and action. The ideas generated by one of us alone are less effective than those that result from dialogue and joint actions with neighbors in our communities. Creating healthier communities by inviting everyone to reflect requires more time, but the ultimate results are real and profound. When we better understand what is happening around us, we can learn how to fix it. When we learn, we expand our thinking with new elements and possibilities. When we take action, we affect the environment. We then learn and have the opportunity to incorporate the lessons into our thinking to create even more effective action. This ongoing reflection and action is vital to transform our communities and sustain changes. Strategic thinking and action should not be the exclusive domain of the privileged few – as if there were a "thinking class." If we want to win real change, strategic thinking and action should be the domain of everyone.

10. We value different cultures and we incorporate them into our work.

Culture may be invisible but it is everywhere. It is just like oxygen; you only notice it when you don't have it. Culture determines everything, from our most trivial routines to our most important life decisions. What do we have for breakfast? What do we wear to work? How and when do we form a family? How do we talk about disease and with whom? How do we discuss death and dying, and how do we grieve? How do we run meetings? How do we structure an organization? Whom do we hire? How do we supervise? How do we create mechanisms for community inclusion? Answers to these and other questions will reveal the dominant culture that is guiding the people and the processes in any institution or organization.

Culture has a central role in our work. At LHA, we create spaces where we can share each other's cultures across ethnic, socioeconomic, and generational lines. The people who are grounded in a certain culture are the ones who design the cultural activities, which we then try to weave into everything we do within the organization and community. Children's activities, fundraising events, holidays, deaths, births, and all events and celebrations are informed and guided by the cultural practices of our participants and by the people who work in our organization.

11. We do not generalize. We honor the self-expression of a person's identity.

People have the right to define themselves. Even though we share similar problems, we believe that every person, no matter how young, is an expert in her own life and can see her own potential solutions.

We come from many places and we have different histories, ways of using language, educational levels, beliefs, religions, spiritual practices, values, sexual orientations, political views, and economic resources. We respect the words people use to define who they are when they share their identities. For example, some may prefer to be identified as Mexican while others prefer to be identified as Latinos or Chicanos. We don't impose labels, nor do we assume people's preferred identities. The Latino community, and for that matter, all communities are neither monolithic nor static. They are always inventing and re-inventing themselves. Youth may self-identify differently from their parents. Neighbors who emigrated from the same village in El Salvador and now live in the same community in Santa Ana may have different ways of describing who they are. Our approach is to allow everyone to be him/herself. We often have problems in common, we analyze particular situations affecting a sector of the population or a geographic area, but we do not generalize. We let people speak for themselves.

The Latino experience in the United States is diverse. We use the word Latino in the name of our organization, Latino Health Access, by choice. In our documents and proposals we describe the community with whom we partner as being predominantly Latino.

The word Latino is used to refer to the community as a collective composed of individuals who come from Latin American countries or who have Latin American ancestral roots. For instance, we talk about Latino communities, Latina women or Latino men, and the Latino vote. However, in our work we let people self-identify as they choose.

12. We work in partnership and solidarity with the community.

Because we believe that the core of our mission is to engage the community in addressing the root causes of suffering, we work in partnership and solidarity with the community. We partner with communities so that they can take a leading role. We are not there to rescue anyone. In the work we do with our families and communities, we hope that they participate, take action, and become key leaders of transformation for change and success. Whether we are talking about a behavior that requires change, families participating in support groups to reduce violence, increasing places where children can play, or increasing the Latino vote, our expectation is that the community becomes an active partner in this enterprise of change and hope. While meeting basic and immediate needs is not part of our core mission, during the course of this work, we occasionally assist our neighbors when they are facing immediate crises. It is possible for us to help people who urgently need food or shelter, or to connect people with other organizations, or to have a small fundraiser because someone needs money for a funeral, but this type of help is an expression of unconditional solidarity and not a model of community work based on charity.

13. We value reciprocity. All give and all receive.

LHA has something to offer and the community also has something to offer. We employ a philosophy of mutual respect and mutual contribution. Our community often wants to help; people want to offer something in return for what they have received. We believe it is a mistake to reject what the community offers, be it a glass of juice, an hour of volunteer work, an apartment where we can meet, cookies for children in the program, or classes in ballet *folklórico*. Accepting what the community offers is a key to maximizing resources and maintaining mutual respect and dignity.

All parties can benefit from such transactions. Traditionally, organizations and charities that work with low-income communities offer goods and services without expecting anything in return. Perhaps service providers feel that it is not fair to ask a person in need to contribute. But then the service provider is treating the client as if he or she has nothing to offer. In our opinion, asking the community to contribute to solutions makes sense because financial resources are finite, because it helps to build community, and because community members often have very good ideas.

Some people have had negative experiences of receiving things and then being used. For example, governments sometimes give favors in order to gain votes, or marketers give perks in order to gain business. These experiences may lead people to distrust our call for reciprocity. But LHA participants soon learn that they are not being used; they are being called to be part of the solution. Sometimes people think they have nothing to give because their talents and skills were not valued before. Once they start to contribute, though, they see how important their talents and skills are for catalyzing action and change.

14. We work in partnership with other sectors and encourage shared accountability.

At LHA, everything we do is in partnership with and for the benefit of local residents. For the community to prosper, however, it needs relationships with other institutions outside the community. We have to build relationships and work with all: business groups, the faith community, the health sector, schools, political representatives, and other public and private groups. We build and improve our community with contributions from multiple sectors, while ensuring representation and active participation of residents. We may work with each sector individually or we may work in multi-sectoral collaboratives to reach collective outcomes.

15. We develop comprehensive responses.

When we include the community in the creation of a strategy, it tends to become very comprehensive. Mothers in our community are not only concerned about their children's weight. They also worry about their education, their emotional well-being, and their relationships with others. Through this way of seeing our work, people who are concerned about housing, food, and education come to have a common cause.

Compared to people in traditional institutions, people grounded in their communities think in a less fragmented way. A mom whose child is overweight will tell us that her son has no place to run and play. This offers us an opportunity to talk about why he doesn't have a place to run and play. This conversation leads to the political question of why we don't have parks. Soon, we are analyzing the root causes of her son's difficulties, not just talking about his body mass index (BMI).

After reaching a deeper collective understanding of the root causes of the problem and the potential solutions, we feel obligated to develop more complete, comprehensive strategies from which solutions consistent with the analysis of the problems can emerge. Additionally, comprehensive responses allow us to work simultaneously on short- and long-term change. For example, in the short term, we can partner with people with diabetes so they can better manage their condition, gain access to medical services, obtain medications, and avoid or manage complications. Meanwhile, we support the family to start eating better. We advocate together to have parks and to be able to use them. We support efforts to have access to health insurance and to health care practitioners, to change school menus, and to make the city safer so people can go outside and be active.

16. We make the health of the organization and each member of our team a priority.

Because we believe that the quality of our work depends on the quality of our team, we invest time and resources into activities that help our team to be healthy and cohesive. We schedule trainings, meetings, and retreats that help the entire team to align with our programs and strategies. We take the duty of the ongoing assessment of our capacity and challenges very seriously. We give staff the space they need to create, innovate, and feel taken care of. We make an ongoing investment of time and resources to understand our individuality, emotions, desires, and problems, as well as to support team members physically, mentally, socially, and spiritually. We work to build team unity by engaging in dialogue and reflection within a culture of respect, mutual aid, and the value of each individual. The principles that guide the organization outside in the community also guide us internally. We are all experts; are all part of the team; all contribute; all have responsibilities and rights. We establish reciprocal and transformative relationships in which everyone learns from everyone else. We create processes that allow us to develop relationships and that respect the experiences and positions of others. We know that sometimes we stray. Sometimes we want to tell others what to do without consulting with them. We know that at times we forget to honor others or their experiences. In these cases, we stop, evaluate, and correct in order to be accountable to each other and the community.

17. We are programmatically accountable, evaluate our programs, and share results.

We dedicate resources and time to evaluating our activities and programs. We create systems that allow us to know whether we are achieving our objectives. We constantly ask ourselves if we are really doing what we say we are doing. All staff members are trained to understand the value of data, and how to obtain it and organize it. We have discussions about the data we collect. We seek, find, and address errors or omissions. We evaluate and correct course when necessary.

LHA is an organization that is constantly learning and trying to analyze the processes and results of what we do, and to incorporate the lessons we learn along the way. We have systems and procedures that allow us to do the job in an efficient and transparent manner, yet still protect the agency. We use the experiences of other organizations and we apply relevant external regulations to help us improve our systems and procedures.

18. We use financial resources responsibly.

Because we take seriously the responsibility entrusted to us by the community, we want to use resources wisely, and we work hard to be financially accountable to and transparent with everyone who is involved in our work, from the funders to the community. We maximize the use of resources by partnering with other organizations, and we welcome in-kind services, donations, and volunteers.

19. We reject invitations for division.

Because we understand that unity is strength, and diversity makes us stronger, we try to avoid the trap of division. Societies, by design, often create reasons for division. For many of us, a way to protect our beliefs, our jobs, our funding, or our truth is by separating ourselves from the "other." This separation is a critical barrier to building common ground. We do not allow ourselves to be distracted from our goals by people who want to divide us, consciously or unconsciously. We recognize the existence of prejudices, even inside our own organization, and make a conscious effort to work on them. We are aware that we have internalized many prejudices simply because we grew up in this society. Our agency is not different. LHA is composed of people who are a part of our society. We acknowledge the risk of division and so are proactive at setting the expectation that we all make a conscious effort to at least tolerate and respect, if not understand and embrace, the differences that we have amongst ourselves at all levels. It is important to remind each other often that we believe in working together across lines of race, gender, age, religion, sexual orientation, national origin, experience, physical abilities, etc. Diversity informs what we do and enriches us. In a proactive and humble way, we remind each other of this principle when we hear or see prejudice in action. When we see hatred or contempt, we try to confront it in a way that helps the person hear and learn. Ignoring the existence of these forces is not healthy. If there are difficulties working with a person or sector of the community, we make an effort to work on the issue and overcome limitations.

20. We recognize the risks that can derail us from our work and from practicing our other principles.

Because doing this work involves many risks, we are careful and attentive so that we can sustain ourselves and adhere to our principles. These risks may include:

Underestimating the oppositional agenda: There are people and sectors whose agenda may oppose or conflict with our work and our agenda of social justice. Often our agenda touches controversial areas in the country's politics, such as those related to health care reform, immigration reform, fair housing, and others. We cannot underestimate oppositional agendas. We are aware that we can also learn from opposing perspectives, and are willing to build bridges when there is a genuine desire to find common ground without compromising our core beliefs in social justice. In order to be stronger and more effective, and to avoid becoming an easy target, we think strategically and in partnership with others who share similar agendas.

Losing our humility: We need to be cautious in two areas: First, in recognizing that university training is a great help in the work we do, but it is not all that is needed. Community experiences and life experiences are of vital importance. At the same time, we need to be aware that just because you live and come from the community you serve, you may not know or represent the collective view. Second, we need to be aware of the risk of believing we are the know-it-alls of building a healthier community or working with *promotores*. We need to remind each other to be humble and open to the lessons we are offered every day from many sources of knowledge, including academia and our community members, and to be open to the challenges that other perspectives add to our work.

Teamwork between the community and university-trained workers, and the ongoing conversation among these partnerships, are practices that protect against academic or community arrogance. We pay particular attention to the relationships between university-trained people and community members without university degrees in our trainings, meetings, and conversations to be sure the environment is safe, non-intimidating, and fosters the free expression of ideas for all.

Losing the balance between short-term services and long-term changes: Managing the balance between short-term work and long-term change is challenging. Sometimes we focus on providing services, and we lose sight of the root causes that created the need for those services. Likewise, sometimes we get very involved in changing policy and power dynamics, and we forget that the community has critical needs that require immediate attention. This is especially challenging because resources are limited, and the pressures of being under-funded, or under-staffed, or short on time can lead to focusing on the easiest projects with the most short-term benefits. Although we may sometimes pick the low-hanging fruit, so to speak, we must continually address the roots of the situation – even if those are harder to get to.

At LHA we live in a constant state of tension between our principles and the need to function in a world dominated by the bureaucratic, corporate model of institutional behavior. Internal tensions can escalate into conflicts that challenge us and force us to re-examine, define, correct, and learn.

LHA is not the community, nor is it an institution separated from the community

LHA is a community institution where we gather together different kinds of experiences, knowledge, and wisdom in order to better discuss, analyze, and make decisions. We firmly believe that we have all kinds of experts among us.

At a typical meeting at LHA, we have representatives of different areas of expertise at the same table. For example, we may have the Director of Accounting; a coordinator with a masters in social work; and a *promotor* who is a father and a former addict, who has diabetes, who has many years of experience working in a burger business, and who is comfortable in our neighborhoods. In this same meeting, we may also have our Director of Evaluation who has a doctorate, and another *promotora* who lives in one of the areas of Santa Ana most affected by poverty and fears for her children every day. This is her first job outside of her home. She is a mom and a brave *promotora* who teaches other families to defend the rights of their children. Next to her is our Director of Mental Health who has several university degrees. Beside her is a *promotora* who lives in the neighborhood with other low-income immigrant families, who completed the sixth grade, and who has work experience cleaning houses. When we first met her, she suffered from depression, but now she has dedicated her life to helping other women recognize their power. This *promotora* has the respect of many women in the community, who see her as a role model.

All of us who work at LHA have roots in communities that are struggling for justice. We are immigrants or children of immigrants, people of color, or people who come from low-income communities. Some of us have been the first in our families to graduate from elementary school, high school, or college. Many of us have been excluded from opportunities because of our race, country of origin, gender, sexual orientation, or mental health condition. Keeping our identities and personal and community experiences alive helps us understand and connect in empathetic and effective ways with the families we serve and with whom we participate.

> *"I am remembering how I came to the agency. It was weird. I come from a history of, 'If you behave well, then you're good and I love you. If you're bad, go away, we do not want you here.' When I came to this place I found Tere, Marisol, and the other moms. I felt weird arriving at a place where there was no one saying what I did wrong all the time. Instead, I was in a place where I felt accepted in my whole being, where no one was indifferent to human pain. When people appreciate you, you can learn to appreciate yourself. And you appreciate others. When you knock on a door, you do not say, 'Señora, I just came to invite you to the park; I don't want to listen to you.' No, I cannot treat people like that. I think our outreach is effective not only because we offer services to people in a program, but also because we invite people to be part of something, to belong to something.*
>
> *"Yesterday, I received a visit from a family that we met ten years ago in a program called FAST [Families and Schools Together]. At that time the daughter was seven years old and now the family returns and the daughter is pregnant. We cannot be indifferent to the situation of that person because she is no longer part of the FAST program. When we go knock on a door, we are making a commitment to that family. We are not just going to invite them to a program, but we are going to listen to them and respect them. We are walking into the life and the history of the people."*
>
> —Sarai, promotora, Community Engagement and Advocacy Program

Our participants are our co-workers

The majority of our *promotores* originally came to request services at LHA as neighbors; they volunteered and now they are part of the paid staff of the organization. Some of the community residents who participate with us and whom we serve are inside the organization. We consider them experts and believe that they have a key role in designing and implementing strategies for LHA.

Promotores bring human and social practices that are non-academic and more rooted in the style of the community. These practices reflect their belonging and understanding of the cultural and social context in which our families live. They have customs, unspoken rules, and ways of interacting that are familiar to the community. These practices that the *promotores* have are what make them so effective when they collaborate with families to create activities in our neighborhoods. However, many of these practices could challenge other people inside and outside of LHA who are accustomed to operating with traditional management models. What is considered informal to institutions can be considered proper to *promotores*. What is considered formal for institutions can be considered ineffective and a waste of time for *promotores*.

Promotores dress in appropriate ways that do not set them apart. They take time to have general conversations that are unrelated to the topic, so that they can strengthen the relationship before getting down to the problem or issue at hand. They dare to share problems and personal stories with participants in connection with their work. They speak using non-technical language. They handle interruptions in a relaxed way. They know how to handle the presence of children while talking with their parents. They make sure they have food in meetings and gatherings. They are flexible with the start time of activities. They help with transportation. They are sensitive to the suffering caused by violence, discrimination, immigration status, poverty, and overwork.

> *"Community people are the experts, ourselves. Sometimes when I'm doing outreach my vocabulary is very 'country,' and I usually encounter people who are like me. I feel a connection when I speak with my simple words. It is there. We have the same vocabulary. I'm not a teacher. I am a mother from the community like them. I give information with my own words, my vocabulary, and they feel that I am really talking to them. Some people have a lot of education, but not many. There are people who cannot fill out a form. I know what it's like because sometimes I have trouble filling out forms. I normally say, 'I'll help you if you like.' I do not ask if they can read or write. When you offer to help, you discover that the person cannot write his name. I think one of*

the things that helps me is remembering that we all have many skills, that people are ready, and that they don't need anything more than an opportunity like the one offered to me. I know I have many things in common with the people I am reaching out to. When they feel confident, they start to open their hearts, their trust, and their doors to us. It is what happened to me when I told my group about the loss of my baby. I saw their sad faces. A mom approached me and thanked me because it had happened to her. And another mom told me, 'I thank you because I lost my baby at four months, and I could not talk about it.' I said, 'That happened to me when I lost my baby. I could not talk about it. I felt that it blocked me.' When someone listens to you without judging, you feel like you are part of a family that you do not know. They open their hearts and they don't judge you. Then you can confide in each other. But if you feel judged, you immediately block yourself. We promotoras, we know about loss and pain, so people feel like they can approach us."

—*Tere, promotora, Emotional Wellness Program*

Tere, *promotora,* tables in a creative outreach activity in the neighborhood.

Validating the community's ways

How many meetings occur in our city per day? Probably thousands. There are meetings within government offices, educational institutions, business groups, community organizations, hospitals, and so on. What those meetings may have in common is a particular way of structuring the conversation. Usually, the meeting will have an objective, an agenda, and time allocated per item. It has a time to start and a time to finish. It may even follow what is known as Robert's Rules of Order, which includes procedures for speaking in order, making proposals, discussing ideas, reaching agreements, showing support, refraining from support, etc. These methods have become the most common forms of conducting meetings in institutions and organizations all over the world. However, at the same time, every day in communities across the planet, people are talking to each other, exchanging ideas, planning, and taking action at different levels. These formal and informal interactions are informed by culture, tradition, history, religion, place of origin, gender roles, needs, power structure, and so on. Understanding how community members talk to each other, reach agreements, and take action is crucial to our work. Many of the methods used by institutions may not be the most appropriate in our communities. In many circumstances, those meeting methods could be intimidating.

The community has its ways of starting conversations. It has its ways of inviting its members to interact, to organize a gathering, to present ideas. Families and communities have ways of reaching agreements about processes. People generate many ideas for immediate action, which fuels enthusiasm to work on what they want to see in the future, and what they want to see in the present.

When *promotores* meet with their neighbors at their homes, it is usually because there is a central issue, for example, increased crime in the area. Very soon, neighbors bring other topics to the table, share personal stories, and then go back to the central theme. It is possible that the meetings do not start on time and do not end on time. Generally, there is food prepared by participants. Kids may be present and interrupt parents often.

Promotores are very tactful in bringing people back to the theme and are very sensitive about respecting the right of people to say what they think is important when they think it is important. There is an art in navigating conversations and reaching agreements at the community level. Notes may or may not be taken and participants may or may not leave with clear responsibilities or specific tasks. This flexible way of convening is not the norm in mainstream institutions and, unfortunately, our neighbors from low-income communities may feel intimidated and inadequate in those settings.

A conversation over coffee between a neighbor and a *promotora* may be the best way for the neighbor to get help in better managing her diabetes. A Sunday visit that includes a walk around the block with a mom and her kids may be the best way to talk about family matters. A meeting at night in the living room of a neighbor may be the best place to feel comfortable and speak your mind about a situation affecting your safety. The *promotor* is the conversational expert in the community the same way the board president is the expert facilitator in the corporate meeting.

This is not to say that community members do not know how to participate or behave in meetings that are recognized as formal by the mainstream, such as those at schools, city councils, and other places. But we are painfully aware that in those meetings, the community attendance tends to be limited; only a few get to speak while most just sit and listen.

Even in our own organization, meetings need to be designed carefully since the institutional mentality and the community mentality co-exist. It is not uncommon in an LHA meeting that a *promotora* or *promotor* will share personal stories, take longer than the time established, or bring other issues to the table that they consider relevant. To balance the institutional and community norms, we hold different kinds of meetings that allow for different kinds of outcomes. For example, we sometimes have short, focused meetings where we are somewhat disciplined about staying on topic. At other times, we hold meetings that are designed to allow extra time for brainstorming, stories, food, and everything else that encourages people to engage, be creative, and commit to results.

In meetings outside of LHA, *promotores* know how to participate in both community and institutional ways. With community members, *promotores* engage in recognized community ways, which make them very effective but could challenge some beliefs about boundaries, how the work needs to be done, how personal staff can be with community members, or how much time needs to be invested in conversations with participants. When it comes to institutional outside meetings, such as steering committees, coalitions, public hearings, or university focus groups, LHA trains and supports *promotores* and community members in how to be effective participants. These institutional meetings may not be as comfortable for our community members, but they are places where decisions are made and we need to effectively participate in them. LHA recognizes the tension between the community ways and the institutional ways in every interaction inside and outside our organization, and we do our best to maximize our effectiveness in all areas.

Protecting the ways of the community

We need to recognize the transformative role of the *promotores*. They are organizers. They use a holistic approach. *Promotores* don't identify an issue, rally people, and then go away. They rally people and keep going because they live in that community, are invested in long-term outcomes, and truly want conditions to improve.

Promotores do not stop participating, advocating, and offering help at the end of their workday, at which point they close their books and go home. Their lives and their work are intertwined in communities where they are partners, moms, dads, and neighbors, and they continue to be organizers, helpers, advocates, supporters, and system navigators after work.

> *"We are told not to give out our cell phone numbers, but how can we not do it? Our participants have problems that need to be solved. The other day, I was just entering my house after a day of work. The phone rang. 'Mrs. Noraima, I do not have a place to sleep tonight.' The young woman who called me is 19 years old, has a four-month old baby, and is pregnant. I called Oscar (another promotor) and told him what was happening. He arrived immediately."*
>
> —Noraima, promotora, *Emotional Wellness Program*

> *"We got in the car with the young woman, her boyfriend, and the baby. The boyfriend was arguing that he does not use drugs. I told him, 'Tell me how is it that you are not consuming drugs and your*

*lips are all burned from the pipe?' We support them, but we also
have to confront them. I called a shelter where they know us, but
where they do not accept children. I did not say anything about the
baby until we all arrived. Fortunately, the shelter accepted them."*

—Oscar, promotor, Emotional Wellness Program

Oscar, *promotor*, marches against violence.

There is a continuum of activities *promotores* can help with.
They can help with education, advocacy, policy, compliance, and
more. But if they are overly regulated and therefore limited in their
roles and distanced from their ways, they are no longer *promotores*.
The magic is lost. They become mini-medical assistants, non-
credentialed case managers, single-focus recruiters of patients into
academic studies, or mere mechanisms for improving quantifiable
outcomes for non-profits.

Promotores' ideas about how to find the community or go about
working on a problem tend to be creative and relevant. For many
institutions working with or wanting to work with *promotores*,
including ours, the risk is to recruit *promotores* that are effective
with the community and then impose restrictions that make them
ineffective. If the *promotora* loses control of her natural way of

relating to others because she has managers who decide how much time she is allowed to spend in the community, or supervisors who say what her interactions in the community should look like, then she will have less of an impact. For example, if the *promotora* is not allowed to share meals while she talks to other women in the community, she will be less effective, if not completely ineffective, because she cannot use her own ways – ways that are familiar and comfortable to her and to the people in the community she is working with.

Areas of tension with our own principles

It is essential that we function consistently within the philosophy and principles of LHA. To compare ways of seeing and doing allows us to open space for critical conversations and reach agreements. Here are some examples of areas of tension that invite us to have ongoing conversations:

We are all experts

Our knowledge and experience inform what we do and allow us to develop effective strategies and problem-solve. We agree that we all should engage each other's expertise. All members of our team have the knowledge and experience gained in their own personal and work life. These include interacting with neighbors from the communities we work with every day; living in the community we serve; sharing a similar background or experiences with those in the community; raising a family in places that may not be safe and that lack opportunities for children; having attended a college or university; having practiced a career for many years in different places or another country; having experience supervising teams; being responsible for computer entry of program data; being the one receiving our daily work reports; being in charge of facilities or accounting; and much more. We agree that we value each other's experience.

If we are all experts, do we treat each other as such? Do we consult each other? Do we ask each other for ideas? Do we include each other in the development of plans and strategies? Do we value one another? How do experts recruit, train, and supervise experts?

We all have power

If leadership is our ability to influence a process, and power is the possibility of influencing through concrete mechanisms, then we all should have the possibility of influencing by using or creating mechanisms to provide or request input, dissent, questions, or pressure. Could we all have the same level of power? Most coordinators and supervisors have university degrees. Also, they have the power of technical knowledge and of administrative hierarchy and authority. *Promotores* have the power of experience, wisdom, and community representation, as well as recognition that they are the engines that drive the organization's community work.

If we all have power, how is this demonstrated in the ways we make decisions? How is influence demonstrated across different areas of work? Are there clear organizational mechanisms through which all sectors inside LHA can express their points of view and be heard? Do all of us have the same level of power? It is important to constantly re-examine and reach agreements about how to recognize and own our power, how to use our power, and how to use our influence in constructive ways.

We want rules to support safety, quality, transparency, and integrity in the workplace

We want to protect and respect our staff and participants. Rules help manage risk. Some are mandatory, such as protective labor laws and health regulations. Some of the consequences of non-compliance are severe, such as fines, lawsuits, and job loss. We put additional rules in place because they help create or improve operational performance, job performance, and communication. This can create tension because the *promotores* know that they need to be flexible with community members who have many immediate needs and often lack time, money, trust in others, and experience interacting with institutions. *Promotores* hold drawings for prizes to collect donations to help participants, are flexible with people who arrive late or do not have appointments, share their phone numbers, receive calls after hours, and are opposed to rules that do not benefit the participants.

For those rules that we create internally, we ask: Who makes the rules? Who approves them? What are the consequences of not following them? Can everyone follow the rules?

Are the consequences fair? Is there an opportunity to make mistakes and learn from those mistakes? Are these rules helping to facilitate community work or are we creating more barriers? What is the role of common sense? In the absence of rules, how do we judge what to do in a specific situation?

Learning and unlearning when we don't get it right

As much as we work to deconstruct power dynamics internally, to recognize and counter the ways in which the dominant paradigms have crept into our own views and actions, we still struggle with this. An example is our recent experience updating LHA's operational policies and procedures.

This was an important task. Our operations manual provides guidance and contains the rules that influence aspects of the organization such as the way we use our facilities, provide babysitting services to support parents, use our vehicles, and develop volunteers. It is crucial that our team understands and can follow these procedures, which have a direct impact on our ability to respond to the community and conduct our programmatic work. One approach we could have taken would have been to review sample policies and procedures from similar non-profit organizations or to hire a consultant, develop updated policies, and then share the results with all staff through a meeting and a written document. But that would impose rules that may not make sense for our agency and may not be understood, embraced, or respected.

So, instead, we formed a committee and invited anyone who wanted to participate. At the time our operations team was convinced that we were forming a very representative committee, and recommended that each person on the committee convene a small group of people within their programmatic team who would be affected by a policy to discuss possible ways to craft that policy.

Despite these efforts, some of the *promotores* did not feel that their voices were being heard at the meetings. They felt a power imbalance. They noticed and called out the privilege of some directors and coordinators. Based on this and similar feedback, we went back to the drawing board. We held a series of retreats to re-align ourselves with our work philosophy and principles. After an intensive five-day retreat, we are setting up a new committee with members voted onto the committee. We are now much more conscientious about the composition of the committee, as well as the need for reasonable time for *promotores* to participate in ways that do not affect their programmatic obligations. More importantly, we have increased our awareness of the need to facilitate the conversation in ways that protect everybody's views, that fulfill our collective and individual responsibilities to hear each other, that raise awareness of our privileges and styles, and that contribute to an inclusive and equitable decision-making process.

Though it is not easy, we are committed to walking our talk. It will take longer than planned to update these policies and procedures, but in the end, they will be very well thought out and responsive. This is our aspiration and we are aligning our practice to allow us all to be co-authors of the new policies and procedures.

We often have conversations about rules and flexibility. Being flexible and being able to improvise and respond in a timely way are very important to our work. Flexibility does not mean disrespecting the rules, being rebellious, being disorganized, or not knowing how to plan. But flexibilty requires a supportive environment where, depending on the circumstances, exceptions to rules are possible, and plans and activities can be changed at the last minute if necessary. We must create an environment where the way we do our work can be questioned and improved in real time to respond faster, more effectively and sensitively, not only towards our participants and communities, but also to our own workforce.

We use appropriate models and locations for meetings

Conversations are not just about their content. In order to be as productive as possible, our conversations need to include a dialogue about content, style, place, and design. In this regard, we ask ourselves: Do we privilege a way of talking and decision-making in LHA? What is the level of complexity used to share information? Is every person in the agency familiar with the procedures in place to reach agreements? Are there inclusive mechanisms to reach agreements? Do we honor the right of our co-workers to be consulted and included in the agreements?

When we create committees to solve problems or create proposals, we have to assure the representation of all sectors within LHA. In order for this to happen we need to accommodate their schedules so they can attend the meetings. It is also important to recognize who within the team is the best representative for the issue to be addressed, based on the context and the group involved. Finally, it is important to recognize when to use parliamentary procedures or academic, business, or community models in meetings and other activities.

The organizational culture of LHA has taught us that when we invest time in conversations and consultations, when we attempt to gather all opinions and process them transparently, we all feel represented with the decisions made and it is easier to implement the resulting agreements. This process requires a high level of investment of time and energy, and often creates tension between those who are more task-oriented and those who are more process-oriented. But we have learned the importance of slowing down.

These are just a few examples of situations in which LHA has struggled to apply our guiding paradigms to our own processes. The first step in identifying what we need to unlearn and learn is to discover inconsistencies between what we think and what we do. If we do not take the risk to unlearn, we will continue to play back paradigms that limit the impact of our organizations and keep our communities and families excluded, in poverty, powerless, with few opportunities, and with high risk of damage to our physical, mental, and social health.

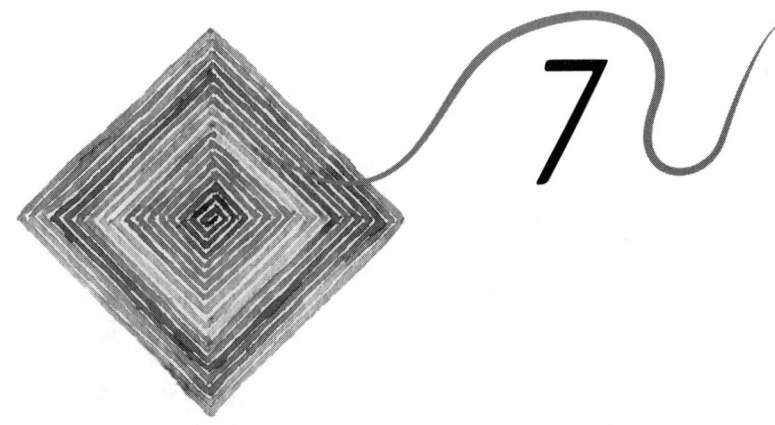

The Personal and Professional

"She tells me, 'If it does not work, it's because you're not a professional. You cannot be a good promotor.' But I don't believe that everything has to be scheduled, planned with a timetable. I say, 'Why does it have to be that way? Why do I need to make an agenda to go with other women from the community to the movie? We will meet there and talk about life.'

Sometimes we say, 'Things are different at LHA.' But are we really on the same page or are the egos winning? I can try my way and you try yours. Then, we can compare because the differences make us stronger. Not that arguments won't happen. Arguments always happen when you work with someone. I want us to recognize and value these differences among us. I always learn many things from everyone, but I say, 'theirs is not the only truth.'"

—*Araceli, promotora, Community Engagement and Advocacy Program*

Being able to realize our vision and mission requires coordination and effective teamwork. When we cannot understand each other, when we hurt, when we don't accept responsibility, when we mistreat others, and when we do not give ourselves the

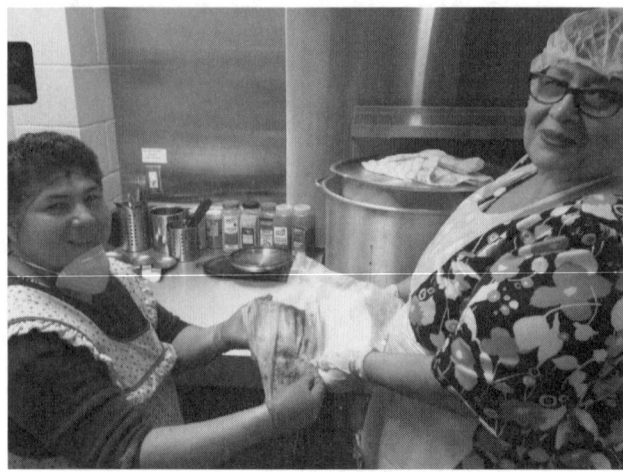

Araceli and Mary
work together on
the annual *Tamalada*
fundraiser.

opportunity or put in the effort to do better, we sabotage our vision
and limit our ability to carry out our mission.

We are all complete beings, each with different stories. When
we arrive at LHA, we don't leave who we are at home. We
don't disconnect from ourselves. Quite the contrary; the passion
that guides us in our work is fed by many of these personal
stories. We understand that as human beings our passion and
our actions are guided by both rationality and emotions, so we
do not want to disconnect from our humanity. What we want
is to take responsibility for creating an environment that invites
teamwork with respect, creativity, and quality at the individual
and organizational levels. We want to create a humanized and
humanizing environment where we have the opportunity to be the
best possible version of ourselves.

The workplace is a place where
we spend part of our lives together

To live with (*convivir* in Spanish) is the act of sharing lives with
others. In our work, we see each other every day for many hours,
and we have to do and accomplish a lot together. In the course
of activities related to our work, we get to see our best and worst
moments. Just as we suggest to the families in the community, in
order to become stronger, we have to take individual responsibility,

as well as group and institutional responsibility, to make co-existence respectful and productive. At the end of the day, we want to go home with thoughts of wanting to return to work. To that end, LHA pays attention to personal and team issues affecting our work environment and the problems of physical health, emotional health, conflict, gossip, destructive behaviors, and dissatisfaction that sometimes arise. We encourage our colleagues to discuss uncomfortable issues with people who can contribute to the solution.

Laura and Rosalia, *promotoras* in the Community Engagement and Advocacy Program

We are a group with members from different religions, socioeconomic backgrounds, sexual orientations, gender identities, cultures, races, countries, interests, talents, experiences, and opinions. Everyone has different tastes and preferences. To work effectively across all these differences, we don't strive to be more similar. But we do strive to talk and listen deeply so we can reach agreements and function respectfully while producing quality work.

We make efforts to give constructive, honest feedback and to focus on behavior, not people. We try to listen to criticism with an open mind but we are not always successful. We also try to be proactive in training and activities that help us learn to prevent and manage conflict, to know what drives us, and to reach agreements.

Importance of stories

"Life is lived as a series of conversations. We are instructed by stories, stories that extend and accumulate over a lifetime: stories that submerge and then re-emerge, sometimes with purpose, other times seemingly out of the blue. These stories contain images as vivid and real as if drawn from the family photo album.

They also contain deeply embedded values like individuality, teamwork, performance, innovation, integrity, and respect for others and oneself.

"These stories or lessons do not respect the boundaries of time or place. They travel with us as they instruct us, and help us make sense of the differing environments we move in and out of each day — at home, at work, or in the community. They beg for consistency and clarity and attempt to bridge the gap between making a living and making a life.

"These are presented here for three reasons. First, in the telling, stories may assist you in recalling your own conversations, some from long ago or as recent as yesterday. Second, stories might encourage your conscious recommitment each day to values that reinforce our better natures. And third, as we listen to and re-tell stories, they will assist you in embracing a positive approach toward leadership in all aspects of your life."

—Mike Magee (Magee, 1995)

We seek ways of embracing the personal stories of each member of the team and retelling the stories of the organization's history and culture, because they make us stronger. Sometimes stories that tell of needs, weakness, or failure can be reframed to help us see our own strengths and the strengths of the organization. We are committed to creating alternative narratives that are centered on the strengths of our co-workers, organization, and communities.

We invite you to think...

Who has not heard expressions such as, "On the job, you should not mix the personal with the professional."? Or, "Don't take it personally." What do these phrases mean? Could there be a way to separate ourselves from where we work, as if we are just a sack of job skills unconnected to our lives, histories, and realities? As if we should only reconnect with ourselves after we leave the office?

Community work touches us at very personal levels. The stories of our co-workers and program participants – their deaths, births, celebrations, defeats, as well as individual and collective dreams – these are not things to compartmentalize and ignore. They are our shared grief and our celebrations. They hold us together. At LHA we seek to create spaces that allow us to:

- grow as humans by recognizing and validating our personal stories and those of others.
- reflect on our emotions, pains, and prejudices as well as their impact on our work.
- overcome fears and insecurities to unleash our creativity and leadership.

"I didn't have a privileged childhood. We had only my dad's salary to support a family with 12 children. My dad worked, but he suffered from alcoholism. My family had many problems and I had to protect myself. Although I loved my mom, I left my house at 14. I had to. I was being sexually abused in my own house.

"I found LHA through an announcement the promotoras made at church. I was curious. They explained to me the services offered there. I went to LHA and received information and health services. I now realize that those were also services for the soul. I became a volunteer. I experienced the protection of this place where I felt respected and able to tell my truth. I remember asking myself, 'Could I ever be a useful person for my community despite the fact that I grew up without tools for life? Is it possible to accomplish anything with my family and in the community despite the life that I have had?'

"I have been developing my ability to listen, when before I could not. I know I can hurt others without wanting to. I know that every human being has the obligation to respect others and the right to be respected. I am aware that no matter how difficult life is, there is always something positive. I have learned to recognize my own strengths, the ones that were invisible at my home. At LHA, I became aware that I am able to manage my emotions and not to leave them to others to manage. I have learned to

have a positive mind, not to be ashamed of being afraid, and to understand that I am responsible to take care of the mental health of my son, of the little girl inside me, and of all children in my community."

—Cathy, promotora,
    Children and Youth
    Initiative and the
    Emotional Wellness
    Program

We recognize that paying attention to aspects of everyone's lives sometimes creates tension among our team members. Almost all who work at LHA, especially the *promotores,* are likely to see opportunities for sharing personal stories as the most honest way to grow, to heal, to appreciate and be appreciated, and to share what we value and what offends us.

However, even within our own organization, some wonder why we should invest in the personal. There are those who think that some of their colleagues hide behind their personal problems as a way to avoid doing their work, or as an excuse for why they don't complete it. Others believe that when you are involved in work activities, you should not have to hear personal stories of co-workers – especially if they are stories of anguish and pain. Throughout the years, we have realized that sharing our stories helps us become better and stronger for ourselves, our families, and the community. That is why, as an agency, we invite our staff to share their stories freely at our retreats and in our conversations. However, we also respect everyone's right to privacy. No one is compelled to tell their story. And if listening to other people's stories is too distracting for some people, or too painful, they have a right to step back.

The responsibility to oneself

Although personal life does not disappear when we come to work, we still have to manage it so it does not interfere with our performance. Each individual is responsible to seek help to overcome or cope with his or her problems and personal challenges.

Each individual must strike a balance between taking care of his or her own needs and getting the job done. We don't leave people alone with this challenge. We have a practice of helping team members when they experience major problems or emergencies. This builds the team, helps us to minimize the impact of a crisis, and regains focus to continue the work. We get to practice helping and being helped. In these situations, common sense is our best counselor for figuring out how to support each other and, at the same time, get the work done.

Management of our personal lives is crucial to our success at work, influencing everything, from what motivates us and inspires us, to fears of change and failure, to how we see the rules, and to our relationships with others.

"Coming here to LHA opened up my thinking about health and responsibility. First of all, I started working inside my home because I felt I could make changes there. Within our home, we started outreach to our own kids because we saw that there were programs for young children. My wife and I saw this need and we realized that alcoholism is an illness that has to do with everyone at home, everyone in the family. So we said, 'Let's work together to have hope so we can do something to change and to live the way we are supposed to.' We united the family that was not united.

"I came to the agency because of my diabetes. And here is where I found out how to be a health promotor. I found that I have knowledge and opportunity and I could live a different life. Now, as a promotor, this is what I feel when I go knocking on doors. I go to give information about a program, but at the same time, I feel that I am responsible for that family or that person, and I want him to find that starting with today, things will be different in his life. The information we have to offer, as well as our own

history and the pain we have experienced, is what counts when we lead with the heart toward someone who is in need of our help."

—*Mario, promotor, Community Engagement and Advocacy Program*

Mario's personal story is intertwined with his work. He brings his own history and pain with him when he knocks on doors to invite people into LHA programs. He may or may not share his story, but the fact that he has lived it helps him reach out with his heart. He is holding his personal and professional life in balance.

Our personal and professional lives are in balance when we:

- Feel passion for the mission of our organization.
- See clearly the personal benefit of our work.
- Take full advantage of every lesson in order to grow and to apply what has been learned in our personal lives.
- Do not do to anyone what we do not like done to us.
- Don't use our private lives as an excuse for not performing our work with quality and on time. Personal excuses are the exception and not the norm.
- Respect the collective physical space. We are discreet about decorating our work spaces. We avoid personal visits and calls during working hours and in the workplace.
- Do not use the property of the organization for personal use.
- Share ourselves and our stories but not in a way that overwhelms others.
- Ask for or seek help when we are consumed by personal problems and these are affecting or may affect the work.
- Behave maturely and proactively, and accept responsibility for following directions and handling differences.
- Present all options to others, even if we have opinions on what is best.
- Respect the choices of others, even if we do not agree.
- Accept criticism at work as a critique of something we did improperly or poorly, and not as a critique of who we are.

- Have decent and cordial relations with everyone at work and in the community although we may not be friends.
- Respect the stories, privacy, and rights of others.

LHA may be somewhat different than some other workplaces in that we believe there is continuity between our personal and professional lives. We encourage and support one another in validating our experiences and in managing our personal lives so that our work lives can be pleasant and productive.

Within the context of the agreement that we are all working on ourselves and supporting each other as we work with and support the community, we also expect certain competencies from each staff member (see chapter 8).

Our Work Performance:
Competencies and Expectations

"To get involved with a place like Latino Health Access is not very difficult. They gave me the opportunity to receive trainings on health, community, diversity, and more. I learned about science, psychology, demography, communication, etc. I could use my computer skills and my talents as an educator, painter, singer, and designer, and I could share a warm welcome in fellowship with all of those who, in one way or another, seek our services. LHA has made me feel loved and important. It is easier to learn in a place where people believe in me, where I'm listened to and accepted with respect for who I am, instead of in a place where emotionally I feel rejected or nullified because I don't have enough formal education, or I don't have as much money, or because I'm Latina. LHA is a school whose classes are invaluable, priceless. Letting me be myself, with my own voice – simple, modest, clear – unafraid to think and to share my thoughts, viewing each situation as an x-ray, looking at what we can improve, how many miles we need to walk to see a tangible 'big difference.' I have taken control of my life in a transparent, simple, and natural way, thanks to the personal growth I have achieved through my work at Latino Health Access."

— *Noraima, promotora, Emotional Wellness Program*

All LHA staff members are expected to work toward full competency in the 18 areas below, regardless of their roles in the organization. We recognize that some of these competencies may take time to develop and may only be partially demonstrated at any given time. We know developing competencies is a learning process; however, we train and coach staff to achieve the highest degree possible of competency within each of these areas, even if their role is not programmatic. The competencies are:

1. Act in a manner consistent with the philosophy and principles of LHA

We demonstrate this competency when we are able to:

- Explain to others how we see community work, our work environment, relationships, and the 20 Principles of Practice that guide LHA (see chapter 6).
- Be alert and open to hearing from others about our personal behaviors that could be in conflict with our principles and paradigms, and actively work to correct them.
- Design activities and programs according to these paradigms and principles.
- Proactively implement activities for reflection and alignment with our team.

2. Create, protect, and maintain relationships with others

We demonstrate this competency when we are able to:

- Appreciate people for their ability to move forward instead of focusing only on their problems or deficiencies.
- Accompany people in discovering their abilities, skills, and self-knowledge.
- Explain the value and purpose of forming relationships.
- Take initiative to meet new people, and start conversations that could allow us to see life from their point of view.
- Listen; appreciate the wisdom, history, culture, and strengths of the other person.
- Use words responsibly and sensitively, adapting to the way the other person speaks and understands.

- Accompany people, offering only what we can deliver and following up on what we promise.
- Act ethically and with integrity.
- Be open to criticism without becoming defensive.
- Know how to offer constructive criticism and how to apologize and repair damage.
- Reciprocate and act in solidarity.

3. Possess the knowledge to do our job

We demonstrate this competency when we are able to:

- Develop our work, bringing all our skills, experience, knowledge, and best efforts to the job.
- Define our roles within the organization clearly and with confidence, as a *promotor*, program evaluator, coordinator, receptionist, assistant, etc.
- Explain the specific tasks, services, and activities we are working on at the present time.
- Refer a participant to another program within LHA by having a strong working knowledge of the initiatives and services we offer.
- Train other staff or volunteers in accordance with the standards of LHA.
- Explain the budget and contribute to the efficient financial management of our program.

4. Plan and document our work

We demonstrate this competency when we are able to:

- Think through and organize activities, individually and as a team, and gather the human and material resources needed to ensure implementation.
- Complete all necessary forms accurately before and after the work according to guidelines and procedures required for each program, and deliver on time.
- Value the importance of numbers and data collection as a record of our progress and of the impact we are having in the community.

Mario and Irma, *promotores*, welcome participants to a training.

5. Implement informative, educational sessions

We demonstrate this competency when we are able to:

- Facilitate an informational or educational session in a way that keeps people's attention, using materials that are appropriate for the learning style of participants, their ages, interests, culture, and state of life.
- Share and adapt presentations and materials, making them interactive and honoring participants' wisdom and experience.
- Speak confidently in public.

6. Plan, organize, and facilitate group sessions with different purposes

We demonstrate this competency when we are able to:

- Convene, organize, have a clear purpose, and have a formal or informal agenda ready in work meetings or in study and support groups.
- Implement the group activity in a pleasant and respectful manner that encourages participation.
- Protect and respect the culture, opinion, and rights of each participant with clear group rules and appropriate consequences if the rules are broken.
- Maintain a network of related organizations.

7. Help, refer, and follow up

We demonstrate this competency when we are able to:

- Provide accurate, relevant, and timely help, in the opinion of the person receiving the aid.

- Promote people's own life experiences, encouraging them to take an active role in defining their needs and how to meet them. Support people in taking steps to find resources and take action.

- Identify helpful resources and assist people in accessing and using services.

- Follow up to find out if the person used the service, whether the service was in fact helpful, and whether additional services are needed.

- Identify personal and organizational limits so that we can be transparent about when we are not able to help someone.

8. Find solutions together in one-on-one conversations

We demonstrate this competency when we are able to:

- Implement one-on-one conversations, which are private conversations between two people designed to help assess situations, consider ways out of problematic situations, find solutions, and implement actions in a respectful way. These one-on-ones can take place with participants, partners, or co-workers.

- Ensure that the people who had a one-on-one conversation feel satisfied with the outcomes and agreements reached.

- Decide when is the appropriate moment to start longer one-on-one processes when the participant or co-worker needs to be accompanied physically, mentally, or emotionally.

9. Find and meet the community, to do outreach

We demonstrate this competency when we are able to:

- Select the geographic area in which we will carry out the activities.

- Decide in advance what kind of strategy to creatively undertake or how to improve an activity to make it appropriate to the needs detected in that zone.

- Capture the attention of people we are hoping to reach.

- Know how to do door-to-door outreach and how to participate in health fairs and mini-campaigns.
- Follow rules before and during activities to protect our personal safety.

10. Build capacity among participants and co-workers so they can use their power to improve their lives, their families, their environments, and their institutions

We demonstrate this competency when we are able to:

- Bring in new volunteers who can do the work to support different programs and initiatives promoted by our organization.
- Train others on how to improve their community.
- Teach others how to advocate and represent themselves and others.
- Offer ideas and help so community members can develop their own projects.
- Organize and mobilize residents of communities for social or political events and to work in groups or committees.

11. Advocate

We demonstrate this competency when we are able to:

- Use our voices and ideas to advocate for others, being sensitive to diverse cultures and ideals.
- Explore different points of view and circumstances that allow us to have balanced points of view about specific topics.
- Present the situation and arguments in a way that increases the chances of success.
- Challenge dominant discourses.

12. Acknowledge job responsibility

We demonstrate this competency when we are able to:

- Meet our assigned tasks and manage work time effectively.
- Honor and follow the rules of confidentiality.

13. Have a commitment to quality

We demonstrate this competency when we are able to:

- Offer effective services and useful activities.

- Identify areas that need improvement. Advocate for and act to bring about those improvements.
- Gratefully accept feedback and suggestions to improve our performance.

14. Know our rights as employees of LHA and know to respect the rights of others

We demonstrate this competency when we are able to:

- Understand and explain the employee handbook.
- Know whom to contact in case of doubt or conflict.
- Know when to use the organizational hierarchy to protect our rights or those of others.
- Make co-workers feel respected.

15. Know and follow administrative procedures

We demonstrate this competency when we are able to:

- Know that all procedures must be approved by the operations team. Procedures related to human resources, financial, fund development, HIPAA (Health Insurance Portability and Accountability Act), and IT (Information Technology) are followed, such as reporting time on time sheets, requesting leaves, reporting absences, reporting incidents and accidents, requesting reimbursements, fees, use of space, accepting donations, and other acts related to the operation of the organization.
- Meet safety standards per LHA safety policies and operations manual.

16. Be accountable

We demonstrate this competency when we are able to:

- Report our work, use of funds, and risks and problems in an honest and transparent manner.
- Accept being evaluated by others.
- Accept responsibility for our actions and their consequences.

17. Be part of the team

We demonstrate this competency when we are able to:

- Accurately explain our role in the LHA team.
- Do the work assigned to us in our programs and activities on time and with quality.
- Take responsibility for the team to plan and carry out activities successfully.
- Help other colleagues to understand their work and improve their job performance.
- Contribute to a harmonious work environment and resolve conflicts that could prevent or delay the planning or execution of our activities.
- Have flexibility to work and to do what it takes to complete the job on time and with quality.
- Take initiative and contribute our ideas to improve and be more productive.
- Act with integrity and loyalty to our team and LHA programs and be worthy of the trust of others.
- Listen to feedback, give constructive criticism, and provide support for others.
- Apply self-discipline and act to improve after we have received feedback.
- Invest time in activities that help us get to know our colleagues.
- Disseminate relevant and proper information within our team.

18. Represent and interact with institutions, groups, or individuals outside of LHA

We demonstrate this competency when we are able to:

- Establish productive and assertive communication with a variety of groups, institutions, and individuals while trying to understand where there may be mutual interests and taking into account their styles, rules, constraints, culture, history, language, and political context.
- Provide clarification and participate in conflict resolution between outside entities and LHA.
- Represent LHA ethically, in a way that is integrated and consistent with our Principles of Practice and paradigms.

- Offer only what we can deliver and follow up on the agreements and tasks.
- Be selective. Know when to engage or not engage in outside projects.

How do we improve, learn and unlearn, and become increasingly competent at LHA?

We travel the paths of learning and unlearning every day at LHA. These paths are full of contradictions. On these paths, we sometimes disrespect, offend, and exclude others. We impose our truths, we avoid conflict, and then we suffer. But it is precisely on these paths where we learn to respect and apologize to each other, to include, value, listen to, and support each other. To learn and unlearn, we discuss books, share testimonies, go camping, attend retreats, and talk in private or in groups. We are accountable to one another. We cry, laugh, and celebrate. We constantly re-commit to change something about ourselves or about our organization. Many times we succeed. Other times, we find it difficult not to repeat behaviors and expressions that we want to give up and are ashamed of; but we keep trying to change.

How do we create an environment where it is safe to challenge our "behaviors and truths?" How do we learn and uphold another way of being and doing?

> *"My family situation reached a crisis point and I decided to call LHA. Two promotores, Oscar and Sol, came to my house every day. They called me several times a day. They saved my life. After that, I became a promotora with LHA. I know that if we help by going the extra mile, we help people get out of holes. Sol and Oscar are my models of what a promotor is."*
>
> —Rosa, promotora, Diabetes Self-Management Program

Development of fundamental skills is a never-ending process. At LHA we use a variety of ways to increase knowledge, to improve our work, and to maintain our balance. These include trainings, field work, peer learning, retreats, receiving and giving support, and monthly team meetings.

Trainings

We design training sessions to work on particular topics. LHA's team may go outside the agency for a training organized by another group, or participate in an internal training. Internally, the coach or trainer may come from outside or may be one of our co-workers. All staff members participate in training throughout the year. Sessions can be either individual or in groups. Below are just some examples of the trainings we repeat to help staff develop various skills.

Laura, *promotora*, explains her conclusions in a training.

Developing skills for community work

- Building healthy cities
- Strategies to conduct outreach
- Adult education
- How to help effectively
- Community organizing
- Improving communication
- Increasing participation
- Building capacity among participants
- How to organize events
- How to do family visits
- How to facilitate educational sessions or support groups
- How to develop one-on-one sessions

Content for health promotion and disease prevention programs

- Prevention and management of chronic diseases
- Obesity and overweight in children and adults
- Nutrition
- Mental health
- Emotional problems
- Helping parents create meaningful relationships with their children
- Domestic violence prevention
- Breast cancer
- Substance abuse
- Child passenger safety
- CPR and first aid
- Poisoning prevention
- How to gain access to services and health insurance

Content for advocacy and leadership programs

- Advocacy in the community
- The U.S. Government
- Leadership 101
- How the budget in your city is developed
- Know your political representatives
- Mobilizing the vote
- Immigrants' rights
- Women's rights

Developing skills to help participants get services from other organizations, including health insurance and health care in clinics and hospitals

- Insurance in the United States
- Health care reform
- Services for those without documents
- Where to find free or low-cost services and what are the requirements for using them?
- How to use service directories
- How to make a referral

- How to track a referral
- What forms need to be filled out?
- Who can and how to enroll participants in health programs?
- How to request a restraining order in court

Developing skills to document our work with participants, measure results, and protect confidentiality of participants

- What is the data or information and what is its purpose?
- What are the most common errors when data is collected?
- Differences between impact and process and outcome objectives
- What are the objectives and what is the expected impact of a specific program?
- How are outreach and contacts documented?
- How to get data from another source?
- How information is entered into our evaluation database
- Laws protecting confidentiality about health information
- How to protect the confidentiality of LHA participants

Use of technology

- Use of computers
- Regulations on the use of computers at LHA
- Using different programs like Word, Excel, and PowerPoint
- Use of office phones, projectors, and other technology

Developing skills for labor rights and duties, including knowledge of administrative procedures

- Study of operations manual policies
- Study of the regulation of financial procedures
- Completing forms for reporting mileage
- How to complete forms to report hours worked
- Preventing and reporting harassment
- Managing and resolving conflict

Developing skills for safety in the workplace

- How to prevent accidents
- How to report accidents
- Disaster preparedness, including fires and earthquakes

- Practicing fire drills
- How to be safe while doing community work, including outreach, home visits, surveys, and the like

Developing supervision skills

- How to supervise
- How to supervise *promotores*
- How to document the behavior of an employee
- How to evaluate a worker
- How to give feedback

Learning about our work

We learn about our work in our interactions on the streets, with participants, and with our own teams. We learn from our work on a daily basis, accumulating experiences that allow us to improve. We share our learnings with each other, discussing what works for us and what does not. When we talk about how and why something worked or failed to work, we try to be honest about our difficulties. We aim to give and accept honest feedback. Sometimes, peer learning takes place when one colleague shares with another colleague his or her mastery of a specific area of work. An example of this could be a *promotora* learning how to conduct a one-on-one session by observing another *promotora* doing her session. Another example is when a *promotora* with more experience teaches less experienced co-workers how to do outreach activities. We also create working groups and committees where all facets of our team, including programmatic and operational team members, are represented. We make sure to include *promotores* in every work group. These working teams are placed in charge of developing projects and improving procedures and practices.

Retreats

Once or twice a year we take two or three days to retreat from the daily work and to focus instead on team activities that strengthen us as individuals and as an organization. A retreat may take place at a campground in the mountains, a quiet and beautiful place away from the office, or in a nearby park. Sometimes we just stop work for two days and stay in our own building. Several times, we have based the content of a retreat on a book that we have read together.

We prepare questions based on the book to guide the discussion. We create spaces for conversational groups, and we always include food and physical activities or entertainment.

We have also had retreats to reflect on who we are and what we do. In these retreats, we share our ways of seeing our work, what we value, what works, and how we achieve our accomplishments. These retreats have allowed us to observe and share stories of transformation and success. They become spaces that allow us to build, align, and strengthen our team.

Receiving and giving support

Besides retreats, people who work at LHA can participate if they wish to in support groups that are offered to the community. This is particularly important for *promotores* who came into LHA through their participation in support groups. Also, we sometimes ask for one-on-one confidential conversations with someone we think can help us. In this private conversation, we discuss our conflicts or problems. In many cases, the conversations are with supervisors, LHA human resources staff, or friends of the organization who are also skilled therapists.

We also help advocate for each other's children. We help interpret for those who don't speak English. And, in some cases, we have sheltered colleagues who have been victims of violence. We help raise money when one of us has a special need, and we stick together through difficult times. We help our colleagues to understand the need for professional help when it is required for social services, health, or legal cases. We maintain an employee wellness program, with activities such as dance led by staff members, and also make sure staff know that they can take time every day to do some physical activity, such as aerobics, walking, dancing, yoga, and meditation.

The monthly staff meeting

Once a month we close the agency and have an all-staff meeting. During that meeting, some departments present their program objectives, report their progress, and share successes and challenges. Each presentation must include creative methods such as drama, testimonies, and questions to engage the audience. The presentations help us learn something new or reinforce previous knowledge.

During these meetings we take the opportunity to welcome new employees, interns, or visitors, or to say goodbye. We have important conversations about strategies, opportunities, dangers, administrative issues, accounting, employee performance evaluations, and many other issues related to our work. We invite outside organizations to present their services. We exercise together at break time, and we celebrate birthdays in culturally specific ways.

How do we validate and defend our model and our work?

"They try to typecast us. They say, 'So, what are you? Community organizers?' I answer that we are promotoras; we are everything; we are what is needed. They do not understand me. Sometimes I feel that I cannot defend myself. I need to be something that they understand. They do not understand that one can be many things at once.

"We have to clarify ourselves, so we can make it clear to those who are wondering. For others to understand us, they have to compare us with something they know, but since they do not know who we are, then we have to break it down so they can understand.

"If we tell them that we provide information, they say, 'Ahh!'

"If we tell them we convene meetings and mobilize people, they say, 'Ahh!'

"If we say we're looking for people to be enthusiastic and involved, they say 'Ahh!'

"If we say we provide classes, they say, 'Ahh!'

"If we say we do raffles to raise money when someone needs help, they say, 'Ahh!'

"But if we say that we can be or do whatever is needed, then they do not understand."

—Sarai, promotora, Community Engagement and Advocacy Program

America, Sarai, and Araceli share ideas.

We are constantly creating a design for a more holistic practice, where we can be whole people working in whole communities and getting our jobs done in a workplace that reflects that balance. We are resisting ways of relating that cause us to dehumanize each other, and we are searching for ways of relating that allow us to be human and to humanize each other.

Who validates our model?

Society at large tests and challenges our principles, ideas, and patterns of thinking and acting. Sometimes, it drains us and makes us doubt who we are and what we do. The dominant discourse may be stronger and noisier at times, and drown us out. What we do may be judged against organizations that operate in more corporate, competitive, and hierarchical ways. What we do and our decisions continuously challenge the values of the dominant society. Outside we are asked sometimes, "Why don't the *promotoras* go to the university to become professionals?" Or, "Why, after going to the university, do the team members choose to stay in the community instead of working in hospitals, universities, and other important places?" What we do and our decisions are continuously challenging the values of the dominant society.

We and our community are the ones who can validate our model. We do this by being clear about the results we get and the impact we are having. Everyone at LHA needs to learn who we are, what we do, and how we do it. At LHA we often stop to talk about ourselves. We recognize the need to observe ourselves critically in order to understand and improve our work and to communicate about it to the outside world. Inside LHA, we consider it a good use of our time to validate our own strategies, models, and methods.

How to innovate?

"We are the community. We live here and we have access to each other every day. Let us use our experience to think creatively about solutions."

—*Soledad, promotora, Emotional Wellness Program*

We are constantly looking for new solutions that could give better results. Unfortunately, we function in a society that constantly asks us to repeat the same strategies even though they may not be effective.

In our daily work, we take risks. Every day we must dare to innovate. We believe that the best innovations arise in meetings and discussions with the community, and they are achieved on the streets and in people's homes, not at a desk. If there is no space to take risks, then there is no room to develop novel strategies. We know that innovation flourishes within groups and organizations where there is time and room for patience and for conversations.

Rescuing common sense

Most of the things we do are guided by common sense. We seek practical solutions to achieve results that endure. Our strategies are not complicated, expensive, or unusual. We do logical things like helping others and being supportive, kind, and respectful. We fight for parks where there are none, bring neighbors together to solve their own problems, believe that people are experts on their lives, and invite them to share their experiences. We believe that having a multi-talented team is better and more efficient. We know there have to be rules and that inevitably there will be conflicts, and we prepare for that. We recognize that common sense is not so common. Common sense may not be as glamorous as some complicated fixes, but we are committed to having quality programs and strategies that are grounded in common sense.

LHA is not a positive and productive environment 24/7. Sometimes, everyone is doing their own work and we mistake that for everyone being aligned. To stay on the same page with each other, we don't shy away from intense interaction. Our meetings provide opportunities for us to align ideas and strategies. We share our dreams and successes, and we remind ourselves about the difference that our organization makes in our lives and in the lives of our participants. When we meet and talk to clarify ideas, we come up with solutions, are filled with optimism, and feel strong.

We can have a lot of disagreements, but we all agree we are not going to renounce the commitment to be better as individuals and as an organization. We constantly seek opportunities to see ourselves with compassion and with a critical mind. Writing this book as a collective has helped us to create more opportunities for reflection and to see each other, appreciate each other, understand each other, and re-commit to this wonderful process of growth and change. The more we work to reflect and improve, the better we will be able to help our families and communities. The process of learning and unlearning is constant; it is a right and a duty for all.

Sustaining Ourselves Financially

"Every department at LHA is an important contributor to helping our organization accomplish its mission. As the Chief Financial Officer at LHA, my work in accounting is black and white. It is about numbers, accountability, discipline, and transparency. I also understand our part in achieving the mission of LHA. I understand the impact that our programs have in the lives of the families we serve and the importance of having a stable and enthusiastic workforce. In addition, I understand my privilege. My parents came to the U.S. 50 years ago. They had to work hard but I grew up within a safe and protected environment.

"At LHA, my team and I work hard to manage resources today and plan for future needs. I am also part of the fund development team. Funding for non-profits is very fragmented and short-term. Every month we have new funding to implement or continue projects. Every year we have to deal with the uncertainty of competing for funding, losing and gaining, and competing again. We create budgets and assign personnel to them. There are projects supported by multiple funders requiring multiple reports. In those cases, one person may be paid by multiple grants. We have people in two or more programs. We often have to transfer

*staff to other programs when their grants end. All must be done
at a reasonable speed so the programs do not stop. We constantly
monitor when grants end to make our best effort to bring resources
to avoid gaps. However, we have to deal with funding gaps
frequently. It is very hard to create a cash reserve when you have
gaps between grants.*

*"In order to accomplish our mission, the programs must do the
work. The Fund Development team is committed to raise money
to support the work. Simultaneously, the Accounting Department
provides the financial discipline for the appropriate management of
funds and the flexibility to assure that programs function in real
time. Our financial work is not directly with the families, but it is
directly related to the mission."*

—Iliana, Director of Finance

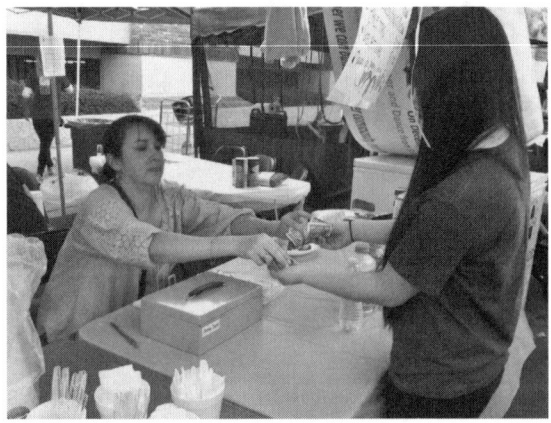

Iliana helps at a
fundraising activity.

People often ask how we have financially supported our work
in the community for such a long time. It hasn't been easy. In
22 years, we've weathered two recessions, donor fatigue, and hot-
button funding trends that don't always align with our mission.
The members of our base, while they are numerous and give
generously of their time, are not wealthy and cannot make large
financial contributions. Meanwhile, Orange County, California,
is a conservative county, home to large and vocal anti–immigrant
groups. While Orange County has been changing demographically
and politically for the past four decades, it still has a reputation of
right-wing activism, homogeneity, and affluence. Richard Nixon,

the John Birch Society, and Ronald Reagan have all been strong influences in Orange County (Romero, Waheed, and Sarmiento, 2014). While our communities have advanced significantly, many government agencies and foundations still, consciously or unconsciously, view our community in a paternalistic way, which is reflected in the way they distribute funding and other opportunites they control.

Yet we have been able to sustain a strong presence in the 92701 ZIP code and in Santa Ana. The two main contributors to our financial stability over the years are: 1) our fundraising strategies, which include grants from private foundations, some government funding, and, to a lesser degree, income from trainings, speaking engagements, consulting, the annual Gala, and smaller donations and fundraising events; and 2) the continuity of our staff and supporters. We have had very little turnover in 22 years: 50% of our staff members have worked at LHA for between 7 and 21 years. Having a dedicated staff and very loyal supporters makes it possible for us to maintain a steady presence in our neighborhoods, whether we are being funded or not. We take the approach that we will find a way to do what we know works.

We have started nearly every project with this attitude, that we will do whatever it takes to improve health and well-being, even if we do not have funding for a specific project, because the ideas for the projects almost always arise from the community. We want to honor their wisdom about what needs to be changed, since they often see the solutions long before funders see them. We want to help them maintain their momentum, and so we support them in launching small projects. These Hope-Energy-Action Projects (described in chapter 3) often then become larger efforts with funding support.

The U.S. has a large philanthropic community and a system to request funding, but it is not easy to navigate. LHA's philosophical view is that funders and those with extra income can and should help relieve disparities for the greater good. Even so, we know that in many places around the world, and in California as well, people are achieving amazing outcomes without any outside funding. We honor and respect that approach and often use it ourselves. However, we seek funding in order to offer living wages to the *promotores* and other people who give their full-time efforts to this work, and to add a level of infrastructural support to the changes being sought.

We don't claim to have all the answers. Still, we have succeeded in employing strategies that have allowed us to attract funding, to adapt, to remain solvent and effective, and to work using a comprehensive, placed-based approach. These strategies include:

1. Partnering with foundations that share our philosophy.
2. Cross-training staff and fostering flexibility in team members.
3. Retaining a presence in the neighborhoods, no matter what.
4. Investing energy in collaborative approaches.
5. Developing diverse means of financial support.

Partnering with foundations that share our philosophy

We have been fortunate to be able to partner with several foundations that respect our approach and share our philosophy. A few foundations have made long-term commitments and offered flexible support to LHA over several years. These foundations have allowed us to plan ahead, knowing we can rely on their funding to sustain the core of our community work. We are then able to layer other complementary or synergistic projects on top of this core.

We have built strong relationships with foundations by working together on a joint commitment to improving community health in low-income areas. Over the years, we have supported their work and invited them to learn about and support ours, further deepening our ability to address issues together. Foundations have asked to hear directly from our community members. We have participated in their trainings, hosted focus groups for them, and offered ourselves as thinking partners, so community input can help to shape funding initiatives. We have been speakers and trainers for their grantees and boards, reviewers, committee members, and board members. Two of these foundations, having seen the outcomes we produce and the reach we have in the community, are now funding LHA to continue what the Institute of Medicine calls the foundational work of building the base of an engaged community in order to produce lasting change (Committee on Assuring the Health of the Public in the 21st Century, 2002).

We have been fortunate to work side by side with foundations that have launched large multi-year initiatives modeled on Healthy Cities. We are extremely grateful for foundations that invest in us because of our track record and the successful strategies we employ. We are grateful, too, for those foundations that provide core support and flexible operational support. It has been a privilege to work with foundations that do their best to mitigate the power imbalance between funder and grantee by showing a great deal of trust and respect for the methodologies we have developed.

One of LHA's major partners has been The California Endowment. Their commitment to the Healthy Cities model makes them a natural partner. Our communities in California have benefited from their long-term commitment to distressed neighborhoods, their dedication to including community members in solutions, and their practice of placing few restrictions on the use of their funds. Other funders that have supported us from the beginning and continue to be wonderful core and project funding partners include St. Joseph Health, Hoag Memorial Presbyterian Hospital Community Benefits, and the California Health Care Foundation. Like other non-profit groups, LHA has an ongoing need for unrestricted funds so we can retain trained staff during funding gaps, take action on issues, and be creative and innovative in real time as opportunities present themselves. The Marguerite Casey Foundation has provided invaluable long-term core support, and we are honored to be considered one of their cornerstone organizations. LHA is proud to participate with Marguerite Casey in the national campaign, Equal Voice for America's Families. Kaiser Permanente has been an amazing partner for providing actual medical care to our community through our inclusion in their medical rotation, for helping us evaluate the Diabetes Self-Management Program among the Kaiser members, and for supporting the writing of this book. We have had many other funders as well who have been genuine partners in the movement to improve health in low-income communities.

Characteristics of the most helpful funding

It is a privilege to work with the community to improve health conditions, and it is very rewarding to achieve significant outcomes in collaboration with the community. This is work we love. Most of us would do it no matter what.

We are extremely grateful when foundations and government entities partner with us. Foundations partner with non-profits to achieve improvements in social and health conditions, providing funding for the non-profit to do the work on the ground. Similarly, government agencies need non-profits because non-profits can do things that government agencies cannot, and can do them quickly. Non-profits have reach, flexibility, and cultural expertise. We assume a great deal of risk that government agencies are not willing or able to assume.

The most helpful types of funding:

- Honor the wisdom of the community.
- Respect the expertise of the non-profit.
- Set broad parameters and ensure that the non-profit is the one to propose the program plan, including the numbers served, the methods, and the outcomes.
- Are multi-year, allowing us to plan.
- Are flexible, with few restrictions on how the funding is spent, as long as outcomes are achieved.
- Offer payment of enough indirect costs to cover administration and other costs of doing business, and to allow staff to have employee benefits, just as foundation and government workers do.
- Are timed so that there are not gaps in funding.
- Are coordinated with other funders so that a concentration of resources can be offered to a distressed community.
- Include core support or unrestricted funds when needed.
- Support infrastructure projects that are necessary but not attractive to other funders.
- Simplify reporting requirements.

Challenges in working with grants and contracts

Supporting the work of LHA with a heavy reliance on foundation funding presents some challenges. One major challenge is the way foundations and governments allocate funding. Usually, grants and contracts focused on prevention and disease are short term and awarded to complete a specific project that addresses one issue at a time. Often, these issues have been identified by the funder, and the issues chosen change over time. HIV, smoking cessation, nutrition, and many other topics have had their moments as intervention subjects favored for funding. When trends change, it can force non-profits to change course in order to stay solvent.

Foundations and government agencies have their reasons for providing such restrictive funding. The health issues they target for interventions may have been identified through epidemiological data. They may face pressure to maximize their "return on investment" and to hold grantees accountable for specific health outcomes. Funders often operate in isolation from each other, may have legal restrictions on their funding that originated with their charters, and may have a limited set of priorities or passion for particular issues. We recognize the critical importance of focusing resources to address a single, pressing issue, rather than diffusing the effort by addressing a range of issues. For many reasons, government and foundations tend not to support projects that have a multifaceted approach to problems created by the intersection of poverty, discrimination due to race and gender, and lack of community control. However, a myopic focus on one health or social issue at a time may be the reason many traditional interventions fail.

Latino Health Access tries to implement an integrated approach to working with the community. In order to do that, our staff must work together so that no matter how a participant gets involved in the agency, he or she has access to all we have to offer. However, categorical funding and funding earmarked to certain programs impose restrictions on how staff can use their time. If a person's position is funded to focus on a particular issue, their time must be spent addressing that particular topic. This type of funding creates situations where one part of the agency cannot cooperate with another part because that is not what staff members on that side of the agency are being paid to do. This works against us in the long term.

Many of us have been university trained in a scientific approach that requires us to isolate issues in order to rigorously test interventions. However, addressing health and social issues in isolation is not how LHA works, mainly because it is not how people in the neighborhoods live, think, learn, and experience health. Threats to health exist within the context of life. They exist in the context of poverty, in the physical design of a neighborhood or city, and in media messages and commercial interests that target neighborhoods affected by poverty. People operate within the context of relationships, work, stress, raising children, interpersonal growth, sexuality, and so on.

LHA engages people through conversations about their strengths, hopes, and dreams, not about threats to their health. It is counterproductive to approach community members by talking about isolated threats to their health and focusing solely on one issue while being blind to the richness of people's lives. It bypasses relationships, trust, and a commitment to long-term, sustainable outcomes. For example, approaching a person about his diabetes will probably not be what motivates him to manage his condition. To address his diabetes in isolation would hamper our creativity and limit the intervention's effectiveness. However, if we approach him about his hopes and dreams for his life, his family, his community, and his neighborhood – now that is a path that is more likely to lead to activating his internal motivation for addressing his diabetes. A socially contextualized approach is also more likely to help him eventually turn his energy toward joining forces with others to change the root causes or social determinants that impede the appropriate management and prevention of diabetes in his community.

LHA's *promotoras* live in the communities they serve. They see life through the same lens as those they reach. Through this holistic lens, the *promotoras* would not consider abandoning a neighborhood because the funding priorities have changed. They are experts at building and sustaining relationships. They refuse to stop working in a neighborhood because there is no funding to do so. They will not deflect conversations about issues that are important to someone just because they are not funded to discuss that topic. To do so would cause loss of their credibility and loss of community trust, both individually and organizationally.

Even so, funding often does require us to address single topics. When we agree to this, it is because the community has already identified the topic as a priority. Community members take more leadership as they become more informed and experienced in addressing issues they themselves identify as important. These issues often become Hope-Energy-Action Projects with community members serving as leaders (see chapter 3). In these cases, we attempt to create our own continuity by making sure each step, or issue focus, builds on previous steps and includes conversations about overall community health and social determinants of health.

Accidentally harmful consequences of certain conditions on funding

We try our best to be careful about what funding to request and accept, based on lessons we have learned over the years. We try to evaluate whether short-term funding, categorical funding, gaps in funding, forced collaborations, lengthy competitions for funding that LHA has a low probability of receiving, one-time funding designed to use a non-profit to promote the funder, and funding subject to other funder-imposed conditions might create unintended harmful consequences. This is similar to when a person goes into a hospital to resolve a health issue and comes out with an infection that was picked up in the hospital.

The same can be said of the consequences of some funding initiatives. We can go in looking for help in one area yet come out with negative consequences as a result of the funding. These negative consequences can include losing trained staff; losing credibility in the community; getting the reputation that when we have money, we come to the neighborhood, and when we don't, we abandon it; diverting staff time away from important work in order to meet the expectations of the funder; not allowing comprehensive strategies to take root and be successful; and forcing collaboration when another partner is not yet ready. Carefully choosing our funding partners, when possible, has allowed us to make lasting, positive changes in the neighborhoods we serve.

Knowing when not to apply

We often choose not to apply for funding. Many times, funders impose limitations on what types of community members an agency can serve. We do not accept money from foundations that restrict funding to certain groups of people. We will not ask participants about immigration status or require proof of income, for example.

We are also careful not to accept subcontract funding when we will not be able to play a meaningful role in the planning of the intervention. About twice a year, we are contacted by universities that have received large government research grants "targeting" the Latino population. The problem is, they tell us, they are not sure where the Latinos are and they cannot "reach" them. These calls usually come with offers for us to participate in projects that have already been defined without our participation and without community input, with little understanding of the capacity of *promotoras* beyond that of inexpensive recruiters of study subjects. We do not accept those invitations. On the other hand, we do participate in research, and we partner with universities when the community recognizes the need for the research. In these cases, we like to have a meaningful role in designing the questions and sharing the data with the community in order to spur or support action or policy-change related to the issue being investigated.

Numbers served over making a real difference

We prefer to have deep, lasting, quality interventions that stimulate real change rather than to reach thousands of people with superficial interventions that look good when funders or government agencies report their numbers, but that are not very helpful in bringing real change to people's lives. In a recent contract negotiation, the funder told us that we needed to increase the numbers served by about 25% even though they were not planning to increase the dollars allotted to accomplish the work. This contract already had us reaching thousands of people with an intervention that we did not consider deep enough to make a lasting difference. We were told in no uncertain terms that the decision makers this person reported to wanted high numbers more than they wanted quality. Ultimately, we negotiated a middle ground in order to keep this contract. We had agreed to the original terms of the contract because there are times when we simply have to serve large numbers in order to attract funding that allows us at least to start a conversation about something that is important to the community. In these cases, we try to pair that funding with other funding that allows a more profound approach to be layered on top of the same or related work. We add layers to the work by using other sources of funding, so that once we reach a participant, we can spend enough time and offer enough resources and opportunities to increase the chances that he or she will experience a real improvement, and might even go on to help others.

Indirect cost restrictions

Another difficult challenge is the restriction placed on allowable percentages for indirect costs. Many foundations expect non-profits to raise additional funds to cover indirect costs; however, that is not always a realistic expectation. Low caps on indirect costs put us in a position of losing money to accept money. If the "cost of doing business" is 20%, for example, but we are allowed to use only 10% of a grant for indirect costs, we will lose money if we take that grant. If a grant pays direct programming salaries only, and doesn't recognize the salaries of the team that makes the programming work possible, we find ourselves running faster to sustain the same level of service. Lack of funding for indirect costs also results in low salaries and poor benefits packages for employees working in the non-profit sector, compared to those working in government and foundations.

Elaine Carpenter, Vice President of Business Development and Communications for ZeroDivide, said in the foundation's e-publication, *Updates from ZeroDivide*, "Given the day-to-day pressures of direct service delivery and the priority many funders give to 'low overhead' as a false metric by which to judge grantees, it is difficult for nonprofit organizations to find the time, resources, and assistance to try new approaches for building capacity and enhancing performance" (Carpenter, 2014).

Non-profits celebrated the federal Office of Management and Budget's new Uniform Guidance (Office of Management and Budget, 2013) that directs any governments using federal funds to pay a non-profit its indirect costs. There remain questions as to whether and how it will be implemented, and so far we have not seen any benefit. We are hopeful the guidance will be adopted by local governments and foundations as well, as this change would allow non-profits to stop subsidizing work they do on behalf of governments and to better invest in technology, staff benefits, and other critical functions that allow us to work efficiently and on a par with business, to which we are so often compared.

Imposed collaborations

Some of our most solid outcomes have resulted from collaborative efforts. These collaborations have been chosen by all parties involved and have been driven by passion for justice and health for all. Funders, having seen the power of collaborative efforts, sometimes require collaboration with preselected partners. This potential imposition by funders has sometimes been harmful. Latino Health Access has multiple programmatic partners in a variety of social sectors. We know which groups we work well with, which ones will deliver, and which ones share a similar paradigm. Forced collaborations can be fruitful, as long as they do not set the non-profits up to compete against one another for funds, pair agencies with vastly different philosophies, require multiple time-consuming meetings for shared outcomes that are unfunded, or hold one agency accountable for another's performance.

Funders involved in program planning

Some funders require that they have input into the program planning process. Because of the power imbalance between the funder and the grantee, honest discussions may not be possible. LHA welcomes funder input, but not at the expense of the community's wisdom and the wisdom of our technical team that is in touch with the community.

Imposed capacity building

Funders sometimes require grantees to participate in activities designed to build the non-profit's capacity. This can include working with external evaluators, policy experts, and others. These opportunities can be helpful when they are requested by the non-profit and customized by the external expert. They can drain the organization when they are not requested or not customized. Often, by the time the external expert learns enough to be helpful, the project is over. And often, the reverse occurs: We have built the "expert's" capacity at the expense of our own staff. We have invested many hours that could have been spent more wisely. In the end, we often receive very generic reports from experts.

Cross-training staff and fostering flexibility in team members

A solution that works well for us to counter categorical funding methods is to cross-train staff. The topic or focus of an educational intervention or an action may change based on funding restrictions, but the *promotoras'* presence in the community and our approach to the community remain constant. *Promotoras* are cross-trained so that when one funding stream changes its focus or runs dry, they are ready to move to another project supported by a different funder yet still remain in the neighborhood.

This flexibility is a key quality we foster within LHA, and we make sure employees understand this before we hire them. We tell them not to get too attached to their workspace, as it may change if it is needed for a more pressing purpose. We ask them to keep a flexible approach to their work, to be creative in how to get things done for their neighbors in the face of limited resources, to collaborate with their co-workers, and to be open to shifting roles as needed.

In the past when faced with a sudden loss of funding, the entire staff reduced work hours and focused on priority areas of greatest need. During both recessions, the entire staff reduced hours to four or fewer days per week. These major macroeconomic shifts are felt painfully at the ground level. Time reductions are painful measures for staff, but the unyielding commitment of the *promotoras* combined with strategic planning have carried us over these tough times to the other side as a cohesive team.

Retaining a presence in the neighborhoods, no matter what

The agency as a whole will still support previous projects if the neighbors want to continue to take action on a particular issue. Because we don't address issues in isolation, we've been successful with this approach. While the primary emphasis may change, often we are able to keep going at some level. For example, diabetes prevention and self-management, heart health, healthy weight, and mental health are closely related and influence one another. Likewise, these and many other topics are closely related to accessibility to parks and safe places to play and exercise. So funding for heart health can still support neighbors working to get more open space for exercise, for example.

Wellness Corridor kick-off to activate public spaces for exercise

LHA participates in Santa Ana's traditional *"Dia de Los Muertos"* event.

Investing energy in collaborative approaches

We have been able to make significant, long-term changes by using synergy to exponentially increase our influence through work with collaborative partners. Latino Health Access engages many community members in coalitions. Community members who work with Latino Health Access also often belong to several coalitions themselves. They are working hard to see changes for their children and their families. By working together with other organizations, we are able to show a groundswell of community will to change a policy or to advocate for resources.

Developing diverse means of financial support

To varying degrees of success, we have developed other means of support to avoid relying solely on foundation and government funds. These include the following:

Trainings

We have long offered trainings for *promotores* and their supervisors and for organizations wishing to begin using or to further develop the *promotor* model. We also offer trainings for organizations wishing to replicate our Diabetes Self-Management Program or any other of our programs. We offer trainings on cultural competency, community engagement, Healthy Cities, advocacy, and others. We customize the trainings to the needs of the organization. We are also asked to speak on various topics related to our strategies and outcomes, and sometimes we are paid for these engagements. We use the money we raise from trainings and speaking engagements to support the otherwise unfunded work in Santa Ana.

Consulting

We have always helped the uninsured in our community learn about health insurance, gain access to it, and use it. Lately, thanks to the Affordable Care Act, insurance companies and health plans have new enrollees who have never before had insurance. We provide a limited amount of consultation and direct service to for-profit organizations, primarily health care organizations. We have expertise to offer the health care system in meeting the community engagement portion of the Institute for Healthcare Improvement's proposed "Triple Aim" (improve health, better care, lower costs), in "patient navigation," and in other areas as well. Consulting and contracting with private health care organizations are important means of diversifying our funding streams. These new contracts allow us to maintain continuity with community members who were previously uninsured and now have private health insurance. Additionally, it allows us to bring a community health perspective to large private insurers and to share our model of practice. They have expressed great interest in what we have learned about community health. We use the funds raised by these contracts to support our programs for the uninsured.

Donations from individuals

Our most successful approach to developing individual donors has been to start giving clubs. A giving club offers a vehicle for board members and staff to ask people to support the agency without directly asking for money. People are asked to join a club. The club has multiple levels of giving. We encourage members to allow us to charge their credit cards monthly so that we can count on a reliable stream of unrestricted funds without the need to ask again every month. We invite club members to parties and events where they can get to know each other while experiencing some of the wonderful things the various Latino cultures have to offer.

Annual Gala

For several years LHA has held an annual event around the theme of celebrating a healthier community. Sponsorship for the event allows us to raise funds for administration and other unfunded and under-funded areas of the organization. The party always includes dancing to live Latin music and a chance to dress up and have fun. Staff members are always included in planning and producing the event. We use the Gala as an opportunity to recognize our community partners as well. Each year, LHA honors two or three partners – for-profits, non-profits, or funding partners – who have made a great difference for the community.

Smaller fundraising events

The *promotores* are eager to raise funds to assist with short-term crises and to alleviate unnecessary suffering experienced by people living in poverty. Resources are always needed to help meet the needs they see on the streets and in homes. The *promotores* have many creative ideas for raising money. Small fundraisers pop up organically when a community member needs to bury a loved one, a woman needs to leave an abusive relationship, or a child's last remaining parent dies. The *promotores* and the community band together to find a way to make ends meet.

America and Tania enjoy the 2015 Gala.

Internally, we have a staff committee that produces smaller events to raise unrestricted funds for the agency. These events usually have the dual purpose of providing a way for the community to come together to have fun, and to have fun without alcohol. They always include children or offer babysitting. Two of the recent events produced by the staff were a *cena baile* (dinner dance) and a show called "*Imitadores*" which involved celebrity look-alike singers. In both cases, community members provided the entertainment. For the dance, a live band played cumbia music. Comedians donated their time for the show. Staff cooked tacos and sold plates of food with salad and a drink. After expenses, these events each generate an average of a thousand dollars. Staff members take advantage of the time with the community to strengthen relationships and announce upcoming events and services.

At times, when the agency or someone in the community has been in dire need of funds, staff members have sold food at soccer games, sold crafts, and engaged in any number of activities to raise

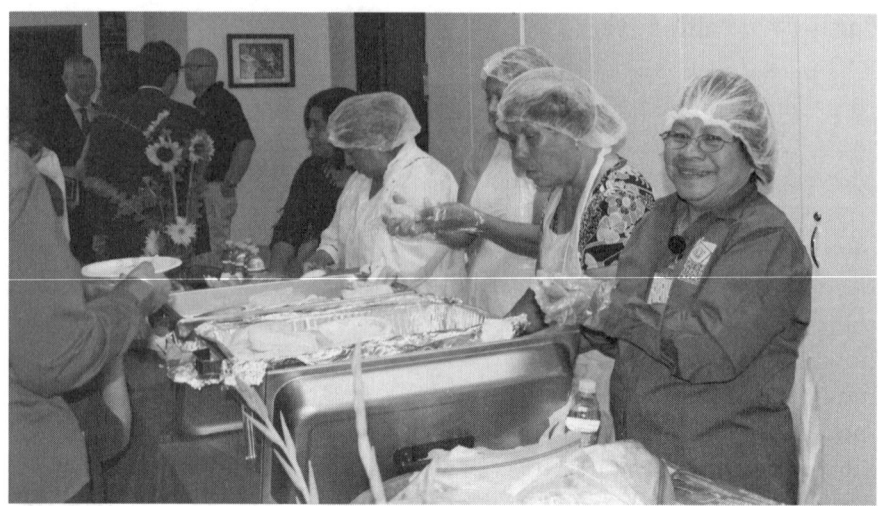

Josefina Bay (right), a founder of the *Tamalada* fundraiser, and other LHA employees and volunteers cook for the annual *Tamalada*.

money. Sometimes these small ideas become big events that we repeat because they have meaning, and because they are successful at raising money and engaging participation. One such event is our *Tamalada*.

The *Tamalada* has a powerful history and brings about powerful results. It is our annual tamale sale. It started in 1993 when America Bracho, our CEO, was teaching the Diabetes Self-Management Program course to one of the first groups of participants. During the course, one of the participants went blind, a common complication of uncontrolled diabetes. America asked the clinic staff where the participant was receiving care and why they had not checked the person's vision. The response was that the clinic could not provide the needed eye surgery, and so they didn't perform a vision test because they did not want to be liable for knowing something they couldn't do anything about. This news was very disturbing to the staff and the participants. America asked the participants if they would like to know if they were going blind, even if they could not afford the surgery to save their sight. They responded that of course they would – partly because it would give them time to figure out what to do about it. They came up with proactive ideas like, "I would sell my furniture to get the money for that surgery," or "I would ask my son to help me." One person said, "I would have that surgery, even if I had to sell tamales." This is a popular saying in Mexico. It means you will do something no matter what – even if you have to sell tamales. That's how Latino Health Access got the idea to sell tamales to create a fund to help people who needed eye surgery due to complications of diabetes.

Knowing that traditional tamales are made with lard, the *promotores* began to experiment with lower-fat versions. They developed a recipe that was fluffy and delicious, and held the first *Tamalada*. We invited elected officials, our partners from hospitals and clinics, and other friends of the agency to join us. Guests had their pictures taken making tamales and then we all sat down to a lunch of healthy tamales, salad, and good music played by our local musicians. Back then, Josefina was the *promotora* who took full ownership of coordinating the tamale-making effort. Josefina died of cancer after 14 years working at LHA. We will always remember her ready laugh and good cheer. The *Tamalada* continues in her honor.

Since then, funds raised from selling tamales have paid for many eye surgeries. Our money goes further than it normally would because the eye surgeries are donated at cost or offered at a discounted price by a local ophthalmologist.

> *"I developed diabetes at the age of nine. I didn't take care of my diabetes. I didn't want to be a person with diabetes. But one day I started to lose my vision. It happened very suddenly. I didn't tell anyone at first, but then it got worse. I couldn't do anything about it because I didn't have insurance, so I tried to get insurance. I bought some from a man who said, 'Sure, just send me $2,000 and you can have that surgery. It will be covered.' I borrowed the money from my mom. But it was a scam. Finally, my husband took me to Latino Health Access. I thought, 'These people aren't going to teach me anything.' But I wanted that surgery so I went to the classes. And you know what? They taught me a lot. I'm very grateful to all of my neighbors for making tamales, selling them, and buying them. I've had three eye surgeries now paid for by the tamales. My vision is not perfect. I'm blind in one eye, but I have 40% vision in the other, and I'm okay with that. I never wanted perfection. Because of*

*everything the community has done for me, I give back. I talk
to my city council members about open space, I volunteer at the
park, I speak to groups about making the city healthier."*

—*Alondra, program participant and volunteer*

Operationalizing fund development within LHA

The fund development function is somewhat horizontal at LHA.
Everyone understands they must play a role.

- **Chief Executive Officer:** The CEO spends a great deal of
  time showcasing the organization to potential supporters. She
  does this as much to share ideas for improving community
  health as to raise funds. This includes meeting with funders,
  providing tours of the neighborhoods, offering trainings, and
  speaking to audiences who might be interested in our work.

- **Development Director:** In 1997, when the organization was
  five years old, we hired a development director to coordinate
  development and communications efforts. Later we added an
  assistant to her team, then a grant writer, and most recently,
  a communications position. There have been times when the
  agency did not have a development director, as is the case now,
  with the Chief Operations Officer filling this role. This has been
  a tricky role to fill, as it requires camaraderie with the staff and
  community, as well as an ability to interface well with funders
  and donors.

- **Staff:** All resource development is done in conjunction with
  staff. In addition to the Staff Fund Development Committee,
  each proposal we write arises from staff members, primarily
  promotoras, reporting a need in the community. Needs statements
  and objectives are written only after meetings with program
  staff to fully understand the approach and rationale. The
  Director of Evaluation is involved in creating the proposed
  outcomes and evaluation plans for each proposal. Drafts go
  back to staff until there is consensus that the proposal reflects
  the need and our capacity to deliver. Staff members are also

involved in hosting visits from potential funding partners and donors. Each staff member at LHA has the capacity to describe his or her work, to give a tour of the community in which he or she works, and to provide opportunities for community members and funders to speak directly to one another. The staff also helps to plan and produce the annual Gala and all events. We provide training to staff members so that they understand the impact that gathering data, meeting their objectives, and completing reports on time has on our ability to seek additional funding.

- **Board:** The Board of Directors, in addition to its governance duties, represents the agency externally. They take the lead on planning the Gala and also assist with introducing potential donors and funders to the organization.

Challenges in the fund development function

While we have been able to sustain our work and to support significant changes toward a healthier community over time, we do struggle with this function. It is difficult to allocate enough resources for fund development. We are aware that if we had more staff in specialized roles, such as donor development, we could raise more unrestricted funds; yet the lack of unrestricted funds prevents this investment. We are woefully underdeveloped in some areas, such as having a high-functioning donor database program, communicating on social media, and others. We are also challenged to participate with funders who do not share our paradigm. This mismatch is not always apparent at the outset and creates tension because the community does need the project or the funding.

For example, we may be funded to do a project, but then also be expected to participate in a collaboration facilitated by the funder that develops paternalistic, simplistic, "collective impact" objectives we do not agree with nor do we think will be effective at addressing the issue faced by the community. Or we are funded to do a project, but then the funder develops tracking tools that would require us to ask people about their immigration status or household income. Great finesse is required in these situations. In spite of the challenges, we do the best we can and are proud of the way the entire team contributes to sustaining the agency.

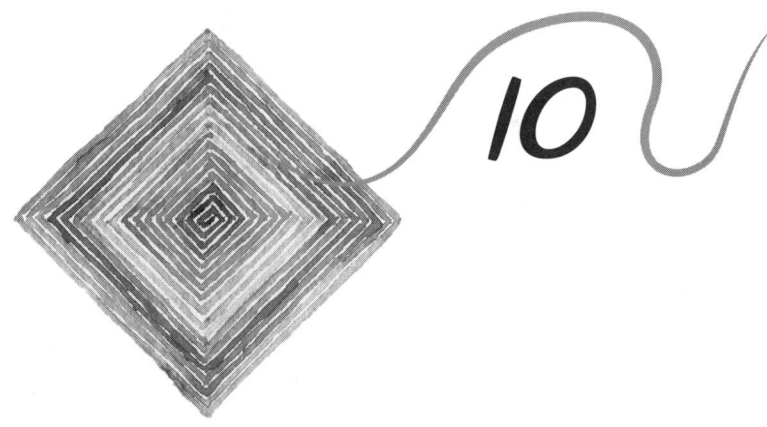

The Tangible
and the Intangible:
Finding New Ways to Measure

*"In our program, there was a promotora who never had her records
complete or on time. I explained to her how to do it several
times, but she did not improve. She would do a lot of things,
but never gave herself time for data. One day we had a different
conversation about the value of data. We talked about the amount
of work that promotores may be doing, but if we do not record it
on paper and we cannot prove it, then no one will know about it,
we will not be able to improve it, we will not be able to learn, and
we will not be able to obtain financial resources to continue the
projects. The promotora reflected over her hard work, the many
things she does, and the results she obtains. She realized that
taking the time to document her work was equivalent to giving
herself a space to reflect. Since then, she always turns in her
documentation on time."*

—Lupita, program assistant, Emotional Wellness Program

Our Evaluation Department was created primarily to assist LHA in demonstrating the value of what we do and how we do it. The second core function of the department is building capacity, as expressed in our Principle of Practice 17: "LHA is an organization that is constantly learning and trying to analyze the processes and results of what we do, and to incorporate the lessons we learn along the way." Early in our organization's history, we made a commitment to create an in-house Evaluation Department that would document and systematize our learning, with the full understanding that evaluation efforts are not simple in any type of organization.

However, we wanted to create a culture of evaluation where all team members could understand, value, and contribute to the evaluation of our collective work. We then started developing appropriate designs, indicators, and validating tools, and we created data collection forms and trained staff members how to use them. The project has not been easy, as our programs are highly innovative and always in motion. However, we have been able to reach uniformity in many areas of our data collection process, and we continue to create new and better ways to demonstrate the value of creative and holistic interventions and strategies.

We are a learning organization committed to understanding what is happening in our partner neighborhoods, the living conditions of our community's families, the problems and issues affecting them, and what works to make things better. Similarly, we are very interested in knowing what does not work and how we can correct and improve. The stories and data come via our *promotores*, who communicate with their program support staff and the Evaluation Department team.

Our programmatic work engages with the entire health of the person, from their basic needs to their long-term dreams. Our evaluation efforts are focused on assessing initial and intermediate behavioral changes, diverse forms of participation, and community involvement in advocacy efforts and policy changes. In addition, our Evaluation Department team highlights the process of achieving those outcomes among participants as well as documenting the efforts on the part of our programmatic team to assist participants to accomplish the desired objectives. Collecting data has a twofold purpose: 1) to be able to share "results" immediately with participants as an educational tool that promotes hope and inspires further action; and 2) to capture changes so that we know whether our programs are working and to be able to communicate that to others, inside and outside the organization.

At LHA, we are grounded in four premises about data collection and evaluation:

1. Evaluation is not research.
2. We value our system of communication across the agency.
3. We use a centralized database.
4. We strive for balance.

Evaluation is not research

Because our programs are not research studies, we have the freedom to change the evaluation plan, the design of the evaluation, the timing of the data collection, and the data collection instruments as needed in the process as our programs progress. While we rarely change our program objectives or outcomes, we pay close attention to the information that process evaluation techniques provide because these are so helpful for determining how well we are carrying out the work. Process evaluation helps us know, for example, if we are reaching the people in the neighborhoods we mean to reach. If not, then we can adjust the in-between steps (our process) to stay on track toward achieving our long-term goals.

LHA has partnered many times with researchers in universities, and we see the value of those studies. However, we have experienced how academic research or rigid evaluation plans can shift our focus from delivering services to engaging participants to collecting data. Academic approaches usually begin with a baseline assessment in the form of a questionnaire. We have observed that some participants feel uncomfortable answering a lengthy survey during our first contact with them. Usually, we use that first contact as an opportunity to build trust, not mine them for information about their personal lives. We understand that it is important to show effectiveness using traditional academic methods. The challenge is to find a balance between serving and engaging the community and collecting data in an unobtrusive manner. At LHA, we make every effort to design the program evaluation in ways that support *promotores* doing what they do best: creating relationships and supporting individual and community improvement.

We value our system of communication across the agency

The Evaluation Department is spearheaded by a Director of Evaluation and an Evaluation Associate. Their job is to plan, organize, and design methods to measure the impact of programs. After analyzing data, they communicate results to the program team. They also train staff on evaluation topics and oversee the centralized database. Each program at LHA has data entry staff, who often are *promotores* as well. They are responsible not just for data entry but also for other tasks, such as providing administrative support to the program and assisting *promotores* with data collection and documentation.

Being embedded in programmatic teams is advantageous because the data entry staff understands what types of data are collected and why, and most importantly, how data contributes to the programs achieving their objectives. This immersion in programmatic tasks facilitates the communication with *promotores* (see diagram below). Data entry staff are part of the program team directly supervised by a program director or coordinator, and are

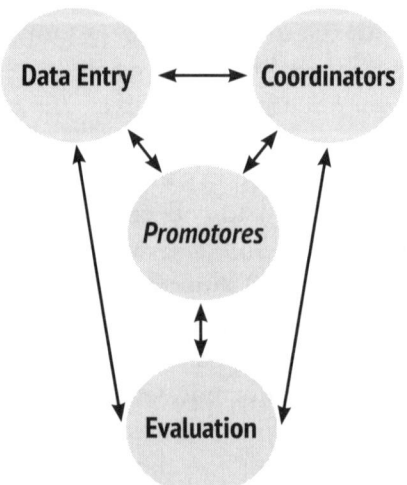

Information flow for data collection and evaluation at LHA

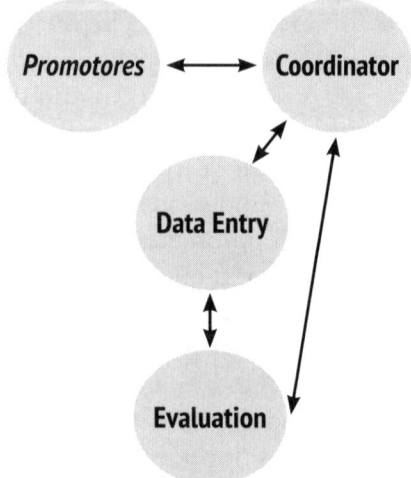

A traditional model, in which data entry is at the center of evaluation activities

knowledgeable regarding program objectives, outcomes, criteria, and evaluation forms. This connection to the team allows them to manage data, not just enter it.

The Evaluation Department supervises the data-related work of the data entry staff and also trains them and meets with them on a regular basis. The evaluation communication system works to to assure a timely and accurate flow of information and decision-making among the Evaluation Department, coordinators, *promotores*, and the data entry staff. This *promotores*-centered structure allows for open and frequent dialogue and helps to ensure that the tools are practical for the *promotores* and the community to use, that they do get used, and that the data collected is relevant and helpful for promoting and measuring change.

> *"Having an evaluation team helps answer my questions about whether something is happening in the community or something is not functioning. It motivates me to know that the work I am doing is being documented. There is proof — reliable and tangible — of what is being done."*
>
> —Charis, promotora, Community Engagement and Advocacy Program

We use a centralized database

When the Evaluation Department was established in 2002, only one program had a structured database to manage data and to produce computerized reports. The rest of the programs relied mainly on Excel for storing their data, and some relied on manual tabulation. Finding and implementing a centralized database became a priority of the Evaluation Department.

With the assistance of Orange County's United Way, we bought and installed a centralized participant management system. This system captures individual data, enrollment in programs, services rendered, assessments, program completion, and outreach efforts. The system also catches duplication, which helps us track the number of unique individuals with whom we work each year, since many participate in more than one program. Little by little, programs transitioned their data into this database. At the same time, we began to increase uniformity of data collection forms. This database has provided the Evaluation Department with the tools to write internal reports that quantify the number of people served per year, services provided, hours of investment per participant, outreach efforts, demographic profiles of participants, and programmatic outcomes. As a result, we now can use our data in our requests for funding.

The centralized database is managed by the Evaluation Department. All data entry and data management training comes from this department. The Evaluation Department team prepares program-specific data entry protocols and programs indicators, outputs, and outcomes in the centralized database.

We strive for balance

Balancing the provision of support and practical services to the community with grant- or contract-related evaluation and data collection requirements has sometimes been a challenge. We improve our opportunity for balance when we openly discuss the impact the requirements of the grants, projects, and funders have on the evaluation approach, design, timing, indicators, and effort required from both *promotores* and participants. We make sure we know ahead of time how much training our staff will need to implement the evaluation plan. As a team, we examine the programmatic strategies, curricula, and training of *promotores*, and then we determine whether the current evaluation plan is appropriate for a particular program. This process can cause delays in submitting a proposal or implementing a program, yet we have learned that not investing this time results in having to backtrack and spend more time later. Having a strong program conceptualization process is pivotal to the development of an evaluation plan.

On occasion, foundations and federal, state, and county agencies have required us to modify our criteria for how to assess a program and have imposed the use of traditional survey tools. While there is room for change and learning in the ways we approach evaluation, we have learned through experience that these imposed methods can be complicated to implement, can interfere with the quality of our services, and can be difficult or intimidating for the majority of our community members who are not academically or linguistically prepared to use them.

Recently, a funder required us to evaluate one of our programs using a survey that consisted of twenty items, some written with double negatives, and a Likert scale of seven response options. We knew that this survey would cause many challenges for our participants and perhaps not even evaluate the program effectively. We explained our perspective to the funder and proposed using an alternative tool that had worked well previously. We achieved a compromise to use both tools; however, this compromise led to a data collection burden.

How do we develop and utilize appropriate methods of evaluation for the type of work we perform?

Our methods and measurement tools depend on the outcomes we hope to achieve. They can be qualitative when we want to learn, for example, the issues that are important to the community and the actual changes being achieved. They can be quantitative when we want to use statistics, for example, to make a case that policies need to change. They can also be clinical when we are aiming for biological or physical changes. Here are some examples of measurement methods and indicators:

Program	Sample Indicator	Sample Measurement
Diabetes Self-Management, an adult diabetes management class series	Reduction in hemoglobin A1C	Pre- and post-hemoglobin A1C values
Breast Health, a cancer screening program	Referral to a mammogram	Referred or not referred
Healthy Weight, a parent-child weight management class series	Reduction in body mass index (BMI)	Pre- and post-BMI values
Community Engagement and Advocacy	Increase level of civic participation	Participation in specific civic activities

Reaching agreements with staff

Reaching agreements with our teams on how programs will
be evaluated and how to collect data requires a substantial
amount of time spent in dialogue, piloting, debriefing, developing
improvements, sharing feedback, implementation, and follow-
up. Our most successful internal effort in this regard was related
to measuring outreach activities agency-wide. Outreach is the
cornerstone of *promotores'* work. *Promotores* engage in vast amounts of
outreach every day. However, in an initial agency-wide assessment,
we discovered that outreach was not consistently documented. The
Evaluation Department team presented these findings to the staff.
We decided we wanted to capture the effort required for outreach
and recruitment, and focus on those already recruited. To illustrate
our investment in outreach, we needed accurate data. To develop
this tool, *promotores* and coordinators identified the types of outreach
they conducted, such as one-on-one, small group, and large
group; and where they did their outreach, such as schools, streets,
laundromats, and apartment buildings. The notes from all of these
conversations were combined into a draft tool by the Evaluation
Department and presented to the *promotores* and coordinators. After

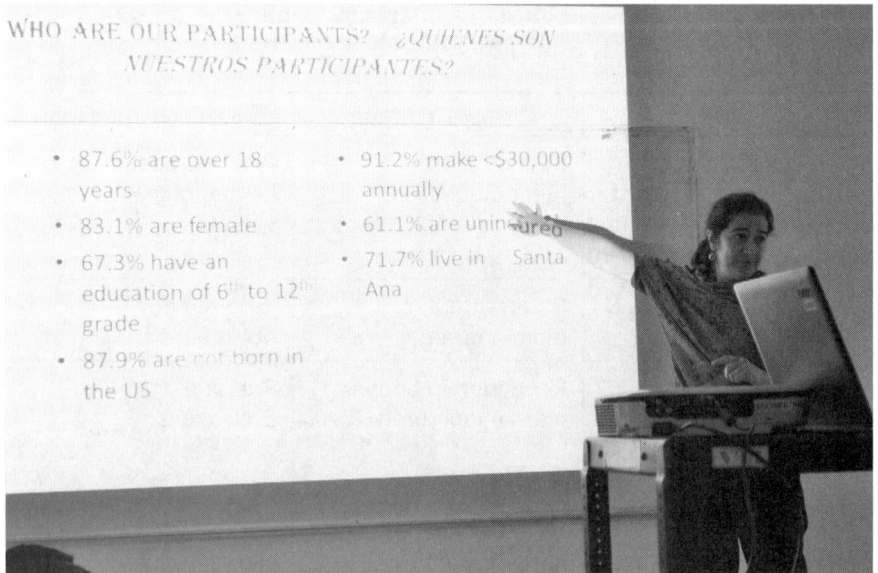

Patricia, Director of Evaluation, discusses data with staff.

incorporating feedback, *promotores* tested the tool in practice sessions until everyone was comfortable. This process was critical to the *promotores* feeling ownership of the evaluation tool. Moreover, this process also ensured that the entire evaluation was relevant to the holistic work of the *promotores*, and responsive to the needs of the community.

The outreach work is now documented. Program teams decide where, when, how, who, what, and why the outreach will take place. They maintain information about the places they have visited and the results of outreach strategies to help make decisions about next steps. We document and organize reports about outreach so we can measure the scope, how much effort we have invested, and which strategies are most successful. This allows us to report to funders our activities and outcomes, compare them with the original objectives, get support to continue our efforts, and demonstrate our ability to reach and mobilize the community. Knowing the results of outreach also helps foundations and sponsors get a clear idea of how much effort and time is spent on these activities. Having this information has increased our ability to understand, appreciate, and communicate the level of effort that must be invested to generate the desired level of community participation. This information is crucial to calculating actual program costs and staff time.

Ultimately, we created an agency-wide internal objective to capture outreach efforts regardless of the funding source or even lack of funding. The number of outreach encounters per program is now presented at staff meetings. Funders and the business sector are increasingly aware of our ability to reach out, engage, and mobilize. LHA has secured a number of contracts solely focused on outreach, which is our entryway to building lasting relationships with participants. Our documented annual outreach has increased dramatically – from 19,133 efforts in 2007 to 94,398 in 2014.

Outcome data: qualitative, quantitative, or both?

Qualitative results provided a wealth of information in the initial stages of *Peso Saludable* (the Healthy Weight Program). To capture the results of our work, we developed a tool that would help us evaluate an eight-week interactive class for children and youth affected by overweight or obesity, and their parents. We chose a qualitative post-test survey. Our focus was on gaining trust and providing the education and skills that families need to have healthier lifestyles. We did not want to burden them with surveys. Parents completed the following statement: "The changes that I implemented as a result of taking the classes were…" and "The changes that I observed in my son [or daughter] as a result of taking the classes were…" The emphasis of these two questions was on actual behavior changes during the class series, not knowledge gained or attitudinal changes. These questions generated many responses that were not in traditional federal and state childhood obesity surveys at that time, such as "not drinking soda" or "does not eat Cheetos" – two common snacks that children and youth had reported consuming. It captured valuable intermediate behavioral changes. The changes that parents and children reported were not always entirely focused on maintaining or losing weight, traditionally the end goal. Many of the reported changes made by parents were implementing healthier eating habits in their household, such as eating more fruits and vegetables, and similarly, parents observed their children consuming less junk food and reading food labels. Responses to these questions allowed us to develop a bilingual checklist of behaviors most frequently reported by parents, and this became our evaluation and follow-up tool. Although the tool is now quantitative, we continue to use a post-test only design.

Outcome data: Policy wins?

We have been fortunate to receive funding from The California Endowment's Healthy Eating, Active Communities, and Building Healthy Communities Initiatives in recent years. We have learned that policy changes or "wins" in improving the built environment are extremely complex and take a long time. However, we concluded that our work in policy is different from other advocacy organizations in that we lead with the work of our *promotores*, who develop relationships with neighbors and support them to influence their environment. As a result, the measurement should also be different. The Community Engagement and Advocacy (CEA) Department team at LHA developed a Participation Continuum schema to illustrate the diverse strategies and activities needed to assist individual participants to progress through the continuum.

(For a complete description of the continuum, see pages 44–47.) This schema and multiple dialogues with the CEA team assisted the Evaluation Department team to create a tracking sheet to quantify resident participation and categorize activities, such as providing education, engaging in advocacy, or mobilization activities. The tracking sheet has had multiple iterations.

> *"The forms change because the nature of our work changes. At the beginning, we tracked [the participation] of leaders; now these leaders are participating in coalitions. [CEA] is creating legislation and policies. Our work has increased and the forms change as we advance. We need a structure of documentation that reflects the work that is being done."*
>
> —Adela, promotora, Community Engagement and Advocacy Program

> *"We want to be able to measure leadership and how that leadership evolves. We want to demonstrate the importance of building relationships and the impact that the process of accompanying our community has in the life of participants."*
>
> —Nancy, Director, Community Engagement and Advocacy Program

We are still in the initial stages of identifying the best processes and tools for assessing participation in different forms, and we are balancing that data with traditional policy "wins." Similarly, we are working with our partners, such as The California Endowment and the Marguerite Casey Foundation, as they themselves are part of the larger trend in the field seeking the best tools for assessing systemic reforms, organizing, advocacy, and other policy change work.

What are the roles of the *promotores* and the community in evaluation?

> *"The way that we evaluate at LHA gives the opportunity for participants to have a voice."*
>
> —Noraima, promotora, Emotional Wellness Program

Promotores at LHA have specific qualities and talents that earn the trust of the community. *Promotores* are the eyes, ears, and voices of the community. They possess critical information regarding the needs and assets of low-income families. The Evaluation Department team and program coordinators, while they may also possess some knowledge of the community, are the main holders of information resulting from university or technical training. Sharing community wisdom and technical information with each other is essential to the creation of practical tools to evaluate *promotor*-led programs. Coordinators meet regularly with *promotores* and together they communicate with the Evaluation Department team about the gaps and strengths of the program and the evaluation tools. In one instance, *promotores* reported needing half an hour to fill out a certain form with community members. According to Hiromi, one of our coordinators, "We found out that the problem was with the language. The community members did not understand." In this process of dialogue and feedback, coordinators and evaluators learn whether the data collection tools are assisting or hindering *promotores'* work, whether there is information that *promotores* have observed that is not being captured, or whether other programmatic strategies need to be implemented to achieve internal, external, or funder-driven objectives.

We have identified five time-sensitive periods where the feedback of the program team is essential:

1. While a grant proposal is being written.

2. Immediately after the grant or contract is awarded.

3. As soon as the tool starts being used and until the team feels at ease with it.

4. When preparing interim reports.

5. At the conclusion of the grant or contract.

The fund development team, the *promotores*, the program coordinator, the evaluation team, and the Executive Director collaborate to write each program's objectives and indicators. This is the time where previous lessons, such as discovering a need to reduce the number of participants served, to increase the number of class sessions, or to remove the pre- and post-test method, are included in the grant application. After the grant or contract has been awarded is the best opportunity for the coordinator and *promotores* to review the program objectives and outcomes, and to meet with the Evaluation Department team to discuss appropriate evaluation tools. Objectives and outcomes they are responsible for achieving are reviewed with the *promotores* who will be implementing the program. *Promotores* are always consulted in the development phase of the proposal, however sometimes different *promotores* will be assigned to the project, or so much time has passed since the proposal was submitted that we all need to refresh our understanding of the project. Once the programmatic team is familiar or re-familiarized with the evaluation tools, they need to use them, provide feedback for their improvement, or receive further training until they feel at ease.

During and after the preparation of an interim progress report to a funder or an internal agency status report, the coordinator, *promotores* and the Evaluation Department team review intermediate results to gauge progress and discuss what can be improved, including the data collection instruments. When programs end, a final review of the results closes the loop. A debriefing among members of the program and evaluation teams serves to share

Promotoras use data collection activities
for learning and unlearning with our youth.

outcome data with *promotores*. Although *promotores* already have observed the impact of the program on individual participants and their families, it is important to provide aggregate data – "the big picture" – and assess whether or not the evaluation tools and outcomes themselves, reflect the changes that *promotores* observed.

In addition to LHA staff, community members play a major and important role in the development of evaluation tools. They provide feedback by answering open-ended questions and by completing qualitative and satisfaction surveys. They also tell us when a particular question on the survey does not make sense. Rosa, a *promotora* with the Diabetes Self-Management Program, reminds us that sometimes the surveys themselves generate doubts and cause confusion. She says, "We notice when something is not sufficiently clear. Whatever participants express, we bring it to the coordinator and this information goes to evaluation."

We rely entirely on participants' willingness to give us reliable data. We believe that their willingness stems from the relationship and trust that *promotores* offer to participants.

We are very proud of our commitment to establishing a culture of learning and unlearning, which has given rise to a culture that is friendly to evaluation, and we are committed to having our own Evaluation Department so that we can measure and validate what the community values as important and the actual changes we are witnessing. We are also aware that this is a very fertile area in which we can continue to grow and learn. Evaluation plays a major role in the sustainability of our organization; therefore, we want to continue to invest in our own organizational development so we can further develop meaningful assessments hand in hand with the people most involved in the work – the *promotores* and the community members.

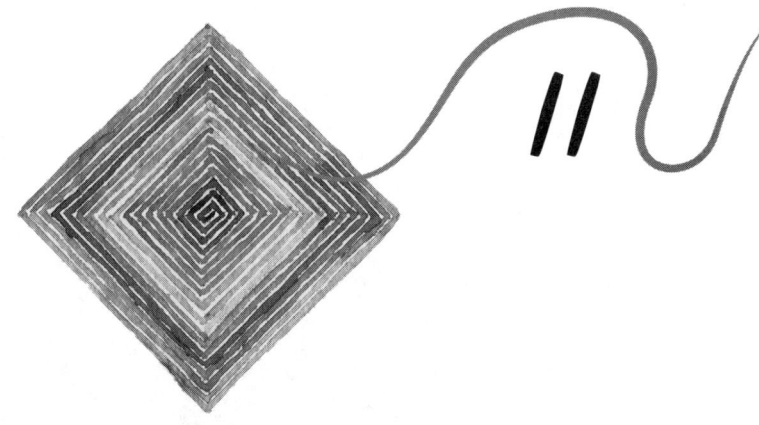

Reflections:
For Institutions Working or Wanting to Work with Promotores

"When I do outreach I think, 'God, lead me to the person who needs me.' Yesterday I was doing outreach with someone who, despite all the difficult things she is living through, has a lot to give. When I met her six months ago, I simply said, 'Hello, how are you?' and started talking to her. When she needed someone, I was there. The trust and affection that people feel is what makes the difference. Our friendship has been slowly growing. I invited her to join me in doing outreach, and she accepted because we are building a relationship of trust and affection. She came with her seven-year-old kid and we did outreach together. The child told me, 'Today is my mother's birthday,' and I said, 'Oh, congratulations! It's such a special day that we are going to share. I am glad to celebrate with you!' We all live painful moments but being able to share them while working together teaches us that we can move forward. I tell her that despite all the problems that life presents us, we always have something to give to people. She says, 'This is my neighborhood. I have been living here for eight years, I know these people.' So now, instead of doing my outreach work alone, I go with someone who knows the neighborhood and has friends here. And we both feel better for it."

— *Araceli, promotora, Community Engagement and Advocacy Program*

Araceli provides health access information at a swap meet.

Much has been published in the last decade about the effectiveness of the *promotor* model.[1] The surge of publications showing improved outcomes in chronic disease management and prevention and education programs have led to a heightened interest in the *promotor* model. Some hospitals, health maintenance organizations (HMOs), health plans, health centers, and other groups across the nation have incorporated, are interested in incorporating, or have attempted to incorporate *promotores* into their prevention and education efforts. While this model provides a cost-effective and culturally appropriate method for reaching consumers, reducing complications from unmanaged chronic diseases, reducing emergency room visits, and improving community health, the model's integration into some organizational structures has proven difficult. We believe that the reason people are experiencing difficulty is that they don't fully understand the depth of the model and its potential. We hope that the stories and insights we provide in this book will help readers understand the full potential of *promotores* and will encourage you to

1 These resources include: Capitman, Pacheco, Ramirez, and Gonzalez, 2009; Cornejo, Denman, Sabo, de Zapien, and Rosales, 2011; Johnson, Sharkey, Dean, and St John, 2013; Gold, 2010; Latino Health Access, *Visión y Compromiso*, Esperanza Community Housing Corporation, 2011; Lehmann and Sanders, 2007.

embrace the model if it is right for you. We hope our observations in this chapter will help you and your organization to make this important decision.

What if we treated communities like institutions?

The power of *promotores* is that they are homegrown community leaders. To understand how they do what they do, we have found it helpful to think of communities as institutions with their own "institutional culture." Just as organizations have directors and managers, the community has residents who are the "leadership" of the community. Just as non-profits have technical experts, the community has neighbors who are experts on various aspects of life in the community. In the same way that institutions have communications teams, communities have networks that spread news and information. Anyone who has ever worked for an organization knows that every workplace has a culture. Some of it is transparent and shared in the form of an employee handbook. Perhaps there is a dress code, a system for celebrating birthdays, some agreement about which holidays to take off, expectations about work hours, and so forth. Some aspects of workplace culture are not verbalized but are still experienced by the people who work there. For example, employees figure out over time if it's common practice to knock on a closed office door, to call informal meetings, to share personal information with co-workers, to look· at co-workers as competitors or as allies, etc. The same is true in communities. There are familiar ways of dressing, of acting, and of convening people. *Promotores* are skilled navigators of communities because they know the culture, the channels of communication, and the leadership networks.

What if organizations that are interested in developing relationships with communities treated communities as institutions? Would it change the unwritten – and unequal – protocols? Would community outsiders be more aware of and respectful of the institutional culture of the community they were hoping to partner with? Would they see the need to have conversations with them prior to reaching decisions about them? Would outside "institutions" work more intentionally to develop productive, inclusive partnerships? Would they have more respect and appreciation for the community experts?

Of course, the community is not exactly like an institution, but thinking the comparison through helps us see the community in a different light. The community operates with unspoken rules and expectations. It has collective wisdom and power. Its leaders have strong opinions about others' credibility, and if they are not thrilled with what outsiders have to offer, they can make sure their opinion is widely broadcast via their unforgiving, efficient, word-of-mouth communication system. These communities, when organized, can mobilize hundreds, even thousands; they have tremendous social and political power.

If you want to develop a successful partnership with communities and their leaders, you will need to carefully consider the reasons to partner. Can you commit to developing common ground, to recognizing the community's unwritten protocols and ways of reaching agreement, and to finding respectful ways of engaging neighbors and leaders? Have you weighed the risks and potential gains for all involved? Not every institution has to partner with communities or include community workers or *promotores* in their strategies. However, if your institution wants to partner with the community, then you need to examine your reasons and ask yourself if your organization has the right leadership and systems for this partnership. If you were meeting with a new funder or considering working in coalition with a union, you would use resources and staff time to learn about this new institution. You would study their leadership, their history in the field, their ways of getting work done, their norms and behaviors, and perhaps even their dress code! The same is true when you decide you want to partner with the community. You need to be sure that your institution has the resources and capacity to interface with the community as a true partner, to treat the community like the complex "institution" that it is.

Some practical advice about managing the intersection of community with institutions

At LHA, our community neighbors are our co-workers. When institutions engage community workers, the community and the institutional world intersect, like a Venn diagram. And that is where we like to do as much of our work as possible – in the middle area, where these two worlds overlap. Of course, there are tensions and conflicts. Sometimes these two worlds don't overlap – they collide.

For example, health care delivery organizations operate within rigid regulatory and financial environments that lead to organizational structures emphasizing patient compliance, staff efficiency, and other results that do not support an approach that views people as partners in their own health (and may well work against it). Within this rigid environment, often the health worker has little power in the relationship with the organization and the supervisor, and is in danger of becoming a part of the *status quo*. Incorporating the *promotor* model into health care delivery organizations in the U.S. can work if certain elements and conditions are intentionally taken into account, including:

- finding a champion in a leadership position at the organization.

- training on the *promotor* model at every level of the organization.

- examining the current organizational paradigm to uncover the role and influence that community and community workers play, inside and outside the organization.

Institutions that successfully integrate promotores:

- Have a history of commitment to low-income communities.

- Have a long-term vision for community improvement.

- Have a definition of community health that is broader than the provision of medical services.

- Have expressed commitment to the reduction of health disparities and/or to achieving equity.

- Work on a variety of strategies guided by that broader definition of community health.

- Have credibility in the community and among other organizations.

- Have a history of collaboration with other sectors.

- Have experience working with people from the community, particularly with low-income residents in programs or projects where the community has had a significant participation in the formulation of the strategy and the decision-making.

- Have a practice of consulting with community members, particularly low-income residents.
- Respect low-income people's right to express their needs, desires, and opinions, and to have a say in how things are done.
- Understand the importance of influencing public policy to achieve long-term sustainable changes.
- Have directors and coordinators with community work experience or who are open to learning about models of community work.
- Ensure that different levels of the organization understand and support the work of promotores, including the board of directors, department directors, middle management, coordinators, and the programmatic and operational teams.
- Have a commitment to maintain quality and to preserve financial resources for the programs.
- Have administrative transparency.

With those conditions in place, an institution is poised to work well with *promotores*. In addition to those general workplace practices, here are some more specific indicators of quality in a *promotor* program:

1. There is a commitment to appropriately compensate the *promotor* and provide full benefits, including health and dental insurance, vacation, sick and bereavement time, etc.

2. The personal needs of the *promotor* are taken into consideration in a proactive way. The *promotor* receives support and understanding to strengthen her emotional, physical, and mental health. This is done with the understanding that by supporting the *promotor*, the team is becoming stronger; therefore, the team can strengthen the community.

3. The *promotor* is considered a community expert who is consulted and whose opinions inform the strategy of the organization.

4. There is a philosophy of respect, patience, and support toward *promotores*, and there are clear consequences if someone disrespects or offends them.

5. The *promotor* is part of a team that is valued and motivated.

6. The *promotor* is part of a team that participates in the creation of its work plan.

7. There are mechanisms to evaluate all the staff, including the *promotores*.

8. There is appropriate supervision.

9. The supervisors and *promotores* have been trained in the *promotor* model to assure understanding and success.

10. The performance evaluation of the supervisors is influenced in great part by the quality of their work with the *promotores*.

11. There are mechanisms to recruit highly-committed *promotores*.

12. There is ongoing training in all areas of competency for the *promotores*.

13. There is cross-training for *promotores*.

14. The *promotor* is considered a leader inside and outside the organization and participates in a variety of training and experiences to deepen and strengthen her leadership.

15. *Promotores* participate in ongoing dialogues about justice, healthier communities, and public policy.

16. There is representation of *promotores* in internal committees in the organization.

17. There is representation of *promotores* in committees outside the organization.

18. It is expected that the *promotor* can help the organization in a comprehensive way.

19. There are multiple opportunities for *promotores* to increase their knowledge and experience inside and outside the organization.

20. The promotores are able to be spokespersons and support fund development. They can present about their own results, participate in site visits, lead tours, and speak to the media.

If you are considering the exciting prospect of including *promotores* in your work, we hope that these reflections inspire thoughtful discussions in your organization. At LHA, we believe that *promotores* have the potential not just to improve health outcomes, but also to mobilize communities in such a way that they address the roots of health inequity, and indeed change the world. For *promotores* to succeed, however, the institutions that they work with need to develop an openness to the *promotor* model. They need to have the capacity to train and support *promotores* in a way that maximizes their contribution. They need to make sure that *promotores'* skills are unleashed, not confined. As one *promotora*, Soledad, reminds us: "A hidden or saved-up talent is of no use; a shared talent fuels more talent." We have told our story in these pages not as a blueprint for finding and unleashing the talents of community leaders, but to offer guideposts for you as you embark on your journey.

Final words: The people of my city

"It is humbling to imagine that someone doing community work somewhere else could be using our learnings to reflect about their own work."

—*Moises, promotor*

"We are not perfect but we work hard to be effective and improve our work."

—*Luzy, promotora*

Fifth grade participant in the Family Literacy Initiative

One Friday at 6:30 p.m., we finished our last retreat before the publication of this book. At the end of the retreat, we shared the excitement of putting what we have learned out into the world.

The following Monday we received news that we were not selected to be funded for a major grant to support some of our programs.

At our little park, the staff and volunteers are selling lunch on Wednesdays and Thursdays to support their activities.

We are getting ready for our largest fundraiser, our Gala. We are sending sponsorship packages, writing the program, and working on the many other details that go into producing a large event.

We received a letter that we got a grant for another program. The amount is not as large as the grant we did not get.

Life goes on at LHA. We share successes, we stress out about work, about funding, about our life-work balance.

We learn and unlearn constantly.

We ask ourselves what the final messages at the end of this book should be and we all agree that with all that is wrong with the world, the struggling organizations, the lack of available resources to do the work, the issues of human rights, the absence of justice that often victimizes our vulnerable communities, and so on, we choose to focus on what is right with the world. We choose the excitement of contributing toward the creation of healthier communities, and from there we deal with the problems. We choose to focus on our hopes for a better world, a better today and a better tomorrow, and from there we deal with challenges. We choose to focus on our collective strengths as members of these communities to which we belong and which we respect. We choose to serve as the fuel to inspire and implement changes that will create the world of justice we hope to leave to our kids and grandkids.

We choose to be grateful to all people that have made our existence possible, grateful for our values, learning, work, resources, results, and faith in ourselves, our communities, and the future.

In particular, we want to express our gratitude to the many neighbors in the communities to which we devote our daily work, communities we belong to, communities we love and that often are stigmatized, neglected, and ignored. There is no better way of thanking them than by sharing with all of you this song written by Moises Vazquez, one of our own *promotores*.

The People of My City[2]

I stand high and tall
When I speak of my people
I am proud and full of admiration for them

My people wake up early in the morning
To begin their journey before the sun comes up
If they are ever mistreated I will defend them passionately

The people of my city are lovely
They are beautiful like no other
The people of my city are strong and wise
They are ready to work and take action

I tip my hat
When I speak of my people
This song comes from my heart
And it is my gift to you all

My people transform themselves into monarch butterflies
And travel long distances in search of a better life
And as strong (violent) as the winds may be
Their color remains brilliant

The people of my city are lovely
They are beautiful like no other
The people of my city are strong and wise
They are ready to work and take action

My people are flavor and melancholy
Nostalgia and joy play a part in our everyday life

The people of my city are lovely
They are beautiful like no other
The people of my city are strong and wise
They are ready to work and take action

---

2 You can see and hear Moises' song here:
https://www.youtube.com/watch?v=V6BuUDxS6PA

These are the people of my city

These are the people of my city

These are the people of my city

—*Moises Vasquez*

❧

Thank you so much for reading our book. We hope it helps to inspire your work. We wish all the best to you and your community.

The Latino Health Access Collective
Santa Ana, California
2016

Bibliography

Alberts, J., R. Bermudez, C.J. Condon. "A Health Assessment of the Latino Community in Santa Ana, ZIP Code 92701." Santa Ana, CA: County of Orange Health Care Agency, Office of Quality Management, 2001.

Ashton, J. "The Origins of Healthy Cities." In J. Ashton, *Healthy Cities*, 1-14. Philadelphia: Open University Press, October, 1991.

Bernstein, Nell. *Lift Every Voice: Movement Building as a 21st Century Philanthropic Strategy.* Seattle: Marguerite Casey Foundation, n.d.
http://caseygrants.org/wp-content/uploads/2012/04/P09642_MCF-BKLT.pdf

Bracho, A. "A Working Model of Community Involvement: The Urgency to Go Beyond Rhetoric." *Minority Health Today*, 2000, 1(4):38-42.
http://calhealthworkforce.org/wp-content/uploads/2011/01/The-Urgency-to-Go-Beyond-Rhetoric.pdf

California Department of Public Health Office of Binational Border Health. *Southern California Promotores (Community Health Workers) Needs Assessment, San Diego And Imperial Counties, 2010–2011.* 2011.
http://www.cdph.ca.gov/programs/cobbh/Documents/Promotores%20Needs%20Assessment22712.pdf

California Health Workforce Alliance. "Taking Innovation to Scale: Community Health Workers, Promotores, and the Triple Aim." California: CHWA. August, 2013.
https://www.phi.org/uploads/application/files/dwjet18q0tvqvzg9iwizi6ts5shmektcxn9tntu7rrp5tugfk5.pdf

Capitman, John A., Tania L. Pacheco, Mariana Ramírez, Alicia Gonzalez. "Promotoras: Lessons Learned on Improving Healthcare Access to Latinos." Fresno, CA: Central Valley Health Policy Institute, 2009.
https://www.fresnostate.edu/chhs/cvhpi/documents/exec-summary-english-final.pdf

Carpenter, E. "Post from Zero Divide: OMB, Nonprofits and Social Impact." Email newsletter. August 22, 2014.

Centers for Disease Control and Prevention. "Community Health Workers/Promotores de Salud: Critical Connections in Communities." Atlanta: CDC, May 20, 2011.
http://www.cdc.gov/diabetes/projects/comm.pdf

————. "Fact Sheet: Health Disparities in Diabetes." Atlanta: CDC, 2011.
http://www.cdc.gov/minorityhealth/CHDIR/2011/FactSheets/Diabetes.pdf

————. "Fact Sheet: Health Disparities in Obesity." Atlanta: CDC, 2011.
http://www.cdc.gov/minorityhealth/CHDIR/2011/FactSheets/Obesity.pdf

————. "National Diabetes Statistics Report, 2014: Estimates of Diabetes and Its Burden in the United States." Atlanta: CDC, 2014.
http://www.cdc.gov/diabetes/pubs/statsreport14/national-diabetes-report-web.pdf

————. "Prediabetes." Atlanta: CDC, 2015.
http://www.cdc.gov/diabetes/basics/prediabetes.html

Committee on Assuring the Health of the Public in the 21st Century. "The Future of the Public's Health in the 21st Century." Washington, DC: The National Academies Press, November, 2002.
http://iom.nationalacademies.org/Reports/2002/The-Future-of-the-Publics-Health-in-the-21st-Century.aspx

Cornejo, Elsa, Catalina A. Denman, Samantha Sabo, Jill de Zapien, Cecilia Rosales. *Scoping Review of Community Health Worker/Promotora-Based Chronic Disease Primary Prevention Programs on the U.S.-Mexico Border.* Hermosillo, Sonora, México: El Colegio de Senora, Spring, 2011.
http://alamo.colson.edu.mx:8085/sitios/CESS/091020_frutosTrabajo/frutos_archivos/2011CornejoEtAl_ScopingReview.pdf

Freire, Paulo. *Pedagogy of Hope: Reliving Pedagogy of the Oppressed.* New York: Continuum International Publishing Group, 1994.

Freire, Paulo. *Pedagogy of the Oppressed.* New York: Continuum International Publishing Group, 1986.

Gold, Rachel Benson. "'I Am Who I Serve' – Community Health Workers In Family Planning Programs," *Guttmacher Policy Review.* 2010, 13(3): 8-12.

Green, Lawrence W., Leslie Sim, Heather Breiner, eds. *Evaluating Obesity Prevention Efforts: A Plan for Measuring Progress.* Washington, DC: The National Academies Press, 2013.
http://www.nap.edu/read/18334/chapter/1

Hayes–Bautista, David E. *Latinos in Orange County: Profile of Demographic and Health Characteristics.* Santa Ana, CA: Delhi Community Center, *Bienestar Familiar* Project, and HERR Coalition, 1993.

Healthy People 2020. "Social Determinants of Health." Washington, DC: U.S. Department of Health and Human Services.
http://www.healthypeople.gov/2020/topics-objectives/topic/social-determinants-of-health

Hilts, Philip. *Rx for Survival: Why We Must Rise to the Global Health Challenge.* New York: The Penguin Group, 2005.

Institute for Healthcare Improvement, IHI Triple Aim Initiative, n.d.
http://www.ihi.org/Engage/Initiatives/TripleAim/Pages/default.aspx

Iton, Anthony. "Tackling the Root Causes of Health Disparities Through Capacity Building," in Hofrichter, Richard, ed. *Tackling Health Inequities through Public Health Practice: A Handbook for Action.* Washington, DC: The National Association of County and City Health Officials, 2006.
http://archived.naccho.org/topics/justice/upload/naccho_handbook_hyperlinks_000.pdf

Johnson, C., J. Sharkey, W. Dean, J. St. John, and M. Castillo. *Promotoras as Research Partners to Engage Health Disparity Communities.* Bethesda, MD: PubMed Central, 2013.
http://www.ncbi.nlm.nih.gov/pmc/articles/PMC3633728/

Johnston, M. P., and S. B. Rifkin. *Health Care Together: Training Exercises for Health Workers in Community Based Programmes.* London and Basingstoke: Macmillan Publishers, 1987.

Latino Health Access, Vision y Compromiso, and Esperanza Community Housing Corporation. *The Promotor Model: A Model for Building Healthy Communities.* Los Angeles: The California Endowment, March 29, 2011.
http://www.visionycompromiso.org/wordpress/wp-content/uploads/TCE_Promotores-Framing-Paper.pdf

Leach–Kemon, Katherine. *The State of U.S. Health: Innovations, Insights, and Recommendations from the Global Burden of Disease Study.* Seattle: Institute for Health Metrics and Evaluation, 2013.

Lehmann, Uta, and David Sanders. "Community Health Workers: What Do We Know about Them?" Geneva: World Health Organization, January, 2007.
http://www.who.int/hrh/documents/community_health_workers.pdf

Magee, Mike. *Positive Leadership.* New York: Spencer Books, 1995.

Marguerite Casey Foundation. *Believing that Change is Possible,* 2015.
http://caseygrants.org/believing-that-change-is-possible/

Marguerite Casey Foundation. Equal Voice for America's Families Campaign, n.d.
http://caseygrants.org/equalvoice/equal-voice-for-americas-families-campaign/

Martin, Philip. "Proposition 187 in California," in *International Migration Review.* vol. 29 no. 1 (1995): 255–263.

Office of Management and Budget. *Uniform Administrative Requirements, Cost Principles, and Audit Requirements for Federal Awards.* Washington, DC: Federal Register, December 26, 2013.
https://federalregister.gov/a/2013-30465

Ovanessian, Vahik. "A Health Assessment of the Latino Community in Santa Ana Zip Code 92701, 1996: In Collaboration with Latino Health Access for the 92701 Project." Santa Ana, CA: County of Orange Health Care Agency, Office of Policy Research and Planning, 1997.

Planned Parenthood Federation of America. "A Guide to Promotora Programs." New York: Planned Parenthood, 2004.

Preskill, Hallie, Katelyn Mack, Matt Duffy, Efrain Gutierrez. *The California Endowment Strategic Review: Building Healthy Communities.* Los Angeles: The California Endowment, November, 2013.
http://consensus.fsu.edu/Civic-Advance/pdfs/BHCStrategicReviewReport.pdf

Rosenthal, E. Lee, project director. *A Summary of the National Community Health Advisor Study.* Baltimore: The Annie E. Casey Foundation, June, 1998.

Rural Health Information Hub. *Promotora de Salud/Lay Health Worker Model.* January, 2016.
http://www.raconline.org/communityhealth/chw/module2/layhealth

Stokols, Daniel. "Translating Social Ecological Theory into Guidelines for Community Health Promotion." *American Journal of Health Promotion,* no. 4 (1996): 282–298.
https://webfiles.uci.edu/dstokols/Pubs/Translating.PDF

Sturgess, Gail. "Skills vs. Competencies. What's the Difference?" Western Cape, South Africa: TalentAlign, December 6, 2012.
http://www.talentalign.com/skills-vs-competencies-whats-the-difference/

Takano, Takehito. *Healthy Cities and Urban Policy Research.* London and New York: Spon Press, 2003.
http://ir.nmu.org.ua/bitstream/handle/123456789/120430/94073c85839d e505748d4f7e2717710e.pdf?sequence=1

U.S. Census Bureau. *Orange County QuickFacts.* Washington, DC: U.S. Department of Commerce, 2014.
http://quickfacts.census.gov/qfd/states/06/06059.html

United Nations Children's Fund. *Getting to the Roots: Mobilizing Community Volunteers to Combat Vitamin A Deficiency Disorders in Nepal.* Kathmandu: UNICEF, 2003.
http://www.unicef.org/rosa/Getting.pdf

Waheed, Saba, Hugo Romero, Carolina Sarmiento. *Orange County on the Cusp of Change.* Los Angeles: UCLA Labor Center, July, 2014.
http://labor.ucla.edu/wp-content/uploads/downloads/2014/07/FINAL-OC-report-for-Web.pdf

Werner, David, and Bill Bower. *Helping Health Workers Learn.* Berkeley, CA: Hesperian Health Guides, 1982, 2012

Wikipedia, "God's eye," (accessed 25 January 2016).
https://en.wikipedia.org/wiki/God's_eye

Wood, C. "The Selection, Training, and Support of Primary Health Care Workers," in *Proceedings, 1981 International Health Conference, June 15-17, 1981.* Washington, DC: National Council for International Health, 1981, 1–7.

World Health Organization. *Building a Healthy City: A Practitioner's Guide.* Geneva: World Health Organization, 1995.
http://apps.who.int/iris/bitstream/10665/62542/1/WHO_EOS_95.10.pdf

————. *Closing the Gap in a Generation: Health Equity through Action on the Social Determinants Of Health.* Geneva: World Health Organization, 2008.
http://apps.who.int/iris/bitstream/10665/43943/1/9789241563703_eng.pdf

————. "Declaration of Alma-Ata: International Conference on Primary Health Care." Alma-Ata, USSR: World Health Organization, September, 1978.
http://www.who.int/publications/almaata_declaration_en.pdf

————. Fifty-First World Health Assembly. "Health-for-all Policy for the Twenty-first Century." Geneva, Switzerland: World Health Organization, May 16, 1998, agenda item 19.
http://www.nszm.cz/cb21/archiv/material/worldhealthdeclaration.pdf

————. *Health 21: The Health-for-all Policy Framework for the WHO European Region.* Copenhagen: World Health Organization Regional Office for Europe, 1999.
http://www.euro.who.int/en/publications/abstracts/health21-the-health-for-all-policy-framework-for-the-who-european-region

————. *International Health Conference* (1946, June, July). Retrieved January 2014.
http://whqlibdoc.who.int/hist/official_records/2e.pdf

————. *Part II: What is WHO's mandate? TMCAM WHO,* (2012, August 18). Retrieved January 2014, from Geneva Foundation for Medical Education and Research.
http://www.gfmer.ch/TMCAM/WHO_Minelli/P2-3.htm#_ftn7

————. *Twenty steps for developing a Healthy Cities project.* Copenhagen: World Health Organization Regional Office for Europe, 3rd ed., 1997.
http://www.euro.who.int/__data/assets/pdf_file/0011/101009/E56270.pdf

————. *World Health Statistics 2014, Part III: Global Health indicators.* Geneva: World Health Organization, 2014.
http://www.who.int/gho/publications/world_health_statistics/EN_WHS2014_Part3.pdf

Hesperian Health Guides

For over 40 years, Hesperian has been the "go to" source for resources about health promotion and community health. All our materials are published in English, Spanish, and a variety of other languages, and are available in print, online, and in several digital formats. Hesperian is a not-for-profit publisher; our work is made possible by your book purchases and donations.

Please visit our multilingual website **www.hesperian.org** for details.

To purchase books or make a donation:
tel: 510.845.4507
toll free in the USA: 888.729.1796
fax: 510.845.0539
email: bookorders@hesperian.org
online: store.hesperian.org

Helping Health Workers Learn, by David Werner and Bill Bower, is an indispensable resource that makes health education fun and effective. Includes activities, techniques, and ideas for low-cost teaching aids, and presents strategies for community involvement through participatory education. 640 pages.

Health Actions for Women, by Melissa Smith, Sarah Shannon and Kathleen Vickery, field tested by 41 groups in 23 countries and provides a wealth of clearly explained and engagingly illustrated activities, strategies and stories that address the social obstacles and practices that prevent women and girls from enjoying healthy lives. 352 pages.

Where There Is No Doctor, by David Werner, Carol Thuman and Jane Maxwell, is the most widely used health manual in the world with information on how to diagnose, treat and prevent common diseases. An emphasis is placed on prevention, including cleanliness, diet, vaccinations, and the importance of community mobilization. 512 pages.